John W. Hilber
Cultic Prophecy in the Psalms

Beihefte zur Zeitschrift für die alttestamentliche Wissenschaft

Herausgegeben von
John Barton · Reinhard G. Kratz
Choon-Leong Seow · Markus Witte

Band 352

Walter de Gruyter · Berlin · New York

John W. Hilber

Cultic Prophecy in the Psalms

Walter de Gruyter · Berlin · New York

♾ Printed on acid-free paper which falls within
the guidelines of the ANSI to ensure permanence and durability.

ISBN 3-11-018440-0

Bibliographic information published by Die Deutsche Bibliothek

Die Deutsche Bibliothek lists this publication in the Deutsche Nationalbibliografie; detailed bibliographic data is available in the Internet at <http://dnb.ddb.de>.

© Copyright 2005 by Walter de Gruyter GmbH & Co. KG, D-10785 Berlin
All rights reserved, including those of translation into foreign languages. No part of this book may be reproduced or transmitted in any form or by any means, electronic or mechanical, including photocopy, recording, or any information storage and retrieval system, without permission in writing from the publisher.
Printed in Germany
Cover Design: Christopher Schneider, Berlin

Acknowledgments

This monograph is an edited version of my dissertation, "Cultic Prophecy in the Psalms in the Light of Assyrian Prophetic Sources", completed in 2004 at the University of Cambridge under the supervision of Prof. Graham I Davies. The original suggestion to apply the Assyrian prophetic sources to some aspect of Old Testament study came from Prof. Davies; and the fruitfulness of this topic, which he suggested before the importance of the Assyrian sources was widely appreciated, is a testimony to his own breadth in Old Testament and ancient Near Eastern studies. Along with his thoughtful and encouraging guidance, he was a model to me of balanced scholarship and gentlemanly demeanour. Others contributed in indispensable ways to my academic growth. Prof. J. Nicholas Postgate and Dr Simon Sherwin invested many patient hours tutoring me in Akkadian and Mesopotamian studies, and Mr Barry Kemp offered immense help in Egyptology. Numerous suggestions for improving the original dissertation came from Prof. Robert P. Gordon and Prof. Alan Millard. Of course, any misconceptions or errors in either the original work or this subsecent monograph are my own failure.

Many others played a critical role during the labours of research and writing. German can be the bane of many English speaking students, but my friends Drs Christian and Hanna Stettler were alongside in the most desperate moments; and were it not for the aid of Dirk Jongkind, many difficult sentences of Dutch would have remained obscure. Dr Charles Echols and Dr Jules Gomes were my fellow pilgrims during the intense years of research — "a threefold cord is not quickly broken"! These friends and many others were part of the great international community at Tyndale House Library, Cambridge, where I learned as much about the world as about biblical studies. The entire Tyndale House staff, under the direction of Dr Bruce Winter, was a source of both encouragement and support, especially the librarian, Dr Elizabeth Magba. I wish to thank the Cambridge Overseas Trust for financial assistance throughout my years of study, and St. John's College showed its characteristic generosity on several occasions. Most important of all has been my family. My daughter, Janice, overcame tremendous challenges when she followed her father across the Atlantic at the age of 14. She is now a young woman launching on her own adventures. How can I begin to thank my wife and companion, Charlotte, without whose partnership and tremendous personal sacrifice this course of life would never have begun let alone come to fruition! I dedicate this work to them both with all my affection.

I wish to thank the editorial board of BZAW for accepting my manuscript for publication. The editor for this monograph, Ms Monika Müller has been a consistent source of encouragement and support.

John W. Hilber
June 2005

Contents

Abbreviations XIII

Chapter 1 Cultic Prophecy in the Psalms: Issues Past and Present 1
1.1 Introduction 1
1.2 Early Discussions 1
1.3 Mowinckel and Gunkel: Classic Formulation of the Debate 3
    1.3.1 Sigmund Mowinckel (*Psalmenstudien*) 3
    1.3.2 Hermann Gunkel 5
    1.3.3 Aubrey R. Johnson 9
    1.3.4 Alfred Haldar 10
    1.3.5 Sigmund Mowinckel (*The Psalms in Israel's Worship*) 11
1.4 Mid-Century Debate: Lack of a Consensus 12
1.5 Late Twentieth Century Discussion 15
    1.5.1 Developments in the Theory of Cult Prophets 16
        1.5.1.1 Jörg Jeremias 16
        1.5.1.2 James G. Harris III 17
        1.5.1.3 Aubrey R. Johnson 18
        1.5.1.4 Klaus Koenen 18
    1.5.2 Uncertainty of Identity of Cultic Functionary 19
        1.5.2.1 W. H. Bellinger 19
        1.5.2.2 Lester L. Grabbe 19
        1.5.2.3 Frederick Cryer 20
    1.5.3 Emphasis on Liturgical Imitation of Prophetic Style 20
        1.5.3.1 Thijs Booij 20
        1.5.3.2 Raymond J. Tournay 22
        1.5.3.3 Hermann Spieckermann 23
        1.5.3.4 Frank-Lothar Hossfeld 25
1.6 Key Issues and Evaluation 25
    1.6.1 The Existence of Pre-exilic Cult Prophets 26
        1.6.1.1 Association Between Prophets and Shrines 26
        1.6.1.2 Priests and Prophets 27
    1.6.2 The Nature of Divine Communication in Worship . 29
        1.6.2.1 Definition of Prophecy 29

      1.6.2.2   Identity and Role of the Functionaries............33
   1.6.3   Post-exilic Cultic Prophecy 34
      1.6.3.1   Prophetic Continuity......................................34
      1.6.3.2   Chronicles 35
1.7   Conclusion and Direction of Study............................37

Chapter 2 Assyrian Cultic Prophecy....................... 40

2.1   Introduction 40
2.2   The Use of Assyrian Prophecy in Old Testament Studies...41
   2.2.1   Definition of Prophecy 41
   2.2.2   True and False Prophecy 41
   2.2.3   Incorporation of Prophetic Material in the OT 43
   2.2.4   Assyrian Prophecy and Second Isaiah 44
   2.2.5   Imagery 46
   2.2.6   Holy War...46
   2.2.7   Kingship Ideology and Covenant 47
   2.2.8   Monotheism...50
   2.2.9   Social Location of OT Prophets............................51
   2.2.10   Summary..52
2.3   The Relationship of Assyrian Prophets to the Temple...53
   2.3.1   Messengers of Ištar...53
   2.3.2   Located at Cult Centres..54
   2.3.3   Cultic Demands by Prophets 56
   2.3.4   Prophets as Temple Personnel..............................57
   2.3.5   Prophecy Outside of the Neo-Assyrian Context......58
   2.3.6   Language of the Prophecies 60
   2.3.7   Summary..60
2.4   The Function of Assyrian Prophecy 61
   2.4.1   Royal Affairs 61
   2.4.2   Cultic Service 62
   2.4.3   Prophetic Response to Inquiry and Lament...........62
   2.4.4   Prophetic Response to Inquiry in Assyrian Sources 65
   2.4.5   Prophetic Response to Lament in Assyrian Sources 66
      2.4.5.1   References to Lament within Oracles..............66
      2.4.5.2   Narrative References to Prophecy as a Response to Lament 68

2.4.5.3   Intertextual Link Between a Lament and a
         Prophetic Message 70
  2.4.6   Summary 74
2.5 Conclusion 75

Chapter 3 Royal Psalms 76
3.1 Introduction 76
3.2 Psalm 110 76
  3.2.1   Authenticity of Prophetic Speech 76
  3.2.2   Formal Unity of the Psalm as a Prophetic Oracle .. 80
  3.2.3   Cultic Setting of Psalm 110 82
    3.2.3.1   OT Cultic Enthronement Ritual 83
    3.2.3.2   Ancient Near Eastern Counterparts 83
  3.2.4   Date of the Psalm 86
  3.2.5   Conclusion 88
3.3 Psalm 2 89
  3.3.1   Authenticity of Prophetic Speech in Psalm 2 89
  3.3.2   Cultic Setting 95
    3.3.2.1   OT Cultic Enthronement Ritual 96
    3.3.2.2   Ancient Near Eastern Counterparts 96
  3.3.3   Date of the Psalm 98
  3.3.4   Conclusion 101
3.4 Psalm 132 101
  3.4.1   Authenticity of Prophetic Speech 101
  3.4.2   Cultic Prophecy in Psalm 132 103
  3.4.3   Limits and Unity of the Oracle 105
  3.4.4   Specific Cultic Setting 109
  3.4.5   Date of the Psalm 112
  3.4.6   Conclusion 114
3.5 Psalm 89 115
  3.5.1   Authenticity of Prophetic Material 115
  3.5.2   Relationship of Oracular Material to the
          Literary Context and Cultic Setting 117
  3.5.3   Conclusion 126
3.6 Conclusion 127

Chapter 4 Asaphite Psalms 128
4.1 Prophetic Tradition of the Asaphite Psalms 128
  4.1.1   Introduction 128

4.1.2 Asaphite Psalms Preserve Genuine Prophetic
    Speech..129
    4.1.2.1 Jörg Jeremias 129
    4.1.2.2 Pieter Schelling..134
    4.1.2.3 Harry P. Nasuti...134
    4.1.2.4 Michael Goulder 140
    4.1.2.5 Beat Weber 141
4.1.3 Asaphite Psalms Imitate Prophetic Style.............143
    4.1.3.1 Hermann Spieckermann..............................143
    4.1.3.2 Klaus Seybold 143
    4.1.3.3 Frank-Lothar Hossfeld.................................146
4.1.4 Conclusion 149
4.2 The Asaphite Psalms in the Light of Assyrian
    Prophetic Sources 150
    4.2.1 Introduction 150
    4.2.2 Psalm 81 150
        4.2.2.1 Psalm 81 as Cultic Prophecy 150
        4.2.2.2 Psalm 81 as Prophetic Imitation or Sermon..151
        4.2.2.3 Evaluation 154
        4.2.2.4 Conclusion...161
    4.2.3 Psalm 50 162
        4.2.3.1 Psalm 50 as Cultic Prophecy 162
        4.2.3.2 Psalm 50 as Prophetic Imitation or Sermon..162
        4.2.3.3 Evaluation 164
        4.2.3.4 Conclusion...166
    4.2.4 Psalm 75 167
        4.2.4.1 Psalm 75 as Cultic Prophecy 167
        4.2.4.2 Psalm 75 as Sermonic Adaptation of
            Prophetic Style..168
        4.2.4.3 Evaluation 169
        4.2.4.4 Conclusion...174
    4.2.5 Psalm 82 174
        4.2.5.1 Psalm 82 as Cultic Prophecy 174
        4.2.5.2 Psalm 82 as Prophetic Imitation or
            "Scribal Prophecy" 175
        4.2.5.3 Evaluation 177
        4.2.5.4 Conclusion...178
    4.2.6 Psalm 95 179
        4.2.6.1 Psalm 95 as Cultic Prophecy 179
        4.2.6.2 Psalm 95 as Prophetic Imitation or Sermon..180
        4.2.6.3 Evaluation 181

        4.2.6.4   Conclusion..184
    4.2.7   Conclusion 184

Chapter 5 Laments, Hymns and Songs of Confidence.. 186
  5.1   Introduction 186
  5.2   Psalm 12 186
    5.2.1   Psalm 12 as Cultic Prophecy 186
    5.2.2   Psalm 12 as Poetic Citation of a Divine Saying....189
    5.2.3   Evaluation 190
    5.2.4   Conclusion 192
  5.3   Psalms 60 and 108 192
    5.3.1   The Question of Intertextuality..........................192
    5.3.2   Psalm 60 as Cultic Prophecy 193
    5.3.3   Psalm 60 as Poetic Rhetoric 194
    5.3.4   Evaluation 196
    5.3.5   Conclusion 201
  5.4   Psalm 91 203
    5.4.1   Psalm 91 as Cultic Prophecy 203
    5.4.2   Psalm 91 as Didactic Style 204
    5.4.3   Evaluation 205
    5.4.4   Conclusion 209
  5.5   Psalm 68 209
    5.5.1   Psalm 68 Contains Cultic Prophecy...................209
    5.5.2   Psalm 68 as Poetic Adaptation 210
    5.5.3   Evaluation 211
    5.5.4   Conclusion 213
  5.6   Psalm 46 213
  5.7   Psalm 87 214
  5.8   Other Psalms 215
    5.8.1   Psalm 14 (53)...215
    5.8.2   Psalm 27 215
    5.8.3   Psalm 62 216
    5.8.4   Psalm 101 216
    5.8.5   Psalm 105 216
  5.9   Conclusion 216

Chapter 6 Conclusion... 218
  6.1   The Central Question 218
  6.2   Cultic Functions of Assyrian Prophets and the OT.....218

6.3 Comparison of Assyrian Prophecies and Psalms 219
6.4 Psalm Composition and Performance 221
6.5 Diachronic Continuity of Cultic Prophecy 225
6.6 Cultic Prophecy in the Psalms 225

Bibliography 227

Index of Texts 252

Index of Authors 265

Abbreviations

AfO	*Archiv für Orientforschung*
AOAT	Alter Orient und Altes Testament
ARM	Archives royales de Mari
ATD	Das Alte Testament Deutsch
BA	*Biblical Archaeologist*
BBR	*Bulletin for Biblical Research*
BHS	*Biblia Hebraica Stuttgartensia*
Bib	*Biblica*
BKAT	Biblischer Kommentar Altes Testament
BN	*Biblische Notizen*
BO	Bibliotheca orientalis
BZAW	Beiheft zur Zeitschrift für die alttestamentliche Wissenschaft
CAD	*The Assyrian Dictionary of the Oriental Institute of the University of Chicago*
CBQ	*The Catholic Biblical Quarterly*
ConBOT	Coniectanea Biblica: Old Testament Series
DJD	*Discoveries in the Judaean Desert*
EA	The Amarna Letters
ExpTim	*Expository Times*
FB	Forschung zur Bibel
FOTL	The Forms of the Old Testament Literature
FRLANT	Forschungen zur Religion und Literatur des Alten und Neuen Testaments
GAG	*Grundriss der akkadischen Grammatik*
HAL	*The Hebrew and Aramaic Lexicon of the Old Testament*
HAT	Handbuch zum Alten Testament
HBS	Herders Biblische Studien
HTKAT	Herders theologischer Kommentar zum Alten Testament
HTR	*Harvard Theological Review*
ICC	International Critical Commentary
JAOS	*Journal of the American Oriental Society*
JBL	*Journal of Biblical Literature*
JCS	*Journal of Cuneiform Studies*

JNES	*Journal of Near Eastern Studies*
JQR	*Jewish Quarterly Review*
JSOT	*Journal for the Study of the Old Testament*
JSOTSup	Journal for the Study of the Old Testament Supplement Series
JSSEA	*Journal of the Society for the Study of Egyptian Antiquities*
LXX	Septuagint
MARI	*Mari: Annales de recherches interdisciplinaires*
MT	Masoretic Text
NCB	New Century Bible
NEchtBAT	Die Neue Echter Bibel Altes Testament
Or	*Orientalia*
OTL	Old Testament Library
OT	Old Testament
RA	*Revue d'assyriologie et d'archéologie orientale*
RB	*Revue Biblique*
RHR	*Revue de l'Histoire des Religions*
SAA	State Archives of Assyria
SAAS	State Archives of Assyria Studies
SBLDS	Society of Biblical Literature Dissertation Series
SBLMS	Society of Biblical Literature Monograph Series
SBLSS	Society of Biblical Literature Symposium Series
SBS	Stuttgarter Bibelstudien
TLZ	*Theologische Literaturzeitung*
VT	*Vetus Testamentum*
VTSup	Supplements to Vetus Testamentum
WBC	Word Biblical Commentary
WMANT	Wissenschaftliche Monographien zum Alten und Neuen Testament
ZAW	*Zeitschrift für die Alttestamentliche Wissenschaft*

Chapter 1
Cultic Prophecy in the Psalms: Issues Past and Present

1.1 Introduction

Since the classic debate between Mowinckel and Gunkel in the early twentieth century, no consensus has been reached on key questions regarding cultic prophecy or its relationship to the Book of Psalms. Recent research into Assyrian prophetic sources provides fresh evidence relevant to this debate, particularly in reference to the preservation of cultic prophecy in psalms. Before examination of the Assyrian sources (Chapter 2) and their application to selected psalms (Chapters 3-5), this chapter surveys the history of scholarship on the subject of cultic prophecy in the OT in order to clarify key issues for this study.

1.2 Early Discussions

The closing decades of the nineteenth century witnessed the onset of modern OT scholarship (Clements 1976: 1); and therefore, this period offers a good starting point for discussion. At the turn of the twentieth century, some commentators affirmed that prophetic speech in the cult was preserved in certain psalms. For example, Delitzsch (1902: 301, 455) argued that in Pss 68:23 and 81:6 the psalmist repeats a divine utterance he prophetically heard (which is subsequently delivered in the cult).[1] Kirkpatrick (1898: 390, 491) also suggested a prophetic phenomenon as one possible explanation for both of these passages,

---

1   Cf. Delitzsch (1894: 8-9, 12, 244-45).

but he held that an older oracle might be cited in some cases (e.g., Ps 68:23). About this same time, other scholars proposed different phenomena to explain what appear to be oracular elements in the psalms. While Hölscher (1914: 143-44, 355) maintained that ecstatic prophets served in the sanctuary under the supervision of the priests and that occasionally a priest emerged as a prophet, he also thought that the appearance of divine speech in psalms was a poetic imitation of prophetic forms (e.g., Pss 2:7-9, 60:8, 68:23, 110:1, Hölscher 1914: 356).[2] In his view, this accords with 1 Chr 25:1-3 where the term "prophesy" is employed to describe the enthusiastic performance of music in a fashion similar to that imagined for older prophetic tradition. Küchler (1918: 285-86, 298-99), who argued that the original function of priests was purely oracular, proposed that instances of divine speech in the psalms stemmed from oracles of divination (e.g., Ps 12:6; 60:7; 75:3; 81:7; 95:8).[3] While Psalm 110 presents itself as prophetic speech, he saw this as an instance of a poet using the form of prophetic speech (Küchler 1918: 299).

Gunkel proposed a similar imitative process for the appearance of divine speech in psalms. In the initial presentation of his form-critical method in Psalms, Gunkel (1913: col. 1933) observed that in the performance of some hymns, a priest might speak words as though Yahweh himself were announcing his own majesty. In songs of lament, the sudden occurrence of the "certainty of a hearing" attests to a divine answer to prayer through the mouth of a priest (Gunkel 1913: col. 1935). However, as is evident from his earlier commentary on selected psalms, Gunkel thought of prophetic elements in the psalms more in terms of imitation of prophetic style than genuine prophetic speech. Writing on Psalm 2, Gunkel (1904: 7) stated that the poet had "taken over this very spectacular prophetic-lyrical genre"; and he called these psalms with prophetic content and form an "imitation of grandiose prophetic visions". Thus, the psalm is only a "reverberation of prophecy in form and content"

---

[2] This interpretation of divine speeches had its mid-nineteenth century antecedent in Hupfeld (1888: 22), who regarded such divine speeches in psalms as poetic fiction.

[3] Duhm (1899: 178) entertained the possibility that Ps 60:8-10 resulted from extispicy, and Delitzsch (1902: 224) thought that the Urim and Thummim might have been the source of Ps 60:8-10.

(Gunkel 1904: 13). The elaboration of Gunkel's view would find expression later in his full commentary and introduction to the Book of Psalms (Gunkel 1926; 1933); but prior to the publication of these works, Sigmund Mowinckel published his studies on the psalms advocating a different approach.

1.3 Mowinckel and Gunkel: Classic Formulation of the Debate

1.3.1 Sigmund Mowinckel (*Psalmenstudien*)

In contrast to Gunkel's model whereby psalmists imitated prophetic style, Mowinckel argued that prophets played a significant role in the cult of ancient Israel and that their oracular speech is preserved in some of the psalms. He criticised Gunkel for stopping short of a full model of cultic prophecy and allowing only a priestly answer to prayer signalled in psalms by the certainty of being heard. Furthermore, Mowinckel attributed Gunkel's position to the older Wellhausenian view that the psalms were non-cultic, individual outpourings of piety (Mowinckel 1922: 2; 1924: 28). In Mowinckel's opinion, the reverse is true, that psalms originated in a cultic context in connection with sacrificial ritual; and only later, after inscripturation, did these psalms become detached from the cult and privatised (Mowinckel 1922: 2-4). He sought to prove that the prophetic form of certain psalms corresponded to cultic reality and that these psalms came from permanent cultic servants with recognized prophetic gifts (Mowinckel 1922: 3; 1924: 37). The fact that OT psalms often looked in form and style like words of prophetic scripture *might* be explained as literary borrowing; but, in Mowinckel's view, a more satisfying explanation was to be found in cultic prophecy (Mowinckel 1922: 1; 1924: 32, 50).

Mowinckel began his argument by relating revelation to the cult and defining what he means by "prophet". He noted that frequently in the literature of his time prophecy and cult are juxtaposed in an antithetical way; and that it is the priest with his Urim and Thummim that is associated with revelation in a cultic context. However, "prophet", in his view, is anyone who stands ready to respond to inquiries about the divine will by virtue of his power to mediate revelation (Mowinckel 1922: 5). For ancient Israel, priest or cult prophet might serve as sacramental mediators; at times they may be one and the same person. However, the personal qualification for the office of cult prophet is having been vested with the power of inspiration which differentiates him from the laity and ordinary priests (Mowinckel 1922: 6-7).

Mowinckel (1922: 9-12) saw an original unity between priest and seer, dual terms emphasising different aspects of the same office (e.g., Samuel). Originally a Canaanite functionary, the prophet gradually took over the role of inspired mediator whereas revelation by technical divination remained the function of the priest (Mowinckel 1922: 15; 1924: 37-38). Yet, priests continued to function in a prophetic way. Not only were some priests prophetically gifted, but as bearers of revelation through technical divination, priests might on occasion answer questions in a way that is richer than the simple binary form (e.g., 2 Sam 5:23-24, Mowinckel 1922: 13). Mowinckel (1922: 17-21) argued for a close association of prophets with cultic acts and sanctuaries. Prophets are active in festival and cultic acts (1 Kgs 18:16-39). The first mention of a prophetic band describes them coming from a high place (1 Sam 10:5) and prophetic organisations had their locus at cultic centres (Ramah, 1 Sam 19:19; Bethel, 2 Kgs 2:3; Jericho, 2 Kgs 2:5; Gilgal, 2 Kgs 4:38). Balaam utilised sacrifice in conjunction with prophesying (Num 23:1, 14, 29). Numerous times prophets are linked with priests (Isa 28:7; Jer 4:9; 6:13; 14:18; 18:18; Mic 3:11; Zech 7:3); and served under the oversight of priests (Jer 29:26), an observation which Mowinckel believed made the institution of temple prophet unquestionable. Jeremiah and Ezekiel were both priest and prophet (Jer 1:1; Ezek 1:3). Regarding 1 Chr 15:22 and 27, Mowinckel chose the view that משא means "oracle", thus indicating an office of one who supervised the prophetic performance of the Levitical singers. This link between ecstasy and singing, he argued, was natural (1 Sam 10:5, 2 Kgs 3:15, Ps 49:5, 2 Chronicles 20, Mowinckel 1924: 49), as was the compatibility between poetic expression and prophecy (Mowinckel 1922: 25-27), especially since Habakkuk and Joel combined prophetic and poetic style in the service of cultic events (Mowinckel 1922: 27-29).

Mowinckel (1922: 7) suggested two primary models whereby prophetic speech might have appeared in liturgical practice. First, the prophet's appearance is set by liturgy, but the content and form of speech is left to the moment of inspiration. Second, the content of the words are fixed in advance, but the rhetorical power in worship (style and form of words) is the product of free inspiration. Mowinckel allowed for a fluid transfer between these two models; however, he thought that when dealing with cult psalms, the second model is most likely involved, especially since these psalms pertain to repeated liturgy. On occasion a third model of the process from spontaneous prophecy to written psalm may apply. In this third type, spontaneous inspiration might have produced an oracle that was so exemplary that it came into written form and was performed on subsequent occasions (e.g., Psalm 60 and most royal psalms) (Mcwinckel 1922: 7-8). He maintained that in the case of a textually prescribed prophecy (the second model and most frequent type), the origin of the psalm from inspiration prior to its performance in the cultic celebration does not nullify its value to the community as genuine prophecy (Mowinckel 1922: 8). Mowinckel's application of these models to specific psalms will be considered in later chapters.

Mowinckel (1922: 21-22) was reluctant to say how early the institution of cultic prophecy became extinct. He suggested genuine, post-exilic temple prophets in Haggai, Zechariah and Joel, and maintained that prophets were resident in the temple at the time of Nehemiah (Neh 6:10-12). By Maccabean times there were no longer institutional cult prophets (1 Macc 14:41). Therefore, by degrees in post-exilic times, cult prophets must have disappeared, having merged with Levitical singers who became merely performers of once inspired and long since fixed prophetic psalms.

1.3.2 Hermann Gunkel

Although Gunkel himself wrote only the first part of the chapter on prophecy in the psalms in his *Einleitung in die Psalmen* (§ 9), Gunkel's student, Joachim Begrich, had an outline, notes and personal guidance from his mentor for completion of the chapter

(Gunkel and Begrich 1933: 5*). While it is no longer possible to disentangle any fresh contribution that Begrich may have made, it is substantially the work of Gunkel (cf. Klatt 1969: 252). As in his earlier work on Psalms, Gunkel's arguments concentrated on the *influences* of prophetic speech on the liturgy. Psalms are "prophetic" which make use of the form and contents of the prophets or depend on them (Gunkel and Begrich 1933: 329). That this excludes prophetic speech originating in the cult and refers to *imitation* of prophetic speech in liturgical composition becomes clear in his ensuing discussion. While Gunkel accepted the place of technical divination in worship by priests, he emphatically denied the existence of cult prophets and was particularly critical of Mowinckel.

The most extensive prophetic influence on the psalms, in Gunkel's view, is thematic, particularly eschatological hope in hymns (Gunkel and Begrich 1933: 330).[4] He also found similar passages with eschatological thought and prophetic forms in individual and community complaint songs, especially in connection with the certainty of being heard (Gunkel and Begrich 1933: 346-47). At the turning point of mood in these psalms, prophetic elements were incorporated (Gunkel and Begrich 1933: 347, 351). The certainty of being heard increases to the assurance of a prophetic proclamation, even taking the same prophetic form, content and claim (e.g., Ps 102:14, 16-19, Gunkel and Begrich 1933: 352-53). If prophetic joy in the psalms approaches prophetic prediction, then it is not strange that the last step be taken so that a prophetic form itself, the oracle, finds entry into the psalm poetry (Gunkel and Begrich 1933: 357-58). Thus, the hymn and those genres which share in the same joyful mood adopted the eschatological faith and style of the prophets (Gunkel and Begrich 1933: 354). Since numerous phrases and ideas in the psalms presuppose, and depend upon, prophetic expectation (Gunkel and Begrich 1933: 358-60), Gunkel argued against Mowinckel's view that psalmody (specifically enthronement psalms) was the place in which eschatology originated and from which the prophets gained influence

---

4   For textual citations illustrating the verbal (i.e., content) links between psalms and prophets, see Gunkel's footnotes (1933: 334-43). For form-critical similarities, see pages 344-46.

(Gunkel and Begrich 1933: 360 n. 6). While not comparable to the influence of eschatology, other prophetic genres show influence on the psalms, such as rebuke (e.g., Pss 50:16-20; 53:1-6; 81:9-12), threat (e.g., Pss 53:6; 95), judgment speeches mixed with other forms (e.g., Psalms 50; 82), prophetic *tôrah* (e.g., Ps 50:14-15, 22-23) and admonition (Pss 81:14; 82 3-4; 95:8-11) (Gunkel and Begrich 1933: 361). However, the passionate rebuke characteristic of eighth- and seventh-century prophets is absent, perhaps consistent with the relatively milder rebuke of post-exilic judgment prophets whom, Gunkel argued, the psalmists imitated (Gunkel and Begrich 1933: 364-66).

Gunkel questioned the appearance of a prophetic speaker in the context of the psalm and the performance of the prophetic word in the cult (Gunkel and Begrich 1933: 368, 370). Because Mowinckel defined "prophecy" with such breadth that priest and prophet are indistinguishable, Gunkel argued that he created a place in the cult for prophets where none actually exists. Gunkel then proceeded to examine the textual sources that Mowinckel cites in support of cultic prophecy (Gunkel and Begrich 1933: 371-72). For Gunkel, 1 Kings 18 only describes the activity of Baal priests whose frenzied behaviour might be characteristic of prophets but whose function was merely sacrificial. The fact that prophets speak at holy sites does not establish their cultic duties; rather, their presence is due to the fact that at a cultic site a prophet was assured of an audience (Gunkel and Begrich 1933: 372).[5] Indeed, the juxtaposition of prophets and priests in Mic 3:11 and Jer 18:18 makes it clear that the common link between the two is *not* cultic, since judges and counsellors are mentioned alongside prophets and priests without the implication that these are cultic officials as well (Gunkel and Begrich 1933: 372-73). Against Mowinckel, who states that Jer 29:26 "unquestionably" establishes the existence of temple prophets, Gunkel observed that the text only affirms that priests were responsible to assure that antagonistic prophets like Jeremiah would be locked up in order to maintain order in temple worship. Gunkel also argued that taking מַשָּׂא in 1 Chronicles 15 as "oracle concerns" based upon the Levitical association with the

---

5   1 Sam 10:5; 19:19; 1 Kgs 18:16; Jeremiah 26; 28; 36; 1 Kings 22; 2 Kgs 3:15; 4:38; Ezek 8:1-3; 11:1, 24.

ark is highly questionable. The priestly descent of Jeremiah and Ezekiel is not certain, and 2 Chronicles 20 merely shows prophetic influence on the post-exilic cult. Gunkel concluded that, on the whole, Mowinckel's argument for cult prophets is very problematic (Gunkel and Begrich 1933: 373).

As an alternative, Gunkel (1933: 373-74) proposed how "cult-free" judgment prophets came to influence the worship service. Since the speech forms found in the mixed liturgies are not identical with that of the judgment prophets, they appear to signal a new element in cultic poetry. After history vindicated the ancient prophetic proclamation of judgment, the cult became open to prophetic content and forms. The content of prophetic speech was easier to adopt than the forms. However, the rhetoric of prophetic rebuke and threat proved useful to priestly exhortation. Gunkel proposed that the priest, who was responsible for articulating the results of the oracle of divination, would also be the one to take up existing prophetic speech forms and employ them in liturgical context. Levitical singers could perform these liturgies as well. But Gunkel explicitly ruled out the prophet, arguing that the prophets' "free inspiration of the moment" (as well as ecstatic behaviour) would preclude them from participating in the more fixed, ritual forms of the cult. Gunkel added that the prophetic psalms were designed for repeat performance, necessitating a fixed content. Citing Mowinckel, Gunkel underscored that if the prophet only contributed the initial wording of the oracle, in the performance there is little that is distinctively prophetic (Gunkel and Begrich 1933: 374-75).

Gunkel's opposition to *prophetic* speech in the psalms may have softened somewhat between the publication of his earlier works on Psalms (Gunkel 1904; 1913) and his later commentary.[6] For example, he considered Ps 60:8-10 as originating from either a priest or "prophet" (Gunkel 1926: 257). Nevertheless,

---

6   Booij (1978: 12, 271 n. 68) notes that Gunkel's later treatment of psalms (e.g., Psalms 91, 95 and 121) shows a greater inclination to connect "prophetic" psalms directly with the cult. This is true of Gunkel's view of psalms and the cult more generally (cf. Klatt 1969: 257). However, in his 1926 commentary, Gunkel still regarded the oracle in Psalms 91 and 121 as a *priestly* announcement and the divine speech in Psalm 95 as an imitation of prophetic style (Gunkel 1926: 405, 419, 540).

his fundamental position against cultic prophets, as non-priestly functionaries in the cult, seems not to have changed and he continued to emphasise the imitative nature of prophetic elements in the psalms.

1.3.3 Aubrey R. Johnson

The next major contribution on the issue of cultic prophecy was that of Aubrey Johnson (1935/36; 1962, monograph first published 1944), who expanded Mowinckel's arguments and articulated them perhaps with more force. He argued that in addition to priests, seers and prophets were also associated with cultic shrines. Originally, the seer was more akin to a Babylonian *bārû*, who maintained control of his faculties (Johnson 1962: 10, 15), while the prophet was an ecstatic whose behaviour was induced through music (Johnson 1962); but eventually the two terms merged.[7] Like the priest and seer, the prophet is found in close association with cult and sanctuary (Johnson 1962: 25-27: cultic feast, 2 Kgs 4:23, sacred tent, Num 11:24-30, Saul and company descending from a high place, 1 Sam 10:5, Samuel's home at Shiloh, 1 Sam 3:21, an altar, 1 Kgs 19:10).

Johnson maintained that the canonical prophets never condemned the function of cultic prophecy, *per se*, but spoke against the abuses of the office of cult prophet and false oracles (Johnson 1962: 30-31); and the relationship of the canonical prophets themselves and the cult is affirmed in Jer 26:7. Coupled with the frequent pairing of priest and prophet,[8] he thought this passage was conclusive evidence that prophets, as much as priests, were officially connected to the cult (Johnson 1962: 61). Other passages supporting this association include Jer 23:11; 35:4 (guild rooms); 29:26 and Jer 27:16, where "your prophets" implies that they enjoyed official status. Priests and prophets alike were slain when the temple was destroyed (Lam 2:20). In the post-exilic period, Haggai and Zechariah were likely proph-

---

[7] He found a significant link between divination (קסם) and the functions of prophets, arguing that divination was one means for obtaining oracles (Johnson 1962: 31, Mic 3:5-7).

[8] Cf. Hos 4:4; Isa 28:7; Jer 6:13; 8:10; 14:18; Lam 4:13; as well as Jer 4:9; 8:1; 13:13; Mic 3:11 and Zeph 3:4.

ets with official connection to the cult. Zechariah spoke of a close connection between the two (Zech 7:1-3) (Johnson 1962: 65-55). However, the failures of the "peace" prophets in the pre-exilic community, coupled with the rise in power of the priesthood, led to the loss of prestige of the cult prophet. Hence, they eventually became merged in a subordinate position to the Aaronitic priests with the rest of the Levites as merely temple singers (Johnson 1962: 66-74).

1.3.4 Alfred Haldar

At the same time as the original publication of Johnson's monograph, Haldar contributed a monograph that focused on comparative Semitic sources in the discussion of cultic prophecy in the OT (Haldar 1945). After studying the various titles and functions of cultic officials in Mesopotamian and in extra-biblical Northwest Semitic texts available at his time, he concluded that ancient Near Eastern religion manifested two general types of oracular officials in the cult: those responsible for technical divination (bārû) and those whose primary function pertained to ecstatic revelation (maḫḫû) (Haldar 1945: 34, 89).[9] Haldar did not differentiate between the terms "priest" and "prophet", and the difference between the bārû class priest and the maḫḫû was more the degree of specialisation than a clear distinction of office (Haldar 1945: 31, 63). Regarding the OT "prophet", he stated that נביא "denotes a cultic functionary whose 'specialty' is ecstasy" equivalent to the maḫḫû (Haldar 1945: 108-109, 114). Thus, despite religious differences, "divinatory associations display a fundamentally homogeneous phenomenology" across the ancient Near East, with prophets holding official functions in the cult (Haldar 1945: 199).[10]

---

9 Haldar cited the Neo-Assyrian prophetic oracle K 4310 as an evidence of a maḫḫû type priest-prophet (Haldar 1945: 24). A priestly equation is not maintained today; however, he is correct in recognising that this oracle represents prophetic speech from a cult prophet.
10 While Haldar was appreciated by contemporaries for helping to dispel the notion that prophets were necessarily opposed to the cult, he was also criticised for going beyond the evidence and for disregarding Israel's religious

1.3.5 Sigmund Mowinckel (*The Psalms in Israel's Worship*)

Subsequent to the studies summarised above, Mowinckel published *Offersang og Sangoffer* (Mowinckel 1951)[11] in which he offered brief comments regarding the contributions of Gunkel, Begrich, Johnson and Haldar. As one might expect, he cited Johnson numerous times alongside his own earlier work (e.g., Mowinckel 1962a: 63 n. 81; 1962b: 54 n. 8, 56 n. 20, 63 n. 41), but he regarded Haldar's treatment as unsatisfying and too adapted to the Babylonian phenomena (Mowinckel 1962b: 56 n. 20). He dismissed Gunkel's and Begrich's criticisms as irrelevant polemics that do not take the texts themselves adequately into account (Mowinckel 1962b: 56 n. 20); and he described Begrich's priestly salvation oracle (Begrich 1934) as clearly prophetic in style without anything "priestly" in style or substance (i.e., *tôrah*, Mowinckel 1962b: 58 n. 28). His general methodological criticism of Gunkel centred on the relationship between psalm composition and cult. In Mowinckel's view, Gunkel departed from his own method when he proposed that psalms are private imitations of the cult (or prophets), with the result that Gunkel went only "half-way" in locating the origin of psalms in the cult (Mowinckel 1962a: 14, 29, 31). Examples such as Pss 81:6 and 85:9 are genuine cultic forms of prophets, not private imitations (Mowinckel 1962b: 60-61). Indeed, the moral emphasis in the cult (e.g., Psalms 15, 24) prepared the ground for the reform prophets more than the rebukes of the reform prophets influenced the prophetic admonition in the cult, as Gunkel had argued (Mowinckel 1962b: 69-70, esp. 69 n. 52).[12]

---

distinctives, Haldar's token disclaimer notwithstanding (cf. Eissfeldt 1948: col. 154; Rowley 1967: 156).
11 Translated into English as *The Psalms in Israel's Worship* (Mowinckel 1962a; 1962b).
12 A similar counter to Gunkel was expressed by Würthwein (1952), who argued that judgment speeches by cultic functionaries (e.g., Psalms 50, 75, 82) based upon covenant law gave rise to the form used by the classical prophets.

1.4 Mid-Century Debate: Lack of a Consensus

Numerous mid-twentieth century scholars wrote in support of the notion of cult prophets or with the presupposition that cultic prophecy existed.[13] Some were predisposed to accept the contribution of prophets at shrines, but were reluctant to accept the existence of prophets as permanent cult personnel. For example, Rowley (1945: 16) observed that it is natural to find prophets, as religious persons, at shrines; but that presence does not make them members of the cultic staff.[14] Porteous (1950-51: 6-7) stressed the same point; and citing Haldar (1945: 199), he argued that the overlap of functions between priests and prophets points to the lack of a distinct class of prophetic personnel (Porteous 1950-51: 8).[15]

Other voices were less positive. Speaking of the evidence mustered by Johnson, Robert (1953: 222) stated that the "hy-

---

13 E.g., G. von Rad (1933: 113-117, wishing to explain the institutional and theological identity of the false prophets, he proposed that the prophetic function was first one of intercession — an idea he wished to add to Mowinckel's discussion, and so institutional prophecy developed within the cult to attend to the national needs for intercession); O. Eissfeldt (1934: 75-76, prophets served together alongside priests in the cult); J. Pedersen (1940: 117, prophets constituted a stable part of the temple staff); R. B. Y. Scott (1944: 43, association of the "great prophets" with the cult was exceptional, but "bodies of 'official prophets'" were common in the cult from early times down to the seventh century); O. Plöger (1951: 177-78, prophets were active in the cult but not as institutional officials); F. Hesse (1953: 52, he approved of studies such as Johnson's that drew attention to the important role of prophets in the cult, but he opposed levelling out distinctions between cult prophets and the classical prophets).

14 Rowley cites personal communication with A. R. Johnson in which Johnson expressed the opinion that cult prophets should *not* be thought of as resident at the shrines (Rowley 1945: 15 n. 81). In this statement, Johnson retreats from his wording that prophets were "stationed" at shrines (Johnson 1935/36: 315).

15 It seems that Porteous misrepresents Mowinckel on this point as insisting on a separate class of prophets that *excludes* priests. In fact, Mowinckel's model allowed for *some* priests to be gifted for inspired speech and thereby be justifiably regarded as "prophets" (Mowinckel 1922: 6-7). Mowinckel himself uses some of the same comparative sources discussed by Haldar to argue that the priest and prophet were at times one and the same (Mowinckel 1922: 11). Strictly speaking, in Mowinckel's view, it is the mode of revelation that distinguishes the diviner-priest and the freely-inspired prophet, not the presence or absence of hereditary distinctives between priests and laity.

pothesis of cultic prophets is absolutely gratuitous". Rendtorff (1959: 802-03, 806) concluded that, at most, one might say there was not a hostile relationship between early Israelite prophets and the cult, but that no firm conclusions could be drawn from the close relationship implied in the numerous texts associating prophets and priests.[16]

Perhaps the strongest statement since Gunkel *against* cultic prophecy came from Quell (1956), who wrote to warn against assuming that cultic prophecy was an established fact. He thought that Gunkel's account of prophetic elements in the psalms was adequate, that Mowinckel's proposal of cult prophets was not justified by the evidence, and that Mowinckel added an unnecessary and confusing element to a historical understanding of cultic practice. In his opinion, Johnson's resort to the use of evidence from comparative cultures was an implicit demonstration that the case for cult prophets *within* the OT was weak. Quell maintained that any thesis proposing prophets as cultic officials was incompatible with the fundamental OT concept of a prophet. The most that was necessary, in his opinion, was that a prophetic word be brought to the sanctuary and scripted as part of the liturgy. This process was more consistent with the likely practices behind the performance of a psalm, such as Psalm 60, which shows evidence of an orchestrated interplay between several parties. The person reciting the divine word in the performance only "mimics" a prophetic function.

In spite of these objections, it appears that by the 1960s many scholars worked from a model of prophecy that included some degree of prophetic activity in the cult. Lindblom (1962: 80) wrote that as a result of Mowinckel's work "there can be little doubt that prophets belonged to the permanent staff of the Jerusalem temple" and contributed the prophetic psalms in the Psalter.[17] Clements (1965: 20-21) maintained that from the earliest days of Israel's worship prophets delivered their oracles in

---

16 Continued scepticism is expressed in *The Old Testament: An Introduction* (Rendtorff 1985: 120).
17 He is also explicit about the institutional source of support for cultic prophets: "There was a special class of 'cultic prophets' in the strict sense, prophets who were more firmly attached to the sanctuaries as members of the ordinary cultic staff, who received their maintenance from the sanctuary, like the priests and other cultic functionaries" (Lindblom 1962: 206).

the sanctuaries, many were permanent functionaries of the cult, and their work can be found in the Psalter. Kraus (1966: 101) confidently asserted that the role of cultic prophets "can no longer be doubted" and that divine speech in the psalms might come through a cult prophet (e.g., Ps 12:6, Kraus 1961: 94).[18] Ringgren similarly considered the existence of cult prophets to be "established", but he preferred to call the functionaries "prophetic priests" and their oracles *"priestly* salvation oracles" (italics his) (Ringgren 1966: 212, 217-18).

But some doubt continued within the field. Writing twenty years after his initial work on the subject, Rowley continued to emphasise that the notion of cult prophets is only a "theory" to which the evidence points (Rowley 1963: 130).[19] He criticised the absolute confidence in the theory expressed by scholars such as Kraus, and he noted that there are still some who question the notion of cult prophets (Rowley 1967: 153).[20] With similar cau-

---

18   Kraus also allowed that the divine speech in this psalm might have come through a priestly voice (after the manner of Begrich's theory of priestly salvation oracles). However, in the revised edition of his commentary, Kraus asserted even more strongly the participation of cult prophets, viewing the entire psalm as the word of a cult prophet (Kraus 1978a: 235)

19   More positively he does state later in the essay, "The view that there were cultic prophets rests not on *a priori* ideas, and forcing of foreign practices on the Old Testament, but on evidence that lies within the Old Testament" (Rowley 1963: 136).

20   In addition to the classic denial by Gunkel and Begrich (1933), Rowley cites Eerdmans (1947: 141), Quell (1956), de Vaux (1961: 384), Motyer (1962: 1042-43) and Klein (1963) among others. It is fair to say that these scholars regard cult prophecy as at best speculative. However, Rowley's use of Vriezen (1958) and Eichrodt (1961) in this regard needs qualification. Vriezen is somewhat inconsistent in his evaluation of the place of prophets. On the one hand, he explicitly rejects the view that prophets had an official function in the cult (citing Johnson in his footnotes as an example of this position) (Vriezen 1958: 261 n. 1). On the other hand, in the same footnote he cites with approval the positions of Rowley and Lindblom, both of whom support a moderate view of prophetic function in the cult. This seems to remove Vriezen from the list of those who categorically deny the existence of cult prophets. Furthermore, Vriezen calls Habakkuk a "cult prophet" (p. 63) and a "temple prophet" (p. 251) and states that a few biblical prophets may have been "temple prophets" (p. 56). These statements remain unchanged in his 1970 edition. Eichrodt's position is also complicated. Rather than deny cultic prophecy outright, he seems more concerned to protect the independence of prophets as charismatic individuals. Thus, he wants to avoid classifying prophetism *as a whole* as a type of sanctuary official (Eichrodt 1961: 1:313-14). The gradual formation of a distinct professional class of prophet led to

tion, Fichtner (1961: cols. 620-21) argued that prophets may have lived in the vicinity of sanctuaries and gave oracles to queries but that an "institution" of cult prophets did not exist as such. De Vaux (1961: 386) maintained that even a moderate view that cult prophets might have left an influence on Psalms is doubtful.[21] Heschel (1962: 481 n. 24) also affirmed the cautions of Rowley and de Vaux over against the position of Mowinckel, Johnson and Haldar.[22]

1.5 Late Twentieth Century Discussion

From the 1970s the emphasis of discussion appears to shift. Throughout the 1950s and 1960s, the debate centred on the existence of cult prophets, particularly whether or not they functioned as cult officials or members of the temple staff. As will be seen, some scholars continued to work with a model whereby institutional cult prophets contributed to worship and psalmody (Harris 1970; Jeremias 1970; Johnson 1979; Koenen 1996).[23]

---

the degeneration of prophetism to a form of temple prophecy, which Eichrodt thinks is represented in many of the psalms, what he calls a "watering down of true prophetic utterance to a priestly exhortation in the guise of prophecy" (Eichrodt 1961: 1:332-33). In this regard, it is odd that he approves Mowinckel's attention to the cultic function of Psalms and yet in the same sentence calls prophetic elements in psalms a "taking over of the prophetic idiom in this religious poetry" (which sounds more like Gunkel) (Eichrodt 1961: 1:322 n. 2). These sections are virtually unaltered from his original 1933 edition (Eichrodt 1933: 1:168, 175).

21 In contrast to Rowley's assessment, de Vaux wrote, "The moderate position [cultic prophecy might have left a trace in the psalms], which does not count the literary prophets among the Temple staff, is itself far from certain. It is unscientific to apply indiscriminately to Israel everything which happened in neighbouring religions, especially where biblical evidence is lacking" (de Vaux 1961: 385).

22 Heschel (1962: 480-81) held the position, mostly abandoned by this time, equating "*nebiim*" with false prophets, who stand alongside priests in the cult in opposition to the literary prophets. Thus, it appears that for him, prophets functioned in the cult but they were illegitimate.

23 Robert Murray (1982: 201) writes, ". . . the evidence is clear that functions that can only be described as prophetic were exercised within the cultic system". Croft (1987: 151-53) largely accepts Johnson's arguments, only he questions the vicarious role of prophets for the lamenting individual and maintains that non-prophetic musicians may also be responsible for some of the psalms attributed by Johnson to cultic prophets.

However, others appear to have emphasised old nuances of debate between Mowinckel and Gunkel. First, the identity of the prophetic functionaries in the cult is opened for re-evaluation (Bellinger 1984; Grabbe 1993; Cryer 1994; 1995). Second the question re-emerges about the origin of prophetic elements in psalms; it is suggested that prophetic elements are merely liturgical scripts that imitate prophetic oracles in style (Tournay 1991; Spieckermann 1994; Hossfeld 1998). Booij (1978) challenges Mowinckel's thesis that prophets, as originally conceived, acted in the cult; rather, the prophetic elements are from singers who composed with a prophetic consciousness that differed from that of genuine prophets.

1.5.1 Developments in the Theory of Cult Prophets

1.5.1.1 *Jörg Jeremias*

Jeremias (1970) wrote to clarify the relationship between cult prophets and canonical prophets. He accepts the existence of institutional cult prophetism in the Jerusalem temple based on the arguments of Mowinckel, Johnson and others (Jeremias 1970: 1, 7). In his view, neither the argument that classical prophecy emerged as a type of cult prophetism, nor models that set canonical prophets in radical opposition to cult prophets, do justice to the evidence (Jeremias 1970: 4, 8). The fact that cult prophets are condemned for failing to announce doom implies that it was to some extent their legitimate responsibility to do so. Focusing on the messages of Nahum, Habakkuk and various psalms containing elements of admonition, Jeremias argues that canonical prophets can be numbered among the cult prophets (Habakkuk but not Nahum) and that genuine prophetic voices of judgment were heard among pre-exilic cult prophets as reflected in the psalms (Jeremias 1970: 49, 110, 195). The critical distinction in message between mainstream cult prophetism and canonical prophets was the extent of judgment. Cult prophets sought to bring restoration to Israel by announcing God's immediate judgment on sinful *individuals* and groups *within* Israel (Jeremias 1970: 195-96). In contrast, the judgment announced by the classical prophets of doom was universal (Jeremias 1970:

196-97). In the message of the cult prophets, Yahweh's salvation of the nation as a whole was assured by the covenant traditions and would be effected by internal purification within the nation. The classical prophets viewed salvation as possible only after universal destruction of the nation and the creation of a new Israel. The function of cult prophets was strongly characterised by the ministry of intercession for the king and the people, particularly at times of national crisis and fasting (Jeremias 1970: 110-11, 195). The resulting cultic form was a lament liturgy in which the prophet uttered the prayer of the people before Yahweh and mediated Yahweh's word back in the prophetic elements recorded in the psalms (e.g., Ps 12:6, Jeremias 1970: 112-13). Judgment against the guilty within Israel is often expressed (e.g., Psalm 14, Jeremias 1970: 115). Thus, Jeremias suggests differences in theology that might have led to a rift in prophetic circles without resorting to the old model of a necessarily fundamental opposition between cultic and classical prophecy.

1.5.1.2 James G. Harris III

Harris (1970) presupposes a cult prophecy model and investigates the theological contribution of those portions in the psalms in which first-person divine speech appears. In his view, third-person speech ("indirect divine speech") is an "imitation oracle" (Harris 1970: 39). After examining Zion Procession Oracles, Oracles of Royal Coronation, War Oracles, and Oracles of Covenant Renewal, Harris (1970: 218) concludes that "prophetic personalities of the official worship institution of Israel introduced and standardized prophetic speeches of Yahwism". Their influence actually paved the way for acceptance of classical prophets, who utilized many of the same forms that were developed in the cult (Harris 1970: 219-220).

1.5.1.3 Aubrey R. Johnson

In *The Cultic Prophet and Israel's Psalmody*, Johnson (1979) attempts a more exhaustive application of his earlier model of cultic prophecy to the text and life-setting of the Psalms. On the basis of his earlier work, he presupposes the existence of professional prophets who are part of the temple personnel (Johnson 1979: 3). He distinguishes "those psalms which were clearly designed from the first for liturgical purposes" and "those which have the appearance of being free compositions which have been adapted for liturgical use" (Johnson 1979: 4); but he explicitly criticises Gunkel for attributing oracular elements in the psalms to a mere imitation of prophetic style (Johnson 1979: 18 n. 4). Like Jeremias, Johnson cautions against dividing canonical prophets and cultic prophets into completely distinct or oppositional categories. However, Johnson prefers to see the distinguishing role of the cultic prophet to be the shaping of the historical, covenant tradition in order to foster faith and so assure the future welfare of the people (Johnson 1979: 30).

1.5.1.4 Klaus Koenen

Koenen explores how the word of God was spoken in an actual cultic situation as well as instances where it is a secondary citation by the psalmist (Koenen 1996: 4). For Koenen, Ps 35:3 illustrates in the most condensed manner the fundamental dynamic of divine word responding to prayer in worship (Koenen 1996: 5). The admonition speeches, such as Psalms 50, 75, and 81, are not the unconditional announcement of judgment as in traditional prophecy; nevertheless they demand change with conditional promises of either judgment or salvation, which may reflect a transformation of prophetic speech similar to Deutero-Isaiah (Koenen 1996: 27). Other psalms (e.g., Psalms 2, 60 and 89) cite divine words secondarily. In these cases the citation functions "aetiologically", by which he means that a past word offers the theological grounds for present hope; but in other contexts (e.g., 68 and 82) an argument from analogy between past and present serves as the basis for hope (Koenen 1996: 69-71). In cases of secondary citation, the divine words are subordinate to the argument of the psalms; but divine words spoken in the present by the psalmist himself are central to the message of the psalm. In these speeches of direct, present address the spirit of prophecy is evident, whereas secondary citation is merely interpretation of transmitted words (Koenen 1996: 72).

1.5.2 Uncertainty of Identity of Cultic Functionary

1.5.2.1 W. H. Bellinger

Bellinger attempts to define more precisely the relationship between psalmody and prophecy, focusing particularly on the psalms of lament (Bellinger 1984: 19). He argues that the "certainty of being heard" in individual laments reflects a "prophetic element" in the sense of anticipating deliverance and judgment. An oracle is not present in these psalms; however, the existence of an answer in the psalm's setting is signalled by a shift in mood, indicating some sort of divine response, whether a woe oracle for enemies or an oracle of salvation (Bellinger 1984: 57-58, 78-79, 81). The presence of an oracle in some community laments supports this idea. Nevertheless, Bellinger is still uncertain as to whether one can speak of cult prophecy in Israel. He insists that it is not the identity of the cultic functionary but the *function* of the language in the text that determines whether the psalm has a prophetic character. While the "anticipatory function of promise" warrants calling these psalms prophetic, the cultic functionaries may or may not be prophets, that is, they could be priests as well (Bellinger 1984: 77).

1.5.2.2 Lester L. Grabbe

Grabbe (1993) discusses the broader sociological roles of various functionaries in ancient Israel. He argues that the roles of priest and prophet blurred considerably in Israelite society (cult functionary, healer, consultant, intercessor, ethical teacher, divinatory functions). He stresses that "The most important dichotomy from a social point of view is often not that between individual specialists (e.g., priest versus prophet) but between level of function, whether at *individual level* or at *state/national* level (i.e., national prophet versus local prophet)" (Grabbe 1993: 45). In his view, both served as cult functionaries.

1.5.2.3 Frederick Cryer

The identity of the cultic functionary as well as the method of revealing the divine will are two major issues in Cryer's study of the nature of divination in ancient Israel (Cryer 1994). In Cryer's view, scholarship has tended to ignore the many manifestations of divination in the OT because it is usually relegated to the lower strata, or popular periphery, of religion (Cryer 1994: 229, 237-38). This is due, he believes, to the influence of deuteronomic theology (esp. Deut 18:9-14) in scholarship's interpretation of the biblical data for actual practices in Israel (Cryer 1994: 231, 242). Partiality for prophecy over divination is set as a presupposition. He argues that the social roles of prophets and priests were not clearly distinct. Therefore, prophets may have performed priestly and technical divinatory functions, including induced dreams, the teraphim, lots, the ephod, the ark and omen sacrifice (Cryer 1994: 250, 292-301). Since none of the forms of divination in the ancient Near East are liturgical actions, he suggests that more evidence is needed than the mere "certainty of a hearing" in the individual psalms before acceptance of temple-divination in Israel (Cryer 1994: 295).

1.5.3 Emphasis on Liturgical Imitation of Prophetic Style

1.5.3.1 Thijs Booij

Booij (1978: 17) investigates the original function and background of the oracles in the psalms, which he defines as those psalms containing pronouncements in first-person divine speech or its functional equivalent. The original function of the divine word in psalms depends on its place within the psalm. Although divine words are central to the message of the psalms, they are not a free-standing element; rather they participate in the distinct language of the psalms and are connected structurally with other parts in a unifying composition (Booij 1978: 23, 26). Nevertheless, the psalms functioned in a real cultic setting, so the divine words are not merely poetic creations but have "actuality" in the setting for which they were composed (Booij 1978: 38-39). For Booij, a prophet is anyone who under inspiration receives a divine revelation and mediates the content without interpreters to another party (Booij 1978: 47-48). In his view, non-official prophetic functionaries participated in cultic activities in their particular ways (Booij 1978: 54-62); however, contrary to Mowinckel and Johnson, Booij rejects a special category of cult prophet. Because a prophet depended on Yahweh's revelation, it is questionable whether such a model is compatible with the agenda-bound performance necessitated by Mowinckel's model and official worship (Booij 1978: 50-51). Even more difficult for Booij is the manner in which oracles are integrated into the psalm as a whole. Such integrated unity precludes the possibility that they resulted from spontaneous prophetic speech as imagined by Mowinckel. One could imagine a revelation received before the gathering and assimilated into song before performance; but, in his view, this hypothesis creates the phenomenon being sought (Booij 1978: 52). Booij (1978: 75-76) suggests that in psalms of praise a subdued form of ecstasy characterised temple singers, and so their service was regarded as "prophesying" by Chronicles (although the phenomenon is evident in pre-exilic texts, e.g., Psalms 68, 75, 81). Divine response through a prophet was expected after seeking Yahweh in prayer, but Booij (1978: 120) doubts that such responses were part of the fixed agenda of worship on feast days. Urgent circumstances, illustrated in 2 Chronicles 20, were probably not normally addressed by institutionally identified prophets (Booij 1978: 128). When divine responses to prayer appear in psalms (e.g., Psalms 60, 85, 132), the integration of the oracle with the whole indicates that the psalm was composed beforehand and performed by the singer. Booij (1978: 146) calls such oracles "singer oracles" because the singer speaks in prophetic terms but it is not an experience that is prophetic in the original sense. Divine reproof in psalms shows a similar prophetic style. For example, Psalms 50 and 95 exhibit "prophet-like speech" but not prophetic speech in the original sense (Booij 1978: 196, 210). The traditional prophetic message is interpreted liturgically through temple singers who were moved by a "prophetic consciousness" to compose their psalms (Booij 1978: 221-223). While royal psalms were not within the scope of his study, Booij suggests that a model of liturgical-prophetic style might be appropriate here as well. For example, the Spirit of Yahweh on the king might manifest itself as royal charisma, that is liturgical prophesying, in Ps 2:7-9 (Booij 1978: 223). In sum, Booij notes: 1) divine words in some cases are merely poetic description (e.g., Pss 35:3; 90:3), 2) in other instances the prophetic consciousness might be blurred with such a poetic functional use (e.g., Ps 46:11), 3) occasionally an oracle is cited secondarily (e.g., Psalm 132),[24] 4) the divine word functioned dramatically without being a priestly or prophetic oracle (as Küchler and Mowinckel had supposed), but the poet was in a certain sense a prophet who inserted divine words out of a prophetic consciousness, mirroring indirectly the characteristics of classical prophetism (Booij 1978: 225-26). Therefore, while Booij does not reject prophetic activity in the cult, he distinguishes clearly between prophecy as originally conceived, where a נביא makes oracular promises directly to a specific situation, and "singer oracles", where a prophetically conscious poet composes divine speech in psalms.

1.5.3.2 Raymond J. Tournay

Tournay's concern is the origin and role of psalms in the religious life of Israel. Since, in his view, extra-biblical comparisons fail to account for this, it is necessary to look more closely at the psalms themselves in light of the writings of the whole OT (Tournay 1991: 24). He looks to the Books of Ezra, Nehemiah and Chronicles as the most valuable data to begin reconstructing the *Sitz im Leben* of the psalms. Against the background of these books, prophetic-messianic themes emerge second only to the feasts as dominating the concern of the psalms (Tournay 1991: 27-28).

---

24 Citation of an earlier speech of God, cited through a prophet or priest, might carry the same "reality value" as the context in which it is placed (e.g., Ps 2:7-9, Booij 1978: 31).

Tournay criticises Mowinckel for improperly extrapolating the information about cultic prophecy provided in Chronicles into the pre-exilic period, and in his view the idea of pre-exilic cultic prophecy is very problematic (Tournay 1991: 30). There is no evidence of cultic prophecy during the period of the monarchy, and material within the psalms is not useful for dating purposes (Tournay 1991: 57-59). Originally, prophecy was linked institutionally with kingship (as at Mari). After the fall of the monarchy and the progressive extinction of prophecy during the exile, the absence of prophecy was compensated for by Levitical singers, who conducted themselves as cultic prophets, claiming David as their model (Tournay 1991: 31, 64).

Given a Second Temple context for cultic prophecy, Tournay proceeds to discuss its features. In the place of the pre-exilic priestly oracle, ancient theophanic traditions were utilized by post-exilic psalmists to preface divine speech in psalms, a form of literary motif reminiscent of earlier material (Tournay 1991: 131, 161). The oracles in the psalms themselves, like the theophanic passages, give the psalms a perceptible prophetic dimension (Tournay 1991: 165). Sometimes the oracles are explicit. Other times the presence of an oracle is only implicit. Evidence of post-exilic cult prophecy is also evident in royal messianism, which began when the Davidic promises became viewed as a covenant (Tournay 1991: 200). He writes, "The inspired sacred writers at the time tried to compensate for the disappearance of the great prophets and to re-animate the faith of believers in the divine promises, in spite of the silence of God" (Tournay 1991: 229).

1.5.3.3 Hermann Spieckermann

Another recent discussion, by Hermann Spieckermann (1994), illustrates the continued support for the view that prophetic speech forms in the psalms are due to liturgical adaptation of prophetic style. Spieckermann argues that, with the exception of kingship ritual (e.g., Psalm 2), most cases of divine speech in psalms occur in post-exilic psalms. In the wake of the exile, the depressive theological crisis and guilt of the people became the dominant theme in psalms. (Spieckermann 1994: 157-58). As seen in the imprecatory and communal lament psalms (e.g., Psalms 137; 44) the community struggled with the silence of God. The theology of guilt was brought into play in the early post-exilic period through Psalm 50 as an answer to this grappling question. Psalm 50 offers an example of a poet utilising prophetic style in order to focus on the guilt of the people in accordance with deuteronomic theology (Spieckermann 1994: 159).[25] Drawing on theophanic traditions the psalmist stresses the universal judgment of God applied to the reform of the sacrificial cult. The psalm opposed the denial of guilt and spiritualised the thanksgiving song (cf. Psalm 95) without marginalising completely the complaint against God characteristic of the exilic period (cf. Pss 74:1, 79:13, 80:2, Spieckermann 1994: 160-62). Spieckermann (1994: 162-63) argues that the composition of Psalm 81 follows that of Psalms 50 and 95, primarily because the thanksgiving song demanded in Psalm 50 is realised in the introductory call to praise of Ps 81:2-4. However, a new element is added, the conditional promise of salvation based upon obedience to law. Psalm 60 reflects an even more positive use of the divine word, to lift the people's discouragement after they have cried out under God's judgment upon their guilt (Spieckermann 1994: 165). In addition to this tradition of an authoritative divine word, there also emerged in the post-exilic period, under deuteronomic influence and promulgated in Deutero-Isaiah (e.g., Isa 40:6-8; 55:10), an emphasis on God's creative word, דבר (Spieckermann 1994: 167-68). For example, in Psalm 33 the word of God comes from him as Creator, in Psalm 105 the reliability of God's word is verified in salvation history, and in Psalm 106 guilt stems from failure to believe this word (Spieckermann 1994: 169). Finally in Psalm 119, God's word in both forms (דבר/אמרה) is undivided in effectively offering blessing. From waiting upon God's word, the way is not far from praise of his word, as almost a hypostasis of God, in Psalm 56 (Spieckermann 1994: 169-70). Thus, reflection upon the pro-

---

[25] Spieckermann criticises Gunkel (1926: 214) at this point for wavering somewhat in his usual, and in Spieckermann's opinion, correct view of prophetic imitation in the Psalms. Gunkel inconsistently, he observes, interprets Psalm 50 as an instance in which the psalmist hears God's word at a "mysterious moment" (Spieckermann 1994: 159).

phetic word has led to liturgical imitation of the prophetic sources of this theology.

1.5.3.4 Frank-Lothar Hossfeld

As introduction to his essay on divine speech in the Asaphite psalms, Hossfeld surveys recent opinions on the question of cultic prophecy (Hossfeld 1998: 223-26). He notes that the hypothesis of Mowinckel and Johnson still finds advocates today; but in his opinion, cultic prophecy theories are falling from favour for two reasons: First, scholars are working with literary formation theories in which divine words in psalms are viewed as a post-exilic echo of an older cult prophetic tradition. Second, the salvation oracle is less commonly viewed as an adequate explanation for the certainty of a hearing in psalms of lament. Thus the activity of a cult prophet (or priest speaking prophetically) is no longer invoked by numerous scholars.

1.6 Key Issues and Evaluation

Since discussions began early in the last century on the issue of cultic prophecy, no consensus has been reached on several key questions. First, while evidence exists associating prophets with cultic shrines in the pre-exilic period, what role if any did prophets play in worship? If prophets served as cultic functionaries, was their relationship to the cult "institutional" (i.e., dependent on the cult for support or regarded as cultic staff)? Second, assuming some place for divine communication in worship, what was the nature of the oracles given? Specifically, were oracles delivered by means of technical divination only (and of what variety, lots or sacrificial divination?), or did non-technical divination (i.e., "prophecy") play a part? In each case, who were the functionaries? Third, what changes in the nature of cultic prophecy might be observable between the First Temple and Second Temple period? Did post-exilic forms bear any phenomenological similarity to pre-exilic forms, if pre-exilic cultic prophecy did exist? Finally, what trace of cultic prophecy is evident in the psalms and what was the liturgical interplay between spontaneous prophecy and the use of written liturgical forms?

1.6.1 The Existence of Pre-exilic Cult Prophets

1.6.1.1 Association Between Prophets and Shrines

Mowinckel and Johnson observed that from the earliest times, the OT tradition associates prophets with cult centres (e.g., 1 Sam 10:5; 19:18-24; 2 Kgs 2:3; 4:38). Particularly informative is the desire of the Shunammite to seek Elisha at a shrine (Mt. Carmel) on a day other than a cultic celebration (New Moon or Sabbath; 2 Kgs 4:23). Her husband's reservations about the journey suggest that the prophet might normally be found only on such occasions (because he had official cultic duties?), but she was persuaded he would be found even on this occasion. Mt. Carmel had already been associated in 1 Kings 18 with the prophetic and sacrificial ministry of Elijah. The association between the destruction of Yahweh's altars along with the killing of his prophets might also imply a regular role of prophets in religious worship (1 Kgs 19:10). However, Gunkel has pointed out that one would expect prophets, as religious zealots, to frequent cultic places. Even the final fate of many prophets in the temple, who were slain with the priests, might be expected given their religious concern (Lam 2:20). If a prophet's motive was to proclaim a message, then a visit to a shrine would guarantee an audience. The fact that prophets might, on occasion, use the temple as a venue for their messages (e.g., Jer 26:7) does not mean that their normal location was in the cult. In the case of Elijah on Mt. Carmel, his sacrifice was an unusual event dictated by the circumstances (mirroring the role of Baal prophets, not Yahweh's prophets); thus, this passage does not suggest a normal cultic role. In short, the frequent presence of prophets at cultic centres does not necessarily imply that they participated as cultic officials or integrated their prophetic ministry with worship at the shrine.[26]

In spite of Gunkel's objection, one might expect a non-antagonistic prophet at a religious festival to participate frequently in a mediatorial role of some kind. The fact that the prophets in 1 Sam 10:5 were *still* in ecstasy while descending from the high place supports the supposition that they had participated prophetically in the worship celebration. While the close proximity of prophets to shrines does not prove an official, institutional connection (i.e., that they were supported by the cult), it suggests at the least a regular role in worship.

1.6.1.2 Priests and Prophets

The frequent coupling together of priests and prophets has been taken by Mowinckel and Johnson to be evidence that prophets served alongside the priests in cultic duties (e.g., Isa 28:7; Jer 4:9; 6:13; 14:18; 18:18; Mic 3:11). Gunkel countered that these passages only identify the prophets as important religious leaders in the nation. The fact that they are listed in some passages with the king and other officials is effective support for Gunkel's contention (e.g., Jer 2:26; 4:9; 18:18; Mic 3:11), since no one would conclude that the king, leaders, wise men or judges were cultic officials simply because they are listed in association with priests. In his view, Jer 29:26 does not imply that a priestly temple officer supervised the guild of cult prophets, only that the priest was responsible for maintaining order in the temple against antagonistic prophets such as Jeremiah. An official cultic role of Jeremiah in the temple based on his priestly lineage (Jer 1:1) is made less likely by the possibility that his family had been cut off from cultic duties by Solomon (1 Kgs 2:26-27).[27]

---

26 A tie between prophecy and singing (1 Sam 10:5; 2 Kgs 3:15; Ps 49:5) is even less suggestive of a link between prophecy and cult, since one would presume that music was pervasive in many different contexts of the culture without necessarily implying a formal link between any of them (e.g., utilising music in a work song or battle march does not in itself make them a part of worship).

27 The priestly status of Jeremiah is problematic (McKane 1986: 1). It is possible that his family was included in a permanent banishment of the priestly

Similarly, Ezekiel's calling came outside the context of temple worship, while he was in exile in Babylon. Hence, his identity as a priest was probably only incidental to his being called as a prophet, even though his priestly training would have equipped him for his prophetic message concerning the temple and its regulations.[28]

However, the likelihood that some prophets lived in temple quarters, the normal domain of priests and temple officials, is not as easy to disregard (Jer 35:4). Even if McKane's (1996: 897) suggestion is correct that this detail is fabricated to create realism in the passage, the supposition that prophets lived in the temple must still be correct to have a realistic effect.[29] The function of prophets ministering in the temple alongside priests is supported by Jer 23:11. The reference in the text to "wickedness" in the temple is clarified later in the context as including, in addition to immorality, a lying prophetic message (Jer 23:14, 16, 21, 25-32). In Jer 23:34-40, these prophets are condemned together with priests for uttering false oracles. So the association of these prophets with priests in this passage sets the ministry of these prophets in the temple. One might also add that the priest Pashhur, the chief officer in the temple, is said to have prophesied (Jer 20:1-6). It is likely his cultic service involved both priestly and prophetic functions. Finally, regarding Jer 29:26, the reference to "every" madman gives the impression

---

family at Anathoth. Even if this is not the case, all indications about Jeremiah's career are that he remained aloof from the official temple leadership generally and held an antagonistic posture toward it. It is perhaps this exclusion from official temple duty that made Jeremiah ironically qualified to announce the temple's destruction.

28 In addition to these objections, B. D. Eerdmans (1947: 142), W. C. Klein (1963: 802) and Booij (1978: 52) questioned the existence of cult prophets based upon the scarcity of legislation regulating the prophetic office relative to the vast literature addressing the responsibilities and support of priests. However, if, as the tradition of 1 Chronicles 25 suggests, the cult prophets were closely (exclusively?) associated with the Levites, then stipendiary issues are addressed to the extent that they are related to the Levites.

29 It could be argued that the actual residents were only sons of the "man of God", and therefore, not prophets themselves (taking "man of God" in apposition to the name Hanan; otherwise, if "man of God" is appositional to "Jigdaliah", they are even further removed as grandsons). But the point of the narrative seems to be that this residence belonged to someone with a godly stature, a prophet himself.

that this occurrence was common. What remains to be seen is whether these prophets announced oracles that formed a part of temple worship or were merely making politically relevant proclamations about the fate of Jerusalem. It is difficult to imagine that such proclamations of well-being for the nation (e.g., Jer 23:17) were detached from liturgical practice.

Thus, evidence favours the existence of cult prophets who contributed to worship and were not merely using the occasion of a religious gathering to proclaim a message outside the context of the liturgy. In addition, at least in the days of Jeremiah, prophets appear to have enjoyed institutional support in the temple. The possible role of pre-exilic canonical prophets in relation to the cult is also important in this discussion, but consideration of this issue is beyond the scope of the present work.

1.6.2 The Nature of Divine Communication in Worship

Mowinckel's definition of the prophetic, that is, any sacramental component of worship whereby God communicates to humanity, was criticised by Gunkel for being so broad that priest and prophet become indistinguishable. Mowinckel's definition is vulnerable to such a critique. However, Mowinckel held that either priest or layman might be prophetically gifted, and so, a distinction did exist in his mind. Nevertheless, a more precise definition of prophecy is needed. It is important to address the nature of divine communication in the cult because it informs how divine speech might be explained in the psalms or operate practically in the context of liturgy. It is also central to any discussion about changes that might have taken place between pre- and post-exilic cultic prophecy. A related issue is the identity of the functionaries who use the various means of divine communication.

1.6.2.1 *Definition of Prophecy*

Based on a broad study of ancient Near Eastern texts, Weippert (1988: 289-90) advances the following definition of prophecy: 1) a cognitive experience, a vision, an auditory experience, or a dream in which the prophet(ess) shares in a revelation from a deity, and 2) an awareness of a commission from the deity to transmit the revelation in speech or symbolic action to a third party who is actually addressed.[30] David Petersen (2000: 39-41) expresses reservations concerning Weippert's definition, arguing that it gives undue weight to the *experience* of the prophet. He would prefer to emphasize observable *behaviour*, since we really have no access to the cognitive state of the prophet, including his awareness of vocation. However, OT texts do convey testimony of prophets to their own conscious awareness of bearing a divine message (e.g., Isaiah's or Jeremiah's memoirs; Isa 6:8; 8:18; Jer 1:6-7; 11:18; cf. 1 Kgs 22:14). If not the authentic words of the prophets, these texts at least express the tradition's understanding of the prophetic vocation, which probably accurately reflects prophetic self-awareness. Such verbal testimony by prophets itself constitutes a form of prophetic "behaviour", a vocal expression of self-consciousness on the part of the prophet; and therefore, Weippert's attention to the experience of the prophet is valid.

On the other hand, behaviour is also important to take into account in any definition of OT prophecy. This extends beyond Weippert's inclusion of non-verbal acts intended to convey the divine message. At times, a verbal form of נבא stresses behaviour, and the individuals so acting are thereby called "prophets" (Num 11:24-30; 1 Sam 10:5-6; 19:18-24). What about their behaviour constituted prophetic action? The narrative of Numbers 11 offers no clues as to the phenomena characteristic of prophecy there. More than musical performance is probably intended in 1 Samuel 10, since the behaviour is eccentric enough for Saul to be regarded by those observing him as having changed into a different man. The incident in 1 Samuel 19 is slightly more descriptive in that Saul's prophesying culminated in stripping off his clothes and lying in that state day and night. The loss of voluntary control is prominent in this passage, since Saul loses the capacity to carry out his mission of capturing David. It is reasonable to assume that some form of ecstatic behaviour

---

30 Weippert's (2001b: col. 197) more recent definition does not differ substantially from his earlier proposal, although Weippert uses the broader term "non-verbal" in place of "meta-speech" ("symbolic action" in footnote).

marked each of these occasions. However, the fact that the individuals in both accounts were normally ambulatory and were performing musically leads to the conclusion that a completely irrational frenzy was not indicative of prophesying. It has long been observed that ecstatic behaviour by Mari prophets did not preclude rational speech. The description of prophets as "madmen" is difficult to assess, since their conscious state did not preclude the utterance of coherent verbal communication (2 Kgs 9:11; Jer 29:26). The important point to observe is that the term "prophesying" might denote ecstatic worship. Thus a broader definition than Weippert's might incorporate some instances where the emphasis is not on the divine message as much as the performance of worship that is perceived by others as being divinely induced. This possibility has important implications for the statements in Chronicles discussed below.

Nissinen (1993: 221; 1998b: 6) underscores an important point in Weippert's definition, that prophetic messages are mediated without the instrumentality of technical means normally associated with "divination". However, he notes the growing tendency in the study of both biblical and ancient Near Eastern prophecy to consider prophecy as an integral part of divination, differing only in the means of mediation. Nissinen (1998b: 87) points to Neo-Assyrian texts where prophecy came in response to a query (SAA 10 294; SAA 9 1.8), a practice he finds paralleled in the OT (1 Sam 9:9; 28:6; 1 Kgs 22:5ff; 2 Kgs 3:11ff; 19:1-7; Jer 21:1ff; 38:14ff; 42:1ff).[31] Van der Toorn (1987: 68-71) makes a similar point, observing that in the OT priestly oracles are sometimes indistinguishable at the literary level from those delivered by a prophet (e.g., 1 Kgs 22:6; Judg 4:14; 20:28; and Deut 20:3-4); and he cites the Mari and Neo-Assyrian evidence to argue that people of these cultures cared little to differentiate between the various types of divination, being more interested in the interpretation of an oracle than in the means of reception. Nevertheless, in principle Weippert's definition that

---

31 Using the account of Esarhaddon's Rise to Power, Nissinen (1998b: 30-34) illustrates the difficulty of differentiating in a textual reference between prophetic speech and an answer through divination.

differentiates between technical and non-technical mediation of the divine will is helpful.³²

Priests practised a form of technical divination through use of the Urim and Thummim. It is also possible that at times officials practised sacrificial divination (Mic 3:6-7; Jer 29:8, although compare the use of קסם in Prov 16:10 where extispicy is not implied). But the argument that omen sacrifice is reflected in the psalms is very weak.³³ Thus, two forms of divine communication may be distinguished, at least in theory if not always in the practice of interpreting texts: 1) inductive, technical divination, and 2) intuitive, non-technical divination, called "prophecy". In addition, the range of meaning denoted by the term prophecy includes in some instances a reference to divinely inspired acts of worship, probably accompanying meaningful verbal speech.

Maintaining this distinction is helpful in discussing the issue of cultic prophecy. One might argue that, in specific texts, discerning the kind of divination behind the divine communication is impossible; but maintaining the distinction between technical

---

32 Technical divination is reported in the form of a short response to a binary inquiry; although an exceptional case might be 2 Sam 5:23-24 (but this could be the summary of a series of divination inquiries or possibly a prophetic expansion of a single inquiry). None of the examples of divination oracles offered by Nissinen or van der Toorn are comparable in length to prophetic speeches, nor do they exhibit the complex form of divine speech in Psalms or prophetic literature (cf. Mowinckel 1924: 50). In spite of the difficulty of distinguishing between oracles of technical divination and intuitive prophecy in some biblical texts, no evidence suggests that technical divination lies behind longer speeches. The form of longer texts of divination oracles collected by Starr (1990) is altogether different from prophetic speech. Assyrian scribes had no difficulty maintaining a distinction between intuitive prophecy and divine communication by technical divination; and as discussed in the next chapter, maintaining a distinction between the two was a matter of professional pride for Mesopotamian scholars. It is very unlikely that prophetic elements in the psalms can be attributed to technical divination.

33 The interpretation of the verb בקר in Ps 27:4 "to undertake an inspection sacrifice" (cf. Mowinckel 1921: 146) is questionable in Biblical Hebrew. The use in 2 Kgs 16:15 offers no support for this translation and the etymological support in HAL only offers a much later Jewish Aramaic reference. The attested usage "to examine, attend to, reflect" (e.g., Lev 13:36; Ezek 34:11) makes good sense, especially in light of the parallelism with חזה in Ps 27:4. Similarly, neither etymology nor context in Ps 5:4 offers any reason to depart from the normal usage "morning".

divination and prophecy makes the question of cult prophecy a meaningful inquiry. First, an important disagreement between Mowinckel and Gunkel revolved around the possibility of prophetic speech intruding into the liturgy. Gunkel permitted oracular response from technical divination by a priest to result in a mood shift in the psalms ("certainty of a hearing"), but he could not reconcile free inspiration with a fixed liturgy. Second, the added complexity of a form of prophecy perhaps characterised as ecstatic praise contributes to discussions about the relationship between prophecy and Levitical music mentioned in Chronicles as well as psalms. Booij, for example, imagines postexilic Levitical singers who "prophesy" while in a subdued ecstatic state. This is discussed further below.

1.6.2.2 Identity and Role of the Functionaries

As noted above, recent scholarship has stressed the fluidity in social roles between various cultic functionaries. This fluidity was recognised even by Mowinckel and Johnson. But from the viewpoint of the OT tradition, the writers appear to have had little difficulty drawing a distinction between priests and prophets (they are frequently juxtaposed in texts). Any confusion appears to be more a problem for modern interpreters than the tradents of ancient Israel. One of the difficulties faced by modern interpreters is that their access to the sociological structures of the ancient culture is primarily through texts, which offer limited data on factors that would have been obvious to the ancient worshiper. One example is the distinction in dress between various cultic officials. Were prophets dressed differently from priests, even as the High Priest would have been easily distinguished from ordinary priests? Another example might be the physical placement of officials at different stations during the liturgy. Such observations would have signalled clear distinctions to someone participating in worship to which we have no access. Nevertheless, our inability to discern obvious distinctions does not obliterate their existence. If the evidence for preexilic cult prophecy is accepted, the possibility remains that on any given occasion either a prophetically gifted priest or "layman" could be the source of the speech, but the fact that it is a priest would not render the speech any less "prophetic".

1.6.3 Post-exilic Cultic Prophecy

1.6.3.1 Prophetic Continuity

Prophets existed in the post-exilic period, as witnessed by Haggai, Zechariah, Malachi and perhaps Joel. The continuity of these prophets with the mainstream pre-exilic and exilic prophets as well as pre-exilic cultic tradition (i.e., Psalms) has been defended by Mason (1982).[34] Narrative report of their presence is found in Ezra 5:2 and 6:14, although the character of prophets was as problematic as in the time of Jeremiah (cf. Neh 6:7, 14, Zech 13:2-6). Whether these prophets served predominantly or even sporadically in the cult is outside the scope of this study. But the important point is that prophecy continued from the pre-exilic period, through the exilic age, and into post-exilic times. Prophecy in the late pre-exilic temple became stigmatised by its characteristic message of salvation, which was proven "false" by the disasters of 598 and 586 (cf. Jeremiah and Ezekiel). However, optimism returned in the prophecies of Haggai and Zechariah. Even if none of these prophets served liturgically, a prophetic message favourable to temple and community restoration would have been welcomed in the Second Temple cult.[35]

---

34 Schniedewind (1997: 206-210) notes that the legitimate sense of discontinuity has been overemphasised in modern scholarship.

35 This casts doubt on the proposal of Johnson (1962: 66-74) that the failure of the peace prophets led to a loss of prestige for cult prophets in the post-exilic period and their subsequent subordination to the institution of Levitical singers (cf. Schniedewind 1997: 209). There is no necessity to "subordinate" the cult prophets at all.

1.6.3.2 Chronicles

Because of the post-exilic origin of Chronicles, its contribution to the issue of cultic prophecy has been set in the present context of discussion.[36] While the Books of Chronicles ascribe temple prophecy to Levitical singers in the pre-exilic period (1 Chr 25:1, 6-7; 2 Chr 20:14-17),[37] the historical reliability of this witness is problematic (2 Chronicles 20); and a question also emerges concerning the nature of "prophesying" ascribed to the singers (1 Chronicles 25).

It is possible that 2 Chronicles 20 contributes nothing concerning actual pre-exilic cultic prophecy. Petersen (1977: 77) views 2 Chr 20:14-17 as a retrojection of Levitical aspirations of the Chronicler's day into the past (cf. Klein 1995: 653), and Japhet (1993: 46, 793) regards the Jahaziel prophecy as a Chronistic composition. However, concerning the credibility of the type of speech portrayed in 2 Chronicles 20, Throntveit (1997: 241) writes, "Thus, while we must remain agnostic concerning the historicity of the address in question, Chr's schematic presentation suggests the historical existence of this form-critical category, which may be of some value in the reconstruction of the context of Israel's liturgical practice" (cf. Williamson 1982: 292-98). Even a fabrication must reflect reality in portraying what the author and his audience expected of the cult in this kind of situation.[38] Therefore, 2 Chronicles 20 may witness to prophetic practice in the First Temple. Alternatively, with the existence of prophets in the post-exilic period, it remains a possibility that the Chronicler is reflecting worship as it was in the post-exilic cult. In either case, cultic prophecy was known in the liturgy.

---

36 Schniedewind (1997: 205) observes that the Chronicler's post-exilic context permeates his composition, and therefore, his prophetic narratives belong to the study of post-exilic prophecy even though he describes the classical period of the monarchy.

37 Mowinckel's view that מׂשא in 1 Chr 15:22 and 27 refers to "oracles" is not likely. The redaction of "prophets" to "Levites" in 2 Chr 34:30 shows the equation of Levitical singers with temple prophets in the author's mind, but this would escape the readers who do not have 2 Kgs 23:2 before them.

38 Balentine (1997: 250-51) argues as much for prayers in Chronicles, which he states must be congruent with social conventions for the time.

The question of cultic prophecy in 1 Chr 25:1-3 is complicated by the unusual description of their "prophesying". Kleinig (1993: 154-57) argues that it goes beyond the evidence of 1 Chronicles 25 to suppose that these singers received oracles. Rather their prophetic function was mediatorial only insofar as they spoke for God to his people in songs of exhortation and salvation (cf. Mathys 2001: 294-95). Williamson (1982: 166) suggests that the Levitical singers are presented in direct continuity with pre-exilic cult prophets; but no activity beyond musical performance is involved, rather the notion of "prophecy" only recalls the early association of prophets with music (1 Sam 10:5, 2 Kgs 3:15, cf. Japhet 1993: 440-41). Thus, in Chronicles, the verb נבא takes on an expanded meaning. Perhaps the Chronicler's change in nomenclature merely reflects a changing interpretive emphasis on the phenomenon of prophecy rather than an actual change in the phenomenon itself. Booij maintains that in *both* temple periods a derived form of prophecy existed in which "prophetically conscious" composer-singers wrote inspired psalms and performed them in a subdued state of ecstasy.[39] Alongside them in the cult an occasional prophet such as Jahaziel might have spoken, but in his view, these generally did not contribute to psalmody (Booij 1978: 128-30).[40] However one conceives of the derived sense of "prophesying", it does not

---

[39] The dates he assigns to these singer psalms extend from pre-exilic to post-exilic times.

[40] For Mowinckel and Johnson, an original distinction between prophetically gifted and ordinary Levitical singers gradually became blurred in the post-exilic period. The significant difference between Booij and the latter two is that for Booij, psalmody should be ascribed only to the singers who composed prophetic psalms in advance of performance. Mowinckel's model calls for cultic prophets to appear at a fixed point in the liturgy. But even Mowinckel thought of musical and poetic "inspiration" as flowing from a "prophetic consciousness" (*prophetisches Bewußtsein*). Cultic prophecy was an extension of the poetic inspiration of singers, from among whom cult prophets were chiefly drawn (e.g., Jahaziel) (Mowinckel 1923: 26-27; 1924: 48-50; 1962b: 92-93). Mowinckel attributes to the prophetic consciousness of singers the list of texts he would assign to cult prophets (e.g., Ps 81:6, 110:1, Mowinckel 1924: 50). At this point, Booij's and Mowinckel's models appear almost indistinguishable. Perhaps Mowinckel had in mind the idea that all poets/musicians/psalmists were "inspired", but not all of them would be considered "prophets"; the latter were a subset of the singers and distinguished as those who spoke for God in first-person divine speech.

preclude the possibility that individuals also emerged on occasion to speak prophetically in the post-exilic cult in the more classical (i.e., oracular) sense. Whether this latter form of prophetic speech became preserved in psalms is the key question of this study. Since many psalms are frequently dated to the post-exilic period, matters of date will receive attention in subsequent chapters.

1.7 Conclusion and Direction of Study

Evaluation of key issues regarding cultic prophecy in psalms results in the following conclusions. First, evidence favours the existence of cult prophets who contributed to worship in pre-exilic times, some of whom may have enjoyed institutional support in the temple late in the monarchical period. However, official institutional status is not an important issue in this discussion, since vocational dependency on the temple is not a prerequisite for contributing to temple worship or psalmody. On the other hand, the existence of cult prophets does not mean that their oracles are preserved in OT psalms. Only examination of the psalms themselves can address this question.

Second, divine communication in the OT takes the form of technical divination (i.e., Urim and Thummim) as well as non-technical divination (i.e., intuitive prophecy); however, evidence is not sufficient to identify with certainty the functionaries responsible for prophetic mediation in the cult, assuming such took place. Probably both priestly officials and non-priestly functionaries prophesied. However, the identity of the functionary is not an important issue in this study, which is interested only in the preservation of intuitive prophecy in the psalms.

Third, post-exilic cultic prophecy is likely on the basis of the continuity between pre-exilic and post-exilic prophecy. The witness of Chronicles is complicated by questions of historical reliability as well as the nature of prophecy described by the Chronicler. Even if the cultic prophecy of Jahaziel (2 Chronicles 20) is the creation of the Chronicler, it must be authentic to the kind of cultic activity known to the Chronicler and his readers. The application of the term "prophesying" to Levitical singers in

1 Chr 25:1-3 suggests a secondary form of cultic prophecy in the performance of temple music; but this does not preclude the possibility that cult prophets occasionally spoke in the manner conceived by Mowinckel's model.

The final issue concerns what traces of cultic prophecy are evident in the Book of Psalms. Not an insignificant number of scholars have voiced doubts about a direct contribution of cultic prophecy to psalms. Gunkel and Quell, for example, questioned whether any form of free, spontaneous prophecy is compatible with the fixed agenda of liturgy. Recent studies recognise the unified literary structure of the psalms containing divine speech and argue that the oracles are only an integrated part of a whole. The composition of the whole must have taken place before the psalm was performed; and therefore, this process excludes spontaneous speech in the liturgical performance of the psalm.

It is the purpose of this study to examine the psalms themselves for evidence of cultic prophecy, utilising a form-critical comparison with Assyrian prophetic sources. The nature and relevance of these sources to the issue of cultic prophecy are the subject of the next chapter.[41] Subsequent chapters examine, respectively, royal psalms, psalms of Asaph, and psalms of lament (together with several other miscellaneous types). In order to limit the scope of the study, only psalms containing first-person divine speech are considered, since this is the most characteristic feature of prophetic (or "oracular") speech, requiring an explanation by either a cult prophetic model or by imitation of prophetic style.[42] After summarising of the results of these chapters, the conclusion returns to questions of compatibility between free prophecy and liturgy as well as the textual

---

[41] On the basis of a failed consensus in the history of scholarship, Haney (2002: 66-67) rejects the comparative method as too hypothetical to help reconstruct the setting of psalms. The priority he sets on the text itself is commendable, but his own method is also too extreme. Similarities and differences between texts and contexts of different cultures must be respected, but comparative studies are an important part of contextual exegesis and should not be abandoned.

[42] Some literature uses the term "oracle" for revelation through technical divination. In this study, "oracle" denotes divine speech resulting from intuitive prophecy unless otherwise indicated.

integration of first-person divine speech within a unified poetic structure.

Chapter 2
Assyrian Cultic Prophecy

2.1 Introduction

The phenomenon of Assyrian prophecy has been known for over 100 years through texts containing prophetic oracles as well as from quotations of prophecy and references to prophetic activity in royal annals and correspondence dating to the time of Esarhaddon and Assurbanipal. In view of the close cultural and chronological proximity of these texts to the period of "classical prophecy" in the OT, one expects important, relevant material for comparative study. However, the Assyrian prophetic texts have received only modest attention in OT studies, and little application of this material to OT studies can be found prior to about 1970. Several reasons might account for this. First, the state of publication of the texts and the fact that they were written in literary Neo-Assyrian made access difficult for OT scholars who had not specialized in Assyriology (Huffmon 2000: 57). The texts were scattered in various editions, individual studies, and anthologies, often only in cuneiform script without translation or commentary (Weippert 1985: 56; 1988: 311-12; Nissinen 1993: 217-18). In addition, the labelling of the prophetic texts as "oracles" confused many scholars, who assumed the material dealt with oracular divination and not "prophecy" (Parpola 1997: XIV). Perhaps, also, interest in the Mari prophecies overshadowed the Assyrian texts and distracted scholars from the attention they deserved. With the recent editions of the Assyrian prophecies by Parpola (1997) and references to prophecy in Assyrian sources by Nissinen (1998b), the relevant material is now readily accessible.[1] Two recent books on Israelite prophecy

---

1   Nissinen has also published an extensive collection of extra-biblical prophetic sources, including the Assyrian texts (Nissinen, Seow et al. 2003).

include significant references to Assyrian sources and signal a change in the level of attention these texts now receive (Ben Zvi and Floyd 2000; Nissinen 2000a).

The purpose of this chapter is two-fold: to summarize the work that has been done to apply Assyrian prophetic material to OT studies and to discuss the social location and function of Assyrian prophecy, particularly in its cultic context.

2.2 The Use of Assyrian Prophecy in Old Testament Studies

Since individual works often address a variety of topics and many studies overlap in subject matter, the following summary is arranged topically rather than chronologically.

2.2.1 Definition of Prophecy

The contribution of Assyrian sources to the definition of prophecy was discussed in the previous chapter, which highlighted the essential distinction of prophecy from other religious phenomena, namely, communication from the divine to the human realm by intuitive means through a human intermediary in contrast to technical or inductive modes of divination. In this regard, Assyrian prophecy contributes to the conclusion that the ancient Near East had functionaries who must be classified in the same way as OT prophets (Weippert 1988: 305-306; Grabbe 1995: 91-92; Nissinen 2000b: 113-14).

2.2.2 True and False Prophecy

Nissinen points to parallels between the OT and Assyrian royal annals regarding the issue of prophetic conflict (i.e., "true" and "false" prophecy). In the *Succession Treaty of Esarhaddon*, prophets are listed as possible sources of insurrection, utilising treaty language similar to Deuteronomy 13 (Nissinen 1998a: 161-63; 1998b: 160-61). The outworking of the treaty stipulations is illustrated in a letter to Esarhaddon in which the king is informed about an insurrection and the role of a prophetess who delivered an oracle against the king (Nissinen 1998a: 163-64; 1998b: 151-52). Only a fragment of the prophecy is preserved in the letter; because it is unfavourable to the king, it would have been destroyed, much like the case of Jehoiakim burning Jeremiah's scroll (Jer 36:11-26) (Nissinen 1998a: 170).

This raises the larger question about authorisation and preservation of prophecy (Nissinen 1993: 250-53). In Assyrian texts, one finds only oracles favourable to the king; but in the OT, the "classical prophets" were largely negative toward the institution of kingship (Nissinen 1993: 250).[2] These texts contrast in ideological outlook, yet both were preserved in their respective cultures to the exclusion of the opposition. In the OT, the triumph of the "classical prophets" (as "true") over the "peace prophets" (as "false") is a result of historical processes. Since their predictions proved "true" and they offered the community a way of coping with the catastrophe and theological crisis of the exile, their message was preserved for posterity. The salvation oracles that remained alive were those which, like the democratised kingship oracles of Isaiah 40-55, proved true in their proclamation of the end of the exile (Weippert 1981: 104-105). In Assyria, on the other hand, only prophecies favourable to the dynasty were archived and so survived. On this point, Laato (1996: 204) warns against assuming that ancient Near Eastern prophecy was only connected with the monarch, since only through the preserved archives in destroyed palaces do we know anything about these prophets. The existence of peripheral prophets, like those known from Mari, leaves open the probability that Assyrian prophets functioned in their local area in ways independent of the institution of kingship. Van der Toorn (1987: 97) stresses the possibility that the differences between the extant OT and Assyrian prophetic sources regarding the criticism of kingship might be due to the particular process of canonical filtering at work in each respective community.

Weippert (1988: 316-17) also discusses the verification principle in Assyrian and OT prophecy. A new oracle is to be be-

---

2   More recently, Nissinen (2003a) has drawn attention to the critical function of prophecy evident in texts outside the biblical corpus.

lieved because the prediction of the deity in the past came true (SAA 9 1.10; Isa 48:3, 6). No signs are offered in either case to verify the reliability of the new announcement if faith is demanded. But only the word that proved true historically was written down. In this manner the tablet collections of the Assyrian prophets as well as the books of the writing prophets had their origin (Weippert 1988: 318).

2.2.3 Incorporation of Prophetic Material in the OT

Based on the view that Assyrian oracles were immediately recorded without alteration, Millard (1985: 142-43) concludes that biblical prophecies were recorded immediately as well, and that this factor must be taken into account in determining the history of the biblical books of prophecy.[3] Barstad (1993: 57 n. 52) qualifies Millard's conclusion, pointing to the presence of material from different periods and of different kinds ascribed to one prophet. Van Seters (2000: 86) likens the collection strategy of Assyrian oracles to the process behind Isaiah 7-8 or Jeremiah's account of the final days of Judah. In similar fashion, Petersen (2000: 43) suggests parallels with collected oracles in Amos 1-2 or woe oracles in Isaiah. Laato (1996: 205-06) notes the following corresponding themes in OT prophetic literature and Assyrian texts: 1) religious criticism of kings; 2) prophecy addressed to the community; and 3) covenant ideology. These "form-historical frames," he concludes, suggest that "OT prophetic literature is rooted in the historical practice of prophecy in ancient Israel". Form-critical similarities between Assyrian oracles and the Nathan oracle suggest that 2 Samuel 7 contains an authentic prophetic oracle (Ishida 1977: 90-92, 115-16; Weippert 1993: 296-98; Laato 1996: 205-06; Gakuru 2000: 71, 93).

Nissinen (2000c: 245, 268) argues that the Assyrian material contributes to a more complex understanding of the process of transmission in prophetic speech. Oracles may quickly have

---

3 Others refer generally to Assyrian prophecy to broaden support for similar conclusions based upon other ancient Near Eastern prophetic texts, particularly from Mari (Barstad 1993: 48 n. 35; Gordon 1995: 68 n. 7).

been recorded, albeit with traces of scribal literary style (cf. Jeremiah 36; Isa 30:8; Hab 2:2).[4] On the other hand, many references to Assyrian prophecy in correspondence and annals suggests that a more complicated transmission process was often involved and that the *ipsissima verba* of the prophet were not of primary concern (Nissinen 2000c: 270).

Ellis (1989: 162-63) maintains that not only are the lines between prophecy and divination report unclear, but that oracles, historical omens, prophecies, royal autobiographies, pseudo-autobiographies and other classes of literary historical texts are all connected; and therefore, modern, imposed literary categories should be abandoned. Rather, these texts should be approached from the standpoint of the genre understood by those contemporary with the documents. Furthermore, because they are a redactional-literary product, OT prophetic books are not parallel to any of these sources in either form or function.

2.2.4 Assyrian Prophecy and Second Isaiah

Harner (1969) describes four elements common to the form of Assyrian salvation oracles and Second Isaiah: 1) direct address (Isa 41:8-9); 2) the assurance formula "fear not" with supporting statements (Isa 41:10); 3) message of salvation (Isa 41:11-12); and 4) self-predication by the deity (Isa 41:13). In his view, ancient Near Eastern salvation oracles originated in times of distress, thereby supporting Begrich's theory that a *priestly* oracular response in the context of cultic lament was the model for Second Isaiah (Harner 1969: 430-31).[5] The oracles are unified, and future references to salvation are an authentic part of the oracle of salvation, not an intrusion from the announcement of salvation (Harner 1969: 431-33). Drawing a similar conclusion,

---

4 Nissinen (1991: 135-38, 146-51, 181-4) employs Assyrian prophetic forms in his work on the redaction history of Hosea 4.
5 Earlier, Gressmann (1914: 289-90) argued that Deutero-Isaiah depended on the pattern of Assyrian oracles. But, as Nissinen (2003b: 123-26) notes, his view became overshadowed by Begrich's theory of a *priestly* salvation oracle, and the prophetic nature of the Assyrian sources was overlooked in subsequent scholarship, including Harner (cf. Zimmerli 1953: 195, 198; 1982: 15, 17).

Dijkstra (1980: 365-69) recognises the consistent phraseology in Assyrian oracles and Deutero-Isaiah but stresses that no particular pattern or choice of verb tense is constitutive of distinct forms. He states that the identity of functionaries behind the Assyrian oracles is vague, therefore he remains uncommitted on the question of whether Deutero-Isaiah imitated a priestly oracle or the form emerged from cultic prophecy. However, he does think that the ancient Near Eastern evidence on the whole supports the existence of cult prophets alongside priestly mantics (Dijkstra 1980: 375-76).

In contrast to earlier studies, Weippert (1981: 110) asserts on the basis of Assyrian prophecies that prophetic kingship oracles, not priestly salvation oracles, are the source for Second Isaiah (cf. Nissinen 1993: 248; 2003b). Even in Jeremiah, where Weippert acknowledges the intervention of a salvation oracle in the context of individual lament (e.g., Jer 20:7-10, 11-13; 11:18-20, 21-23; 15:10-18, 19-21), he prefers to see a temple prophet rather than a priest as the one contributing the oracle (Weippert 1988: 313-14). Weippert (1988: 314-15) notes the similarity in speech between Deutero-Isaiah and Psalms, but he does not commit himself to a position on the relationship between their respective *Sitze im Leben*.

Weippert (1997) also compares self-reference of a deity in Assyrian prophetic texts and Deutero-Isaiah (SAA 9 3.3; SAA 9 7 with Isa 48:12-16; 42:5-9; and 41:21-29). In each case, the pattern of promise/fulfilment in the past is used to strengthen the faith of the audience in divine promises yet to be realized. This reference to past prophetic fulfilment was particularly important in the case of Deutero-Isaiah, where historical circumstances might give the appearance that Yahweh was dominated by foreign deities; a problem not faced in the Assyrian texts where circumstances were clearly favourable to the king who lived under the blessing of Aššur. The homogeneity of prophetic style in Isaiah 40-48 and Assyrian oracles, over against the lack of similar forms and phrases in Isaiah 49-55, suggests that an outline of individual authorship can be ascertained for Isaiah 40-48 that isolates this core from later accretions in Isaiah 49-55 (Weippert 2001a: 55-57).

2.2.5 Imagery

Weippert (1985) discusses speech imagery in Assyrian prophetic texts and parallels in the ancient Near East, including the OT.[6] The common "Mother and Nurse" metaphor finds true parallels only in Old Akkadian and Sumerian texts, where connotations of divine kingship contrast with the later Assyrian use which only implies a functional role of the deities in protective relationship to the king (Weippert 1985: 72-73).[7] Nissinen notes, however, that in the OT the protective parental role of Yahweh is not exclusively directed towards the king but extends to the people (Nissinen 1991: 280-94; 1993: 246). In comparing "Nature Images" with OT texts, Weippert (1985: 79-82) cautions that similarities are frequently only superficial. Nissinen (1998b: 74 n. 325) notes the common expression for putting the enemy into the king's hand (e.g., SAA 9 2.4; Judg 20:28; 1 Sam 23:4; 1 Kgs 20:3; 22:12, 15).

2.2.6 Holy War

Weippert (1972) critiques von Rad's thesis that "holy war" was a theologically centred, defensive undertaking unique to Israel's tribal confederation. Assyrian prophetic texts support a broader ancient Near Eastern ideology in which there is no distinction between "holy" and "profane" warfare or between "defensive" and "offensive" campaigns. Van der Toorn (1987: 79-85) expands upon Weippert's contribution showing that promise of victory, divine presence in the midst of battle and divine participation that eclipses human action are all part of a propagandistic func-

---

6   Others have observed various parallels without undertaking a comprehensive investigation, e.g., Tadmor (1975: 43) appealed to the "Fear not!" formula to support the possible influence of West Semitic prophetic phenomena on Assyrian prophetic speech; Keel (1978: 223) noted the "shield" metaphor in comparison with Gen 15:1 and Psalms; and Ishida (1977: 90-92) discussed dynastic nomenclature.

7   Parpola (1997: XXXVI-XLI) prefers to maintain the semi-divine status of the Assyrian king, partly on the basis of this metaphor, and he suggests a similar ideology existed in the form of Asherah in eighth-century Israel.

tion of prophetic oracles of victory in the OT and the ancient Near East (cf. Oded 1992: 16-17 n. 21 and 26 n. 48).

2.2.7 Kingship Ideology and Covenant

Ishida (1977) draws attention to the contribution of Assyrian prophecies to understanding OT kingship ideology. He notes that Esarhaddon sought oracular permission to repair Aššur's temple; and Assurbanipal received a negative dream answer on the night of his inquiry, both similar to the story in 2 Samuel 7 (Ishida 1977: 85-86). Assyrian prophetic oracles, he argues, encompass most of the themes in 2 Samuel 7 except temple building (Ishida 1977: 91-92). In support of the idea that there was a three-fold relationship between Yahweh, David and the people, he cites SAA 9 3, suggesting that it, too, may have established a three-way dynastic treaty. In SAA 9 3.3, one finds the covenant tablet between Aššur and Esarhaddon which, on his interpretation, is a different covenant from that of SAA 9 3.4 between Esarhaddon and the people, witnessed by the deities (Ishida 1977: 116).

Weippert (1981) examines the ideology and function of Assyrian prophetic oracles and OT prophecy with regard to the establishment of kingship, noting that both 2 Samuel 7 and 1 Kings 11 are prophetic initiatives establishing the kingship of an "outsider" (Weippert 1981: 105-106; cf. Nissinen 1998b: 76 n. 332). A post-exilic recurrence of this ideology can be found in Haggai and Zechariah, who put their hope in Zerubbabel as the revitalization of the Davidic monarchy (Weippert 1988: 314); although a different development is found in Second Isaiah (e.g., Isa 45:1-7) (Weippert 1981: 108; 1985: 58). An original form of the Nathan prophecy in 2 Samuel 7 that excludes the temple building motif is supported by comparable kingship oracles containing dynastic promises from Assyria (Weippert 1993: 296-98).

Gakuru (2000) also makes a form-critical comparison between SAA 9 1.6-1.7, SAA 9 1.9-1.10 and 2 Samuel 7 and concludes that Nathan's oracle is a "Dynastic Oracle of Salvation", which he argues was associated with cultic festivity, not enthronement. While this genre fits well in connection with bringing the ark into Jerusalem, it excludes the temple building motif from Nathan's original oracle (Gakuru 2000: 67-70). In contrast to Ishida, Gakuru argues that Nathan's original Dynastic Oracle of Salvation had no explicit covenant associations. He concludes, "The Davidic covenant is not a historical event as such but a cluster of interpretations about the dynastic promise developed over the years under different social and historical circumstances" (Gakuru 2000: 234).

Laato (1996), focuses the covenant ideology of SAA 9 3 on 2 Samuel 5 and especially 2 Kings 11, outlining the following comparison: 1) the covenant legitimises Joash's kingship, taking place in the temple to unite deity, king and people (cf. Ishida 1977: 116); 2) a covenant between the king and the people accompanies the coronation; and 3) there are stipulations to maintain the cult of the deity (Laato 1996: 274). He suggests that Psalms 2 and 110 are connected with this type of coronation ritual and Psalm 132 reflects the king's covenant duty to maintain the cult.[8] Furthermore, perhaps Deut 17:14-20 emerges from the covenant background of such occasions; and Isa 8:16-23a might refer to such a covenant document (Laato 1996: 277). Laato (1998: 94, 99-100) argues, therefore, that covenant traditions associating enthronement and cultic reform lie deep in the early history of the Davidic monarchy and are not dependent upon deuteronomic innovations.

Nissinen's comparison between Assyrian prophecy and OT kingship ideology begins with Psalm 21. Ps 21:2-8 describes the splendour and long reign given to the king by Yahweh, while verses 9-13 treat the destruction of the king's enemies (e.g., SAA 9 1.6; 1.10; 2.3) (Nissinen 1993: 232). In the Assyrian dynastic promise, he finds similarities with 2 Sam 7:12, 16 and Ps 89:5, 30, 37. The king's filial relationship to the deity is also parallel (2 Sam 7:14; Pss 2:7; 89:27-30; Isa 9:5). While questions arise concerning deuteronomic redaction of the Nathan oracle, Nissinen judges that the critical verses are original to the oldest form (Nissinen 1993: 233-34). The problem of tracing the development of kingship ideology in the OT from pre-exilic to post-exilic time is complicated. The themes of divine love and election for

---

[8] On the basis of SAA 9 3, van der Toorn (1987: 88) earlier suggested that prophetic oracles in the OT were used regularly in the enthronement festival (e.g., Psalms 2; 110).

the king are clearly represented in the Assyrian texts, but in the OT, the concept of elective love is best seen in deuteronomic literature. In the post-exilic context, the divine relationship with the king is democratised (Isa 55:3). Here, Nissinen follows Weippert (1981) in relating the motifs and forms of Deutero-Isaiah to Assyrian royal prophecy. As an example, he cites the oracle to Cyrus, which still retained its individual kingship function, yet in the previous oracle, the same form is democratised (Nissinen 1993: 234-36).

Regarding covenant, Nissinen cites SAA 9 3.4 (where he suggests vassal kings are present on the occasion of Esarhaddon's enthronement and participate in a treaty created on that occasion) as a point of comparison with the OT. Many expressions are shared between the two, mostly from deuteronomic texts (Nissinen 1993: 237-38). Such ideas, he argues, are easily transferred from the Assyrian overlords into the vocabulary of their vassals; and in the case of the OT, Yahweh became the object of covenant verbs. However, he notes a distinction here. In an Assyrian treaty the Assyrian king is, in theory, an equal in a bilateral agreement to which the gods are witnesses and enforcers. In the OT, Yahweh is presented explicitly as the superior who is not only a treaty partner but also its witness and the one who enforces sanctions (e.g., Hos 4:1-10; 12:3; Ps 89:35-36) (Nissinen 1993: 238-39). However, he notes that Ištar appears to institute the treaty in SAA 9 3 which was used regularly in the enthronement festival of Esarhaddon (Nissinen 1998b: 165-66). In the OT concept of covenant, Nissinen again finds the process of democratisation of what was originally the prerogative of kingship. In the OT, the people represent themselves in the covenant, whereas ancient oriental treaties were concluded only between kings (Nissinen 1993: 240). Concerning the eternality of the Davidic Covenant (2 Sam 23:5; Psalm 89), Nissinen sees the preservation of the covenant ideal either figuratively, in democratisation, or through reference to a concrete messianic figure (Nissinen 1993: 241).

Starbuck (1999: 211-12) argues for a process of democratisation during the time of the exile in shaping the royal psalms for inclusion in the Psalter. He observes a striking contrast between ancient Near Eastern royal hymns and prayers and the royal psalms of the OT with regard to the inclusion or absence of regnal or personal names; and he cites SAA 9 1.6 in support of his primary examples from hymns and prayers (Starbuck 1999: 72 n. 19). He further questions the common view that royal psalms had their *Sitz im Leben* in the royal cult and were reused repeatedly as an integral part of Israel's worship (Starbuck 1999: 104, 206-208). Thus, Starbuck's conclusions stand in contrast to those of van der Toorn and others noted above.

Ringgren (1983) offers a form-critical comparison between Psalm 2 and SAA 9 7, and more recently, Steymans (2002) has done the same for Psalm 89 and Assyrian oracles. Their contribution will be treated in the examination of royal psalms, which also reproduces the study by Hilber (2003) of Psalm 110.

2.2.8 Monotheism

Religious criticism of the king is found in Assyrian prophetic texts as well as in the OT. However, Nissinen (1993: 250) notes that at worst, Esarhaddon is reproached for paying insufficient attention to the cult. Unlike the Israelite prophets, the reproach is not followed by judgment, rather renewed promise of the trustworthiness of the deity. Laato (1996: 205) adds that criticism for *religious apostasy* is unique to the OT. After comparing OT prophets with their ancient Near Eastern counterparts, Gordon (1995: 86) concludes, "In the end the difference between Israelite prophecy and the rest may simply have to be expressed in terms of its conception of its God." Nissinen (1993: 236, 239) suggests that Assyrian treaty ideology underwent a theological-monotheistic adaptation in Israel, evident as well in the emergence of a "monotheistic manifesto" in Deutero-Isaiah (e.g., Isa 43:11; 45:5, 21).

In contrast, Parpola (1997: XXI-XXVI; 2000), argues that the theology reflected in Assyrian prophets and the OT may not be dissimilar. This stems from his theory that the Assyrian pantheon may only be comprised of various manifestations of the one deity Aššur, and that the monotheism of ancient Israel was, in fact, characterized by a plural diffusion of the divine essence of Yahweh. Van der Toorn (2000b: 79), however, disagrees with Parpola's conclusions. He argues that when a prophet(ess) of Ištar speaks on behalf of other deities, Ištar is not "putting on new masks," rather the same prophet(ess) is simply functioning as an agent for a different deity at that moment of speaking. Others have criticised Parpola's interpretation of Assyrian religion on broader, methodological grounds as well as in particulars (Porter 1999; Cooper 2000; 2000; Lambert 2001/2002; Weippert 2002).

2.2.9 Social Location of OT Prophets

Writing before all of the Assyrian prophetic sources were accessibly published, Wilson (1980: 119) suggested that some Assyrian prophets functioned at the periphery of society acting to reform religious and political practices, while others who advanced the king's interests had a social locus in the court. This analysis supports his sociological model of prophecy for the OT, whereby prophets functioned at the periphery of social institutions to advance the interests of their constituency or else served in official capacities to maintain established power structures. Nissinen (1993: 223) also notes that both the content of the oracles and their preservation in the royal archive point to the *influence* of the Assyrian prophets in the court politics of their day. However, regarding social location, he follows Parpola and argues that the Assyrian prophetesses were permanent members of the Ištar temple-community (Parpola 1997: XLVII; Nissinen 2000b: 95-102). Parpola observes that these prophets addressed the masses, and that their potential to influence masses of people effectively in support of, or in opposition to, the king is indicated in the texts (cf. Laato 1996: 205). Van der Toorn (1987: 90-91) suggests that ancient Near Eastern kings may have tolerated a degree of criticism by prophets because they conveyed the sentiment of the people and therefore often enjoyed much popular support. It would be politically expedient to give opportunity for *some* voice of the people. Nissinen (2000b: 112) also calls for an end to the caricature of Israelite prophets as purely reformers who were hostile to establishment, priestly functionaries; and he questions the historical reality of prophets as innovators altogether. The impression of prophets as reformers is the result of centuries of interpretive literary tradition, when in fact, Israelite prophets may have looked mostly like the establishment cult and royal prophets of Assyria (Nissinen 2000b: 113; cf. Weippert 2001a: 34).

2.2.10 Summary

Oracles of intuitive prophecy and reports of prophetic activity preserved in Assyrian sources provide a portrait of prophetic activity very similar to that found in the OT. In terms of social function, Assyrian prophets served the interests of the court; although their social location appears to be more closely associated with the cult, and minor criticism of the king is evident in an effort to promote cultic interests. Some evidence exists, however, for greater peripheral prophetic activity in opposition to royal interests and hence a tension of prophetic authority similar to the OT. The Assyrian sources provide a glimpse of the process from oral delivery to written text. This, coupled with the similar form-critical elements in OT texts, suggests that the OT preserves authentic prophetic speech, although redactional activity in the OT over a longer period may have resulted in a more complex text. The most striking similarities are found in Second Isaiah, although royal psalms and oracles of victory share many similarities. Much work has been done on the ideology of kingship expressed in Assyrian sources, which bears similarity to that expressed in processes of enthronement and legitimisation of the king in the OT. OT dynastic oracles have much in common with Assyrian prophecy, which centres on the relationship between deity and king, and features a covenant ideology uniting the deity, king and the people. The most prominent difference between the Assyrian prophets and those of the OT appears to be the fundamental commitment of the latter to the exclusive worship of one god. Because social location and function of Assyrian prophets has important implications for the possibility of cultic prophecy in the OT, the following section examines more closely the evidence for Assyrian cultic prophecy.

2.3 The Relationship of Assyrian Prophets to the Temple

2.3.1 Messengers of Ištar

As Parpola (1997: XLVII) and Nissinen (2000b: 95) emphasise, Assyrian prophets speak almost exclusively in the name(s) of Ištar/Mullissu.[9] Furthermore, several prophets bear names reflecting their affiliation with the worship of Ištar/Mullissu.[10] This does not necessarily mean that they served in official capacities within her cult or spoke within the temple context. But this close affinity between prophecy and Ištar is consistent with other evidence, discussed below, that links the social location of prophetic service closely with the cult of Ištar.[11]

---

9   SAA 9 1.1 i 11-12, 18, 20-21; 1.2 i 36-37; 1.4 ii 30; 1.5 iii 4; 1.6 iii 7, iv 6, 21; 1.8 v 12; 1.9 v 27; 1.10 vi 1, 4; 2.3 i 36; 2.4 ii 30, 38; 3.4 ii 33; 3.5 iii 16, iv 8; 5:1, 3; 6:1; 7:2; 9:1-2. On occasion the prophets speak for Bēl (SAA 9 1.4 ii 17), Nabû (SAA 9 1.4 ii 38), and Aššur (SAA 9 3.3 ii 13-14, 25). The distinction between the Ištars of the various locations and Mullissu appears inconsequential, as they not only appear interchangeable in the voice of the prophets, but the names Ištar and Mullissu are also set parallel to one another in the texts (SAA 9 2.4 ii 30; 5:1, 3; 7 r. 6; 9:1-2, r. 1; cf. SAA 3 7:11-12). Nissinen (1993: 228; 2001: 191-95) opines that these goddesses are fused, with Mullissu appearing as one of the many manifestations of Ištar (cf. SAA 10 284 r. 4-8). In SAA 9 1.6 iii 7-15, Ištar (singular) speaks in jurisdiction over four different cities at which there are Ištar temples (cf. Nissinen 2000b: 95 n. 36). Outside the corpus of Assyrian prophecies in SAA 9, deities other than Ištar are also involved. For example, Nissinen (2000b: 99) notes that when a Babylonian scholar cites prophecy, it is the word of Bēl (SAA 10 111; SAAS 7 5.3), and events in the city of Harran are addressed by Harranean deities, Nikkal and Nusku (SAAS 7 6). It is not possible in these cases to ascertain the affiliation of the prophets who have spoken.

10 *Issār-lā-tašīyaṭ* ("Do not neglect Ištar"; SAA 9 1.1); *Issār-bēlī-da"ini* ("Ištar, strengthen my lord", SAA 9 1.7); *Mullissu-kabat* ("Mullissu is honoured", SAA 9 7); *Urkittu-šarrat* ("Urkittu is queen", SAA 9 2.4: Urkittu is an appellative of Ištar/Mullissu, as in SAA 3 13); *Sinqīša-āmur* ("I have seen her distress", SAA 9 1.2: distress is frequently associated in contemporary texts with Ištar's distress) (see Parpola 1997: L-LII). Outside the oracles of SAA 9, there is a prophetess named *Mullissu-abi-uṣri* ("Mullissu, protect my father") in a letter to Esarhaddon (SAA 13 37; SAAS 7 4.2) (Parpola 1997: CVI n. 259).

11 In addition, Nissinen (2000b: 90-95) summarises the lexical data concerning *raggimu/raggintu*, the intermediaries of the Assyrian oracles, and the designations for other prophetic functionaries. He concludes, "They found their nearest colleagues among practitioners of noninductive divination and among people whose more or less frenzied behaviour, eventually perceived

2.3.2 Located at Cult Centres

Some prophets were active outside of temple contexts. It is likely that they served in the court of the king, as is evident in one letter from a scholar to Esarhaddon complaining that the king had summoned prophets and prophetesses instead of him (SAA 10 109, SAAS 7 5.2).[12] Another text names a prophet, Quqî, in a lodging list of high ranking military officials (SAA 7 9 r. i 20-24; SAAS 7 3), suggesting to Nissinen (1998b: 65) that prophets accompanied the king on campaign as part of his divinatory apparatus (cf. reports of prophetic messages in the annals, SAAS 7 2.1, 2.3).[13] In oracle SAA 9 1.3, a prophetess speaks in the name of Ištar of Arbela, but her location is an unknown mountain village (Nissinen 1993: 228; 2001: 206-207). On one occasion, a spontaneous prophetic word comes to two men facilitating the repatriation of the Marduk statue during the reign of Esarhaddon (SAA 10 24). This incident shows that prophecy was not confined to the temple or even to professional functionaries (Pongratz-Leisten 1999: 90-91).

While these references show prophetic activity away from cult centres, the oracles collected in SAA 9 (with the exception of SAA 9 1.3) originated from cities with major Ištar or Mullissu

---

as odd by the majority of the population, corresponded to their role in the worship of the goddess [Ištar]" (Nissinen 2000b: 95).

12 De Jong (2001: 19-20) notes that Parpola's translation hinges on restoring a lacuna in line 9, which he suggests can alternatively be translated: "Why has [the king not] paid [attention] to the prophets and prophetesses?" (restoring the end of line 9 as [LUGAL *la iš-ši*] as in line 16; and interpreting the idiom *rēša našû*, "to lift up a head", as "pay attention to" rather than "summon into service"). On the basis of this alternative interpretation, he argues that the passage cannot be cited as evidence for prophets being summoned to court by the king. With respect to interpretation of the idiom, the context involves Bel-ušezib requesting a formal relationship with the king as an advisor; therefore, the connotation of a royal service is more appropriate than merely "paying attention". Also, the immediate context of lines 8-16 is a complaint on the part of Bel-ušezib that the king has not called him into service in spite of all he has done in the past. A contrast between lines 16 and 9 is more consistent with this complaint than a mild admonition to the king for not listening to the words of prophets. In short, Parpola's reconstruction and translation of the text is preferred.

13 However, these oracles could have been delivered by messengers (de Jong 2001: 37 n. 196).

temples.[14] With one exception, whenever the colophon of an oracle is preserved it includes the name of the prophet and his or her residence.[15] Of the fourteen colophons preserved, nine originate from prophets of Arbela,[16] two are from the "Inner City" (Assur)[17] and one is from Calah.[18] The colophon of one oracle names the prophetess without specifying location (SAA 9 1.7), but it may be Arbela because the oracle shares a similar theme with the next oracle in the collection (SAA 9 1.8) which did originate from Arbela.[19] In another prophecy, the location of the prophetess is not specified, but her name is at the heading of the oracle and not in a colophon (SAA 9 7:1). The purpose of the colophon was to indicate responsibility for the oracle; and so, in addition to the prophet's name the colophons denote the residence of the prophet and, by implication, the location at which the oracle was given. This is evident from SAA 9 6 where the colophon expands the usual formula ("PN of GN") to a more explicit statement of origin for the prophecy itself:

Tašmetu-ereš, a [prophet of ....],
Pro[phesied] (this) in the city of Arbela. (SAA 9 6:11-12)

Even if the lacuna specifies a GN (as opposed to a DN) that is different from Arbela, the scribe's resort to a circumlocution to specify the place of the prophecy would establish the rule.[20] The

---

14 Menzel (1981) mentions temples for Ištar in Arbela, her major cult centre (p. 6); in Assur, where she was venerated in many manifestations (p. 70) and possibly merged with Mullissu, who was worshipped there as Aššur's consort (p. 63); and in Calah (pp. 93 and 103), where Mullissu was venerated as well (p. 94). Nineveh also contained major temples for Ištar of Nineveh (p. 116) and Ištar of Temple Kidmuri (p. 121), whose major centre was in Calah. But Ištar of Nineveh does not appear in the Assyrian prophecies, except possibly the reference in SAA 9 1.6 iii 9. Parpola (1997: CIV n. 238) opines that this absence is purely coincidental (cf. Nissinen 2001: 191-93).
15 In eight oracles the tablet is broken where one might expect a colophon (SAA 9 1.6; 1.9; 2.5; 2.6; 4; 5; 10; and 11). SAA 9 8 is intact but contains no colophon.
16 SAA 9 1.1; 1.2; 1.4; 1.8; 1.10; 2.2; 2.3; 6; and probably 9 (nine oracles from seven different prophets in all).
17 SAA 9 1.5; 2.1.
18 SAA 9 2.4 (this prophetess speaks in the name of both Ištar and Mullissu (line 30, 38).
19 See Parpola's discussion of the prophetess's name, Issār-bēlī-da"ini (Parpola 1997: L).
20 Nissinen (2000b: 92) translates the text differently from Parpola:
    Tašmetu-ereš, the [prophet], prop[hesied this i]n Arbela.

case of the prophetess from an unknown village also reinforces this interpretation of the colophons:

> I rejoice with Esarhaddon, my King! Arbela rejoices!
> By the mouth of the woman Remutti-Allati of Dara-ahuya, a town in the mountains. (SAA 9 1.3 ii13-15)

It may be that the prophetess was a resident of Dara-ahuya but delivered the prophecy in the Ištar temple in Arbela. But if the prophetess spoke from her resident village, which is probably the case (cf. Nissinen 2001: 207), then this colophon is consistent with the view that the prophetic colophons designate the identity of the prophet, his or her residence, and by implication, the location where the prophecy was given.[21] In each case, the prophecy is associated with a major cult centre of Ištar/Mullissu. In addition to the evidence in SAA 9 there are three letters from priests of Arbela which cite prophecy (SAA 13 139, 144 and 148).[22]

2.3.3 Cultic Demands by Prophets

Exhortation to the king to support the cult is a notable theme of Assyrian prophecy. Two oracles place cultic demands on the king (SAA 9 3.5 iii 26-37; 2.3 ii 24-27), and Assurbanipal claims authorisation from prophets to restore temples (Assurbanipal Prism T ii 7-24; SAAS 7 2.2). A letter from a temple official in Arbela contains a report of a prophetic rebuke to the king for a cultic misdeed (SAA 13 144).[23] Another letter locates the origin

---

However, his reconstruction does not account for the space on the line lost in the break, according to Parpola's transliteration. If Nissinen's reconstruction is correct, then the problem of a different GN does not present itself. Nissinen (2000b: 92 n. 18) notes that the professional determinative precedes whatever signs were in the first lacuna, hence the title "prophet" proposed by both Parpola and Nissinen is reasonable.

21 Hunger (1992: XXII) argues that when locations are cited after the name of scholars in the colophons of astrological reports it is probably to identify the place of observation.
22 See Karen Radner's notes in SAA 13 144 linking it with 145 in Arbela (cf. Nissinen 2001: 180).
23 Nissinen (2000b: 98) cites this text as proof of the reasonable assumption that prophecies were uttered in the temple of Ištar of Arbela.

of a cultic demand from a prophetess explicitly in the Aššur temple:[24]

> The prophetess Mullissu-abu-uṣri, who took the king's clothes to Babylon, has prophesied [in the] temple: "[The t]hrone from the te[mp]le [...]" (SAA 13 37; SAAS 7 4.2)

Pongratz-Leisten (1999: 83) cites this as confirmation that prophecy was a temple institution.

2.3.4 Prophets as Temple Personnel

Several texts demonstrate the existence of prophets as temple personnel. The colophon of one prophetic oracle (SAA 9 1.7) identifies the prophetess as a votaress who probably resided at the Ištar temple in Arbela.[25] Similarly, a fragment of a priest's letter, which probably once contained a portion of a prophetic message, names a certain votaress of Ištar of Arbela (SAA 13 148:2).[26] In the letter SAA 13 37 (SAAS 7 4.2), the important role played by the prophetess in the substitute king ritual makes it likely that she was part of the temple personnel.[27] Prophets played a role in the Akitu festival along with other cultic personnel (SAA 3 34:28, SAA 3 35:31, cf. Parpola 1997: CIV n. 242; Nissinen 2000b: 100). A document dating from 809 B.C. specifying provisions for the Aššur temple lists prophetesses in a section concerning the expenditure for the "divine council" (SAA 12

---

24 On the basis of the priority of the names Aššur and Mullissu in the letter's introduction, Parpola argues that this prophecy was probably given in the Aššur temple (Parpola 1983: 329; cf. Nissinen 1998b: 78).
25 Parpola (1997: L) groups this oracle with the next, SAA 9 1.8, which is from Arbela.
26 Nissinen (2000b: 96 n. 37) notes that the oracle may only have been conveyed by the votaress and not actually spoken by her in a prophetic capacity.
27 On the other hand, her demand is not immediately accepted by the temple official, therefore, her relationship to this temple might be questioned. Nissinen (1998b: 81) suggests that the prophetess's request exceeds her normal authority on this matter, and therefore, the temple official defers to the king's judgment of the oracle. In another letter regarding the substitute king ritual, a divination priest draws upon the words of a prophetess to support his claim about the effectiveness of the ritual, although the setting of the prophecy appears to be in the public assembly, not the temple (SAA 10 352:22-r. 6; SAAS 7 4.1).

69:29, cf. Nissinen 2000b: 99-100).[28] One might include the *Letter from a Forlorn Scholar* as evidence of prophetic activity in the temple (SAA 10 294; SAAS 7 5.1). In the context in which the scholar claims to have consulted with a prophet, he reports that he had visited the Ištar temple in Calah (SAA 10 294 r. 13-14, 23, 32). Finally, Nissinen (1998b: 79, 123; 2001: 205) draws attention to Esarhaddon's reception of what may have been a prophecy in a temple of Sîn at Harran (SAA 10 174:10-14). While these last two examples only show prophets functioning in the cult, they complement the more explicit references to prophets who were institutionally supported.

2.3.5 Prophecy Outside of the Neo-Assyrian Context

Many references to prophetic speech in the Mari letters locate the prophets in a temple.[29] Nissinen (2000b: 100-101) points out that some of the deities were local manifestations of Ištar. Van der Toorn (2000b: 80-84) postulates that Mari and Assyrian prophecy differed from each other on the issue of temple association. He argues that the Mari prophets appear to be more closely related to practices of divination (a temple activity) than is the case for Assyrian prophecy and that there is no evidence from Mari that prophets ever functioned *outside* temple contexts, as was the case for Assyrian prophecy. However, Mari letters ARM 26 206 and ARM 26 371 report prophetic speech in the city and palace gates respectively, and the gathering of prophets reported in ARM 26 216 was probably not in the temple but in a court setting.[30] Therefore, prophecy at Mari was not

---

28 As Nissinen (2000b: 100 n. 57) observes in this regard, the "divine council" is an important concept in SAA 9 9 .
29 A.1121+A.2731 (Lafont 1985); ARM 26 195, 196, 202, 209, 212, 213, 214, 215, 219, 227, 233, 236, 237. In addition, see the ritual texts cited by Nissinen (2003: 81-82).
30 Roberts (2002: 165) notes the similarity between this gathering and that reported in a court setting in 2 Kgs 22:6. Van der Toorn (2000a: 222) writes, "When a prophet delivers an oracle outside the sanctuary, at the residence of the royal deputy of the city for instance, it must be assumed that he repeats an oracle revealed to him in the sanctuary" (cf. ARM 26 212 5-12, r. 10-11). While this may be the case is some instances, the evidence just cited calls his general assumption into question.

exclusively a cultic affair; and in the light of the above cited Assyrian evidence, van der Toorn overstates the case for the *degree* to which Assyrian prophecy should be disassociated from temple contexts. Contemporary with Mari is a prophetic text from the temple of Kititum (a manifestation of Ištar) at Eshnunna which exhibits similar royal ideology to the Assyrian prophecies.[31]

There is significant evidence from the Middle Assyrian period as well. Parpola (1997: XLVIII) notes that a prophetic oracle of Ištar of Nineveh dating from the fourteenth century is preserved in the Amarna correspondence (EA 23). This letter concerns a visit to Egypt by the goddess (i.e., her statue), which would have necessitated authorisation and cooperation by temple personnel. It is reasonable to infer that a temple prophet uttered the oracle indicating the goddess' will in this matter.[32] Texts from thirteenth-century Emar mention prophets in association with the Išhara (Ištar) temple, including rations for their support (Pongratz-Leisten 1999: 54, 58-59; Lion 2000: 22). Prophets are also included on a royal maintenance list for the Ištar temple at Kār-Tukulti-Ninurta.[33] Pongratz-Leisten (1999: 54-55) has identified a Middle Assyrian citation of an Ištar oracle by the *šangû* of this same temple.[34] Lion (2000: 23, 28) discusses the possibility

---

31 For translation and analysis, see Ellis (1987), who suggests that the oracles preserve actual prophetic speech rather than reflect the product of literary creation (Ellis 1987: 250, 256). Moran (1993) also argues cogently for the oral nature of this document. Pongratz-Leisten (1999: 203-204) argues that the function of FLP 1674 is similar to divine letters. However, the boundary between divine letters and oracle reports is fluid, particularly when the time reference of the letter is future (Pongratz-Leisten 1999: 211). A good example of an Assyrian text classified as a divine letter that is indistinguishable from a prophetic report is SAA 3 47 (cf. Pongratz-Leisten 1999: 232). Another Old Babylonian oracle may have originated in a temple setting, although the circumstances of the divine words emanating from the temple door are unclear (van Dijk 1962: 61-62; translation in Pritchard 1969: 604; discussion in Pongratz-Leisten 1999: 49-50).
32 The use of the introductory speech formula (*umma*) in line 13 implies prophetic speech rather than an inductive oracle (or at least prophetic interpretation of divination results). For text, see Adler (1976: 170).
33 Parpola (1997: XLVII, CV n. 244), Nissinen (2000b: 94; Nissinen, Seow et al. 2003: 185), Lion (2000: 23).
34 The citation is introduced with the direct discourse markers (*mā*) and Pongratz-Leisten notes that the expression *abata ša* Ištar (lines 5 and 6) is simi-

that the *āpilu* receiving goods in connection with temple service at Nuzi had prophetic functions similar to those at Mari.[35] This evidence fills the temporal gap separating the prophetic citations in Mari letters and the Assyrian oracles (Lion 2000: 31-32; cf. Nissinen 2000c: 238). It appears that temple prophecy constituted an ongoing part of the cult in Mesopotamia.

2.3.6 Language of the Prophecies

Parpola (1997: XLVII-XLVIII, CV n. 246 and 247) and Nissinen (2000b: 97-98) summarize the textual affinities between the Assyrian prophecies and the literature of the cult, which strengthens the link between the prophets and cult. In particular, one text (SAA 3 13, *Dialogue Between Assurbanipal and Nabû*) places a prophetic oracle (lines 24-26) within the context of the king's lament in the temple (lines 3, 12, 15, 23) and is discussed below. On the basis of the metaphors used in the oracles, Weippert (1985: 87) argues that the prophets were located in the temple rather than at court. However, the lack of metaphors drawn from court does not necessarily mean that the oracles were not delivered in such a context; rather, the prophet may simply have been more familiar with nature schemas due to the setting from which they originally came.

2.3.7 Summary

The prophecies collected in SAA 9 evidence a close association between prophets and Ištar/Mullissu, and they originated from cities that were important cultic centres. This in itself does not prove that the prophecies were delivered in the temple nor that the prophets were temple personnel. Indeed, there is evidence that prophets served outside of temple contexts. But several sources place prophets and prophecy explicitly in the temple.

---

lar to that used in the oracles SAA 9 2.4 ii 30, 38; SAA 9 3.4 ii 33; 3.5 iii 16; SAA 9 5:1, 7:2.

35 Nissinen (2003: 9) does not include the references from Emar and Nuzi in his collection of prophetic sources because he judges that the identity of the functionaries is too unclear.

This includes the title "votaress" attached to prophetesses, the inclusion of prophets in ration lists for temple personnel, the citation of a Middle Assyrian prophecy probably delivered in the temple, and a Neo-Assyrian letter citing a prophecy as given in the temple. Prophecy seems to have functioned in service of the king, but also frequently in the support of temple interests, as one might expect of prophets whose primary allegiance was to the temple community. On the whole it seems reasonable to conclude that the temple was a significant location for prophetic activity and that the primary identification of prophets was with the cultic community. Because the colophons in SAA 9 identify the prophets with major cult centres, it is likely that these prophecies originated in a cultic context.

2.4 The Function of Assyrian Prophecy

2.4.1 Royal Affairs

All of the extant Assyrian prophecies were found in the royal archive at Nineveh and consequently are concerned exclusively with royal affairs. According to Pongratz-Leisten (1999: 288) all forms of divine communication, including prophecy, were utilised in royal documents to help the king secure and hold power.[36] It substantiated the king's access to divine knowledge, thereby proving his competence to rule as a wise custodian of world order. At the centre of kingship ideology expressed in these prophetic oracles is the role of Ištar as the divine patroness of the king. The goddess nurtures him, destroys challengers, goes before him into battle and guides him into divinely authorised action in military and cultic affairs (Pongratz-Leisten 1999: 92-94), all themes that are reflected in the prophecies.

---

36 For occasional warning to the king, see Nissinen (2003a).

2.4.2 Cultic Service

Evidence shows that prophets also served more diverse needs within the society, including the maintenance of the cult, as discussed above. Nissinen (2003a: 9) has suggested that the cult in ancient Near Eastern society served a role in social welfare, so that advocacy for the cult was tantamount to advocacy for the poor as well. At times, the prophet's duty toward royal affairs overlapped directly with cultic ritual, such as the role of prophet in the substitute king ritual (cf. Nissinen 1998b: 68-81). Royal maintenance of prophetic functionaries at the temple suggests they had permanent duties; however, there are no extant descriptions of their tasks within the cult.

2.4.3 Prophetic Response to Inquiry and Lament

A clear distinction between inquiry and lament is difficult to make. Even queries by extispicy were presented in the most solemn, penitent mood and, at times, with an attitude of lament.[37] Nevertheless, when a text stresses an anguished emotional state or an attitude of complaint on the part of the supplicant, it moves the inquiry beyond the desire for information to a solicitation of action on the part of the deity. For example, the mood of an inquiry whether or not to appoint a certain person to an administrative post, or to find a lost object (e.g., 1 Sam 9:6-20), might be qualitatively different from a dying supplicant who desires to know whether or not he will survive (e.g., 1 Kgs 14:5; 2 Kgs 1:2-4; 19:2-20:2). In the latter case, an element of desperate hope that the deity will intervene favourably is present, so that invocation of the deity is motivated by more than a desire for

---

37 The formula used in divination queries petitioned the deity to disregard numerous improprieties that might negatively affect the willingness of the deity to respond, including improper attitudes such as anger. Ritual incantations were known as "prayers" (Starr 1990: XXI-XXVI). Two examples reflecting a lament background are outstanding. In SAA 4 196, Assurbanipal had been continually "moaning" (*nazāzu*) over whether or not to attend to cultic duties at various shrines. Sennacherib's prayer over the sin of Sargon expresses both lamentation and a change of mood, comparable to many biblical psalms, that was effected by a positive answer from the gods through extispicy (SAA 3 33).

information. Military campaigns would always be charged with high emotion. However, there are varieties of risk levels and assessments of circumstances that evoke different moods on the part of a king contemplating whether or not to engage in battle (e.g., 1 Kgs 22:5-12; 2 Kgs 3:11-12; 2 Chronicles 20). Therefore, differentiating inquiry and lament can be meaningful if it helps to clarify the mood and expectations of the supplicant.

Texts outside of the Assyrian corpus illustrate how inquiries and lament could be answered through prophetic agency. With respect to the Mari prophets, some oracles appear to have been unsolicited (Huffmon 1968: 105; cf. ARM 26 196 and A.1121+A.2731 in Lafont 1985). However, oracular response to a query stands in the background of texts ARM 26 207 (unspecified male and female intermediaries; cf. ARM 26 208) and ARM 26 212 (an *assinnum*).[38] The gathering of a group of prophets [*nabî*]) in ARM 26 216 for the purpose of prophetic inquiry was probably combined with extispicy, with the prophets augmenting the inquiry taken by a *bārû*.[39] In ARM 26 209, a prophetic response is given by an *aplûm* to a sacrifice offered "for the life of my lord [i.e. Zimri-Lim]" (lines 4-5), which may be a petition for general well-being rather than an inquiry concerning his future. It is, nevertheless, a prophetic response to one seeking the deity

---

[38] Lack of clarity regarding the drink ritual used to induce the prophets (see Nissinen, Seow et al. 2003: 41) does not weaken these texts as examples of inquiry made independent of extispicy. The prophetic message mentioned in ARM 26 212 might coincide with inquiry by extispicy (Durand 1988: 394); however, as Pongratz-Leisten (1999: 69-70) notes, this is not evident in the text. What is clear is induction of prophecy through drink.

[39] Pongratz-Leisten (1999: 69) suggests that the phrase *têrtam epēšum* in ARM 26 216 line 8 is a general expression for obtaining the divine will, not necessarily restricted to extispicy. That *têrtum* by itself can designate a prophetic speech oracle is illustrated by ARM 26 197 line 5 (speech of an *assinnum*), ARM 26 200 line 6 (speech of a *muḫḫūtum*) and ARM 26 203 line 28 (speech of a *muḫḫûm*) (see Durand 1988: 379-80; Fleming 1993: 180). However, as Fleming (1993: 179-80) observes, the full idiom *têrtam epēšum* has not been demonstrated to indicate anything other than examination of entrails. Fleming interprets ARM 26 216 as parallel to A.1121 where an *āpilum* gives a message in conjunction with extispicy. Durand (1988: 378) suggests the possibility that *nabûm* and *bārûm* are equivalent terms in Mari Akkadian; but given the likely cognate use of נביא for prophet in the Old Testament (see Pongratz-Leisten 1999: 69) and the attested complimentary function of the *āpilum* to extispicy, Fleming's interpretation of the function of the *nabûm* in ARM 26 216 is most likely.

(cf. also ARM 26 215 [*muḫḫûm*] and 219 [*āpilum*]).⁴⁰ In two Hittite prayers, the supplicant expected that his inquiry into the cause of a plague might be answered through a prophetic intermediary (cf. Weippert 1988: 297-99; Pongratz-Leisten 1999: 54 n. 56; Singer and Hoffner Jr. 2002: no. 4a §§6, 11 and no. 11 §11).⁴¹ Prophetic response reported in the Zakkur inscription is well-known and frequently discussed (cf. Nissinen, Seow et al. 2003: 203-207), and an oracle from Amman is reminiscent of other salvation oracles delivered during military crisis (cf. Nissinen, Seow et al. 2003: 202-203).⁴² Nissinen (2003: 9-10) draws attention to an example of prophetic response to a lament in a third-century Aramaic-Egyptian text, *Papyrus Amherst 63* vi 1-18 (Steiner 1997: 313).

---

40 Van der Toorn (2000a: 224-25) maintains that the *āpilum* is an "interpreter" of extispicy who works in association with a *bārûm* (cf. A 1121+A.2731, Durand 1988: 389; Ellis 1989: 136 n. 36; Fleming 1993: 180). But to argue, as van der Toorn does, that there is no hint of a trance or sudden illumination does not do justice to the fact that an intermediary (the *āpilum*) distinct from the diviner (*bārûm*) speaks for the deity. It appears that intuitive inspiration provides the interpretive expansion of the outcome of the query (see Durand 1988: 386).

41 These are close to corporate lament in that they are uttered by a representative for the community, i.e., the prince-priest or the king. Mentioned in the same context as dreams and extispicy is inquiry through a "seeress" in one case and a "man of god" in another. Nissinen (2003: 9) warns, however, that the prophetic identification of these functionaries is not entirely clear.

42 It is possible that the Mesha inscription reports prophetic speech in response to campaign inquiries (lines 14 and 32), but a response through extispicy is equally likely. This is a problem vexing interpretation of many OT passages as well (e.g., 2 Sam 2:1-2). The verbal form of divination inquiries lends itself to a response that might *appear* to be prophetic words, whereas in reality the response is merely a parroting back of the wording of the originating inquiry with an affirmation of the request. This complexity is discussed by Victor Hurowitz (1998), who cites SAA 4 81 as an example in which great detail of a battle plan is incorporated into the inquiry. The problem of differentiating between prophecy and response to a divination query is also highlighted by Ellis (1989: 162-63). The lines of distinction are even more difficult with regard to prophecy and dreams (Parpola 1997: XLVI-XLVII; Nissinen 1998b: 167).

2.4.4 Prophetic Response to Inquiry in Assyrian Sources

In Assyria, inquiry through a prophet was a means of discerning the divine will in addition to omen observations and extispicy. In a letter from Bel-ušezib to Esarhaddon, the astrologer complains that Esarhaddon has summoned prophets and prophetesses for divine revelation instead of him (SAA 10 109; SAAS 7 5.2).[43] Other correspondence between this individual and Esarhaddon suggests that the issues of inquiry concerned political matters, including war and appointment of high officials (Nissinen 1998b: 89-90), and so it is reasonable to suppose that these topics were part of the content of the prophetic response to Esarhaddon's inquiries. While there may have been "professional competition" between scholars and prophets (cf. Nissinen 1998b: 93-94), there is good evidence that individuals sometimes sought the divine will through both agencies.[44] Nissinen's suggestion that prophets may have been part of the king's divinatory apparatus on campaign has already been noted (Nissinen 1998b: 65, cf. SAA 7 9 r. i 20-24, SAAS 7 3). Prophetic words also played a part in granting divine permission for the restoration of temples (Assurbanipal Prism T ii 7-24; SAAS 7 2.2). However, this particular exhortation may have come at the initiation of the prophet and not in response to an inquiry (cf. SAA 9 2.3).

An instance of prophetic response to the need for information is implied in the letters of Nabû-rehtu-uṣur to Esarhaddon (SAAS 7 6). Concerned over a conspiracy against the king and a

---

43 See note 12.
44 Solicitation of prophetic messages and divination queries were not mutually exclusive practices. On the contrary, individuals availed themselves of both resources under the same circumstances. That this practice was customary is implied by the presence of a prophet in the military camp, who must have shared intermediary functions with the divination priests. The divine response to Esarhaddon's call for help in the civil war against his brothers came from both prophets and diviners (SAAS 7 2.1). Under these same circumstances, Naqia sought the will of the gods through prophets (SAA 9 1.8 and 5) as well as through divination priests (SAA 10 109, Nissinen 1998b: 23-24, 89-95; Melville 1999: 27). Since a colophon dates SAA 9 9 to the rebellion of Šamaš-šumu-ukin, then this prophetic message was received under the same circumstances in which Assurbanipal sought an extispicy report recorded in SAA 4 279. Pongratz-Leisten (1999: 86) notes that the positive pronouncements of prophets played a role alongside divination inquiries (Mannean war of Assurbanipal; Prism A iii 4-7 and SAA 4 267-69).

prophecy uttered in support of a potential usurper, Nabû-rehtu-uṣur experienced a counter-prophecy in a vision.[45] The texts do not cite the exact contents of the vision nor do they offer explicit information about what prompted this oracle; however, the fact that a deity responded with information to a needful circumstance illustrates general cultural expectation regarding such revelations.

2.4.5 Prophetic Response to Lament in Assyrian Sources

In contrast to the above inquiries, the following examples from Assyrian texts reflect situations in which the request for divine aid arises from the desperate state of the petitioner.

2.4.5.1 References to Lament within Oracles

Several Assyrian prophetic oracles refer to the lament of the supplicant. In SAA 9 1.8, Ištar responds to the complaint of Esarhaddon's mother, Naqia: "Because you implored me (*maḫāru*), saying . . . ". The oracle quotes the complaint of Naqia that Esarhaddon's brothers appear to be favoured by the goddess in their illegitimate occupation of the throne in disregard to Esarhaddon's rightful claim. The prophetess assures Naqia (and the king, presumably in absentia) that the kingdom is Esarhaddon's (Melville 1999: 27-28). In another oracle to Naqia, likely alluding to the same circumstances of Esarhaddon's exile, the goddess acknowledges that she has heard Esarhaddon's "lamentation" (*killu*; SAA 9 5:3). While Naqia was receiving prophetic oracles during Esarhaddon's exile, the crown prince himself was

---

45 The term used, *diglu* (CT 53 17:10 = SAA 16 61; CT 53 938:10 = SAA 16 60) also describes the prophetic oracle in SAA 9 11:6, although de Jong (2001: 31-32) may be correct to question Parpola's reconstruction and interpretation. Nabû-rehtu-uṣur uses phrases from the word of the goddess in his letter that echo affirmations from extant oracles in SAA 9 (Nissinen 1998b: 119-20). Thus, while the divine word came in a vision, the formula of introduction, "this is the word of Mullissu" (CT 53 17:8-9; CT 53 938:8-9), indicates that he considered this a form of prophetic revelation, particularly as it countered another prophecy.

in a state of lament, receiving prophetic oracles that encouraged his ambitions to avenge his father's death and seize the throne. The prophecy, SAA 9 3.3, records the outcry of Esarhaddon:

> Now then, these traitors provoked you, had you banished, and surrounded you; but you opened your mouth (and cried): "Hear me, O Assur!". I heard your cry (*killu*). I issued forth . . ."[46]

In this context "hearing" might only imply that the deity answered his prayer in the form of intervening action. However, inscriptions describing Esarhaddon's lament at the news of his father's assassination also report that he was urged on by divination reports.[47] In other words, Aššur "answered" him by way of revelation. The technical terms in this text denote an answer by extispicy (Nissinen 1998b: 33-34). However, the existence of prophetic oracles alluding to this historical context link a prophetic response to Esarhaddon's lament as well (SAA 9 1.2, which refers to securing Esarhaddon's succession, and SAA 9 1.6, which probably alludes to crossing the Tigris on his return from political exile to capture Nineveh).[48] SAA 9 1.2 also alludes

---

46 SAA 9 1.1 i 24-27 refers to Esarhaddon's paralysis and woe, and SAA 9 2.3 ii 12 describes his condition as one of anxiety and trembling.

47 The text emphasizes the lament of Esarhaddon at this time:
> I Esarhaddon, who with the help of the great gods, his lords, in battle turmoil never turned back, as soon as I heard their evil deeds, cried "Woe!," tore my princely garment and broke out in lamentation; I became enraged like a lion, and it enraged my disposition. In order to occupy the rightful kingship of my father's house, I beat my hands together. To Aššur, Sîn, Šamaš, Bēl, Nabû, and Nergal, Ištar of Nineveh, and Ištar of Arbela I lifted my hands, and they heard my words. With their firm "Yes" they sent me repeatedly this encouraging oracle, "Go without ceasing, we will go beside you and kill your enemies." (Esarhaddon Nin A i 53-62 in Borger 1967: 43). See also Nissinen (2003: 139).

48 See Parpola's reconstruction of the historical circumstances behind this oracle collection (Parpola 1997: LXVIII-LXIX) as well as the discussion by Nissinen (1998b: 24-34). De Jong (2001: 22) questions Parpola's reconstruction of the historical reference to crossing the river, since river crossings are commonly mentioned in campaign descriptions and therefore this reference could be to any of Esarhaddon's military campaigns. In support, he argues that Esarhaddon is already viewed as king in SAA 9 1.6. However, Esarhaddon is also viewed as king in SAA 9 1.8, which de Jong himself acknowledges to originate from the pre-accession period (cf. de Jong 2001: 20). The promises in SAA 9 1.6 refer to the security of Esarhaddon's kingship within the central cities of Assyria, possibly implying that internal security was the sole issue of this oracle; and therefore, it would not refer to a later campaign crossing (SAA 9 1.6 iii 9-10, iv 14). In contrast, other oracles which appear

to prayer in the question: "What [.....] I would not have heard you?". Esarhaddon reported that such prophetic oracles were an encouragement to his heart (Esarhaddon Nin A ii 6-7 and Ass A ii 12; SAAS 7 2.1). While the context is seriously broken, the phrase "I heard and" in SAA 9 6 appears to refer to answering prayer; although, unlike the previous examples, the historical circumstances are not known in this case. The important point is that when the deity "hears", she not only intervenes with action, but at times answers with a word through a prophet as well.

2.4.5.2 Narrative References to Prophecy as a Response to Lament

One of the clearest texts illustrating the relationship between lament and prophetic response is Assurbanipal's description of the Elamite crisis:

> Ištar heard my desperate sighs and said to me: "Have no fear!" She made my heart confident (saying): "Because of the 'hand-lifting' prayer you said, your eyes being filled with tears, I have mercy upon you." (Assurbanipal Prism B v 46-49; SAAS 7 2.3)

Later in the text Assurbanipal recalls the encouragement he received through omens, dreams and prophetic messages (Assurbanipal Prism B v 94-95; SAAS 7 2.3).[49] While there is no reference to prayer in the oracle itself, SAA 9 8 probably originated under these circumstances. A commemoration of the defeat of Elam (SAA 3 31) records a prayer of Assurbanipal offered at this time and possibly paraphrases an actual oracle (Nissinen 1998b: 53):

> When I heard [this piece of insolence], I opened my hands (in supplication) to [Ištar, the lady of Arbela], saying: "I am Assurbanipal . .

---

in collections SAA 9 2 and SAA 9 3 explicitly concern and name foreign enemies or vassals (cf. SAA 9 2.3; 2.4; 2.5; 3.2). Several oracles in collection SAA 9 1 can be dated to the early crisis phase of Esarhaddon's succession (SAA 9 1.2; 1.7 and 1.8 [Naqia's intervention]). Therefore, Parpola's reconstruction is most plausible.

49 The effect of the oracles is reflected in the words, "I trusted . . . in the unchanging message of Ištar"; "the great gods, my lords, encouraged me with good omens, dreams, speech omens and prophetic messages."

. . I have [come] to worship you; why is [Teu]mman fa[lling] upon me?" [Ištar sa]id to me: "I myself [...] . . . I made him fall [.....]."

Divine letters are another type of divine communication together with extispicy, dreams, visions and prophetic oracles (Pongratz-Leisten 1999: 202). One divine letter from Aššur to Assurbanipal (SAA 3 45) commends the king for continually approaching the god during the Elamite crisis.[50] Together, these texts portray a reciprocal relationship between lament of the king and prophetic oracles as part of the divine response to the situation.

Two texts illustrate that non-royal individuals might consult prophets in times of distress as well. In SAA 10 294 (SAAS 7 5.1) a disenfranchised scholar writes to Assurbanipal begging to be restored to the king's service. He shows the depth of his despair by reporting that he, an expert in divination, resorted to prophetic help: "I turned to a prophet (but) did not find any hope, he was adverse and did not see much". In his discussion of this letter, Nissinen (1998b: 85-88) observes that it is difficult to conclude what Urad-Gula expected of this prophet: whether an inside influence with the king or an oracle of personal encouragement. Allusions in this letter to *Ludlul bēl nēmeqi* underscore the author's role as righteous sufferer. This consultation probably took place at the temple, and it illustrates the broader cultural expectation that a deity might respond to lament in the form of prophecy. One Neo-Assyrian text specifies an offering for prophets in a healing ritual, and their role is related to that of an intercessory cult functionary named in the text (Nissinen 2000b: 94; Nissinen, Seow et al. 2003: 136, 175-77). This illustrates the role of prophets in response to lament as well as their attendance to the needs of non-royal individuals.

---

50 Livingstone (1989: XXX), following Weippert (1981: 71ff), notes that these divine letters are of a different genre from the prophetic oracles themselves; although, as Pongratz-Leisten (1999: 232) argues, at least one divine letter (SAA 3 47) is formally indistinguishable from a report of prophecy. Both divine letters and prophetic reports were part of a complex communication system between the king and the gods, and SAA 3 45, while formally not a prophecy, attests to this ongoing interaction pattern of which prophetic oracles played a part, in this case, during the Elamite crisis. SAA 13 139 records what is probably an oracle from Aššur to Assurbanipal (note first-person divine speech with "Fear not" formula), which is followed by a report that the king responded with prayer, illustrating an ongoing communication between the two parties.

2.4.5.3 Intertextual Link Between a Lament and a Prophetic Message

The two previous sections have noted prophetic oracles that refer to answered prayer and non-prophetic texts that refer to prophecy in response to a lamentable situation. A third line of evidence is provided by a pair of texts that might be regarded as a lament with prophetic response (SAA 3 13, *Dialogue Between Assurbanipal and Nabû*) and a prophetic response to what was likely the same lamentable situation (SAA 9 9). Parpola has observed that both texts share many affinities and that it is likely they both emerged from the same historical situation. Both tablets were written and edited by the same scribe (Nissinen 1993: 219 n. 8; Parpola 1997: LXXI; Pongratz-Leisten 1999: 75). To my knowledge, no one has elaborated these similarities, but the following table highlights some of the textual affinities between the two tablets. Neither text follows any established form-critical structure. Therefore, the similarities are arranged topically without regard to their placement within each respective text:[51]

---

[51] Parpola (1997: LXIV-LXV) has noted that the Assyrian oracles share common structural and thematic elements, but that they are combined freely without a consistent form (cf. Dijkstra 1980: 164). The *Dialogue Between Assurbanipal and Nabû* is a unique composition, combining elements of complaint, petition, responsive divine speech, dream report, and narrative explanation. While not purely of the genre "lament," the *Dialogue Between Assurbanipal and Nabû* contains large sections that are predominantly report of lament.

	Dialogue (SAA 3 13)	Prophetic Response (SAA 9 9)
Deities Concerned	in temple of Queen of Nineveh (3, r. 2, 6, 7) in house of Emašmaš (=Ištar temple, 12)	
	prayer to Urkittu (=Ištar, 13, r. 3) lap of Mullissu (21)	Mullissu (1-2, r. 1) Lady of Arbela (r. 1, 4)
	Nabû (esp. 1, 3, 5, 19, r. 11, 15)	favourite of Nabû (22)
	The distinction between the Ištars of the various locations is inconsequential, as they appear almost interchangeable in the voice of the prophets (cf SAA 9 1.6, lines iii 7-15; 2.4, lines ii 30, iii 18). The free interchange between the words of Nabû and Ištar is illustrated in SAA 9 1.4.	
Blessing in Assembly	Assurbanipal: I praise you *in the assembly of the great gods* (1)	I have ordained life for you *in the assembly of the great gods* (16)
	Deity: I will bless you *in the assembly of the great gods* (26)	*in the assembly of all the gods* (23)
	not come to shame *in the assembly of the great gods* (r. 2)	
	you will stand before the great gods (r. 11)	
	The phrase "in the assembly of the great gods" is only found among the prophecies in SAA 9 9.	

Creation by the Gods	the figure I (Nabû) created (15) in Ištar's lap, suckling (6-8) deposited in the lap of Mullissu (21)	creation of their (Ištars') hands (5, r. 2) arms and shoulders carry (17-18) sending love (i.e., maternal) (4)
	Unlike the previous phrase, "assembly of the great gods," the concept of divine sonship is common (cf. SAA 3 3; SAA 9 1.6; 1.8; 1.10; 2.1; 2.4; 2.6 and report 7). Nevertheless, it is a shared concept between these two texts, and the term "creation" of Assurbanipal in SAA 9 9 is unique among the prophecies, except possibly for the epithet "Creatress" in SAA 9 2.1.	
Concern for Life	ill wishers take possession of *life* (2) prolong the *life* of Assurbanipal (18) my *life* is written before you (20) I will give you long *life* (24-25) do not abandon my *life* (r. 5)	for the sake of his *life* (6-7) desiring your *life* (8, 25) I have ordained *life* for you (16) demanding *life* for you . . . your *life* you shall increase *life* (20-21)
	One of the predominant themes in Assurbanipal's laments is the concern for life, which finds a correspondingly dominant echo in the prophecy as well.[52] Guarding the physical well-being of the king is common to the other prophecies, but the term "life" only occurs in SAA 9 9.	
Promised Destruction of Enemies	destruction of enemies (r. 9-10)	destruction of enemies (26)

The shared themes (in some cases terms uniquely shared in comparison to the other extant prophecies), coupled with the

---

[52] The logogram TI.LA (*balṭu*) is used throughout SAA 9 9, but SAA 3 13 employs both TI.LA and ZI (*napištu*).

identical scribal hand and possibly common historical circumstances, suggest that these two texts are related.[53] The prophecy would have been delivered in response to the same prayers of lament recorded in the *Dialogue*.

The *Dialogue* itself preserves words of encouragement using the "Fear not!" formula so characteristic of speech in the Assyrian prophetic corpus (SAA 3 13:24).[54] The encouragement oracle within the *Dialogue* is said to come from either a dream god or perhaps a professional intermediary who prophesies (*zāqīqu*, line 23).[55] In the absence of allusion to incubation, perhaps the latter is more likely here. If the *Dialogue* is a composite of Assurbanipal's experience in this situation, it might be suggested that its composition postdates and *summarizes* the substance of the oracle preserved in SAA 9 9 (see Pongratz-Leisten's suggestion discussed below). But the absence of the "Fear not!" formula in SAA 9 9 would seem to preclude this possibility. However, the link between the *Dialogue* and SAA 9 9 does not hinge on the inclusion of a summary of SAA 9 9 within the *Dialogue*. The oracle of SAA 9 9 may simply be a completely separate oracle delivered by a prophetess in response to the laments of Assurbanipal recorded in the *Dialogue*. If these two texts share the same life setting, then the sequential link between lament and prophetic response is well preserved.[56] Pongratz-Leisten (1999: 273 n. 37) argues that SAA 3 13 is a fictive dialogue, similar to the literary technique used in the exchange of letters between deity and king. However, she proposes that be-

---

53 The prophetic oracle, SAA 9 9, is unique in one other way. It was preserved on an archival tablet of the type used for the oracle collections in the same corpus (i.e., a library copy rather than simply a report); and the oracle is clearly the only one intended for this tablet (Parpola 1997: LIII-LIV, LXI). This suggests a particular importance in comparison to other individual oracles that were written on tablets for temporary recording.
54 Weippert (1981: 72) suggests this text might contain prophetic speech although diverging from other Assyrian prophecies due to its dialogue structure.
55 Butler (1998: 82-83) argues that *zīqīqu* can denote either a dream god or professional intermediary (cf. de Jong 2001: 15 n. 56).
56 One cannot say that the lament portion of this sequence is preserved in total, since the *Dialogue* is a composite of lament and words of encouragement. We do not know what other prayers of lament were offered at this time, especially in view of indications that Assurbanipal's lament was ongoing (cf. SAA 3 13:16-18, r. 1).

hind the exchange of letters, there is an actual sequence of events in which the king reports his campaign results to the deity and the deity signals approval of the campaign by issuing a prophetic oracle (Pongratz-Leisten 1999: 274). Consequently, even if SAA 3 13 does not recount a specific instance in which Assurbanipal received an oracle during a visit to the temple, the text reflects an actual exchange of lament and oracular response that characterised the general situation (cf. Nissinen 2003b: 154).[57] The literary dependence of the *Dialogue* on prophetic speech (such as SAA 9 9) supports the idea that such prophetic responses existed in the cult.[58]

2.4.6 Summary

In addition to royal and cultic service by prophets, there exists strong evidence that prophetic response played a significant role in situations of inquiry and lament in Assyrian religious life and the cult. Many prophets appear to have functioned in the temple environment, where they would have been accessible to a supplicant. This is depicted in Assurbanipal's dialogue with Nabû, the scholar's plea for a divine word from a prophet, and the reference to prophets in a healing ritual. Access to prophetic services was not the exclusive right of the king. The Queen Mother, a disenfranchised scholar, and beneficiaries of the healing ritual all sought help from prophets in time of need.

---

57 Dijkstra (1980: 147-48) thinks that it is a collection of unconnected oracles with their corresponding prayers, yet related to an historical event and composed as a sort of psalm.

58 Parpola (1997: LXXI) suggests that *Assurbanipal's Hymn to Mullissu and Ištar of Nineveh* (SAA 3 3) was a praise corresponding to the oracle of SAA 9 9, which itself was a prophetic response to the *Righteous Sufferer's Prayer to Nabû* (SAA 3 12). It seems uncertain on what basis the latter suggestion could be substantiated, and the thematic links between SAA 9 9 and SAA 3 3 are not as strong as those between SAA 9 9 and SAA 3 13. One important concept found in the *Hymn* ("Palace of Succession", line 11) suggests a link to SAA 9 7 (line 6), which is related more to the general transition of kingship in Assyria (cf. the promise to Esarhaddon in SAA 9 1.2). The *Hymn* appears to be a praise hymn reflecting upon the whole of Ištar's blessings upon Assurbanipal, rather than in response to any specific situation of deliverance. Therefore, Parpola's suggestion regarding the link between this hymn and the context of the *Dialogue* and SAA 9 9 appears improbable.

2.5 Conclusion

Although the social location of Assyrian prophets in the cult has been argued for by others, because of the important implications of this for prophecy in psalms, this chapter has described in much greater detail the evidence for Assyrian cultic prophecy. Assyrian prophets were closely connected with temples, and cultic prophecy contributed to the display of Assyrian royal ideology and served as an important source of divine response to worshippers seeking their deity. The role of cultic prophecy in Assyria and the broader ancient Near East supports the argument, based on OT texts discussed in the previous chapter, that prophets functioned in similar ways in ancient Israel. The following chapters explore more closely the contribution of Assyrian prophecy to understanding the nature, form, and ideas of prophecy expressed in certain OT psalms.

Chapter 3
Royal Psalms

3.1 Introduction

Because the extant Assyrian prophecies concern the king, the royal psalms are their closest counterpart in the Psalter, corresponding not only in form-critical style and thematic content but also in function. Among the royal psalms, Psalms 2; 89; 110 and 132 exhibit first-person divine speech and therefore are the most likely to preserve cultic prophecy. Psalm 110 presents itself as an oracle and so is examined first. Very similar to Psalm 110 is Psalm 2, both pertaining to cultic enthronement. Consideration of the commemorative Psalm 132 and the royal lament Psalm 89 follows.

3.2 Psalm 110[1]

3.2.1 Authenticity of Prophetic Speech

On the basis of the introductory formula, נאם יהוה, commentators generally affirm the presence of prophetic speech in this psalm.[2] While some suggest the speaker is a cult prophet (Anderson 1972: 767; Kraus 1978b: 929; 1989: 346), others prefer to assign the oracle to a court prophet (Weiser 1962: 693;

---

1 This is a slightly abbreviated version of Hilber (2003).
2 Gerstenberger (2001: 264) observes that this term is almost exclusive to prophetic literature. Num 24:3-4, 15-16 concerns a prophetic figure. Gerstenberger posits general human speech for Prov 30:1, 2 Sam 23:1 and Ps 36:2. But in 2 Sam 23:2, Yahweh speaks through David, denoting a prophetic oracle, and in view of the concern of God's word in Prov 30:5-6, Prov 30:1 might indicate a form of divine word for Agur's address (cf. 2 Sam 16:23).

1987: 476; Seybold 1996: 438), or simply to speak of a court poet who adapted a prophetic revelation (Allen 1983: 86). Gunkel's customary position, over against Mowinckel, is that prophetic elements in psalms are liturgical adaptations of prophetic style (Gunkel and Begrich 1933: 370-75).[3] With regard to Psalm 110, he recognises the prophetic style but proposes that here a singer announces an oracle before the king, perhaps in the sanctuary (Gunkel 1904: 17; 1926: 481, 483). He cross-references his own discussion of Psalm 20 where he accepts the existence of sanctuary singers who felt inspired by the Spirit (Gunkel 1926: 82-83). He also observes that Psalm 110 bears a similar introductory formula to that found in Assyrian oracles, and he notes a similar expression in Psalm 110 and the Assyrian prophetic text currently referred to as SAA 9 1.4, both of which speak of the deity at the king's right hand (Gunkel 1926: 481). Nevertheless, he prefers to identify the psalmist simply as a poet or an "inspired singer" (who receives a "divine revelation"), without explicit use of the term "prophet" (Gunkel 1926: 481, 483).

The introductory formula marking the psalm as a prophetic oracle is supported by the numerous similarities to Assyrian prophecies:

1) introductory formula "word of DN to Esarhaddon (SAA 9 3.4 ii 33-34; 3.5 iii 16-17)[4]

---

[3] A good example is Gunkel's view of Psalm 2, for which he argues that the poet borrowed the hope and style of the prophets (Gunkel 1904: 8-9, 16; 1926: 5).

[4] Other possibilities are SAA 9 2.4 ii 38-39 and SAA 9 5:1, but the texts are broken. Parpola (1997: LXV) observes, "This element corresponds in every respect to the biblical *dbr yhwh*, 'the word of Yahweh'" (cf. his biblical parallels in p. CVII n. 290). The correspondence is not exact in most instances. The Hebrew expression, דבר יהוה, is accompanied with the preposition אל to designate the recipient of the oracle, normally the prophet. Parpola cites two examples where this preposition introduces the party for whom the prophecy is intended, as in the Assyrian oracles (Zech 4:6; Mal 1:1). But Psalm 110:1 employs the expression, נאם יהוה לאדני (preposition ל). Perhaps the best parallel between Psalm 110:1 and Hebrew prophetic literature would be Isa 30:1, which illustrates of the use of the expression נאם יהוה with the preposition ל to introduce the addressee. Of the two Hebrew words, דבר and נאם, only דבר is semantically equivalent to the Akkadian (*awātum*); but both Hebrew expressions are functionally equivalent to the Assyrian as introductions to the divine word of prophecy.

2) subdivision of oracle with a second introduction formula (Ps 110:4, נשבע יהוה). This is comparable to SAA 9 2.4, where a single oracle (bracketed by horizontal scribal divisions and colophons) is subdivided by parallel formulas within the oracle introducing the divine word within the oracle:

Part 1-
- Address to king (topical introduction-answering the rebels) (ii 29)[5]
- "word of (*abat*) Ištar" . . . "word of (*abat*) Queen Mullissu" (ii 30)
- Announcement of divine intervention (ii 31-37)

Part 2-
- "word of (*abat*) Ištar" (ii 38)
- Address to king (warning about rebels) (iii 1)
- Announcement of divine intervention (iii 2-6)
- Address to king (no need for him to answer the rebels) (iii 7-11)
- Announcement of divine intervention (iii 12-15)
- Address to king ("fear not") (iii 16-17)
- Colophon (iii 18)

3) change in person, both of the addressee and the divine speaker:

Examples of change between second-person and third-person addressee are illustrated in SAA 9 1.2; 1.6; 2.2; 2.4; and 2.5. Such a change supports the possibility that the king could be in view in Ps 110:6 (as in verse 7), even though the king is addressed in the second person throughout the oracle up to this point.[6] More significant

---

[5] On the basis of the form displayed in the second half of the oracle, one might expect the announcement of the divine word to introduce the oracle with the address to the king following (cf. SAA 3.4; 3.5; SAA 9 5). However, the style of oracle introductions varies, and an opening address to the recipient is used in several cases (cf. SAA 9 3.2; 3.3; SAA 9 9).

[6] Booij (1991: 403-405) attempts to maintain consistency of referent between verses 6 and 7 by arguing that verse 7 continues the description of Yahweh's actions from verse 6. However, his interpretation of the imagery in verse 7 is improbable, particularly with respect to Yahweh drinking from the wadi. De Regt (2000; 2001) argues that shift between second and third person in prophetic speech can alter the rhetorical sharpness, with third person being more distant and softer than second person address.

for the unity of oracular speech in the psalm is the change between first-person divine speech and third-person reference to the deity. This style is observable in SAA 9 3.2 ("I" [i 35, ii 1], "Aššur" [ii 3]); SAA 9 3.4 ("my" [ii 35], "she" [iii 2-3], "me" [iii 13], "I" [iii 15]); SAA 9 5 ("my" [2], "Mullissu" [3], "I" [8, r. 2], "we" [r. 5], "Mullissu" [r. 6]); SAA 9 9 ("they" [3-7], "I" [8-26], precative invoking names of deities from line 1 by the prophetess [r. 2-3]); SAA 9 11 (first person speech of both the deity and the prophet occur in the same oracle).[7] The implications of this for Psalm 110 are discussed below.

4) legitimation of relationship between deity and king[8] - "at the right hand of Yahweh" (Ps 110:1) affirms his privileged position (1 Kgs 2:19; Pss 45:10; 80:18), similar to the Assyrian king seated on the lap of the deity (SAA 9 1.8 v 15-16; 1.10 vi 29). It may also suggest the concept of heir (cf. Gen 48:17-18). The Assyrian oracle, SAA 9 1.6 iv 6, 20-21, associates sonship with royal legitimacy. Although this latter Assyrian example does not employ a physical metaphor (i.e., sitting at the right hand or on the lap) for the concept of heir, a similar ideology is present in both the Assyrian text and Psalm 110, even without the variant reading, ילדתיך, in Ps 110:3.[9] Esarhaddon was

---

7   Person shift also appears in Assyrian treaty language (e.g., third to first person and third to second person in SAA 2 2 iv. 29-v. 4 as well as first to third person in SAA 2 5 iii 2-4).
8   In this regard, the similarity between Psalms 2, 110 and the Assyrian prophecies has been noted by numerous scholars (e.g., van der Toorn 1987: 88; Oded 1992: 22; Nissinen 1993: 233; Laato 1996: 276; 1997: 92; Parpola 1997: XXXVIII).
9   The variant, which yields a parallel to the divine birth theme of Ps 2:7, has the support of some of the textual evidence (see *BHS*, ad loc.). But the traditional text should be accepted here on the basis of the more difficult, but not impossible, reading. A New Kingdom royal text from Luxor might offer a conceptual parallel in support of the difficult MT reading:
    The elite rejoice when they see him,
    and subjects perform a dance of celebration
    in his form as a youth
-translation from Baines (1998: 42); for full text see Parkinson (1991: 38-40). Hence, the theme of divine relationship is not expressed in verse 3. Rather, this difficult line continues the theme of military brilliance with images of majestic splendour and youthful prowess. Perhaps it is also relevant to Psalm 110 that this Egyptian hymn also extols the king's priestly role.

said to place his son Assurbanipal on his right hand, who was to succeed him in Assyria, and his eldest son Šamaš-šumu-ukin on his left, who was to take the secondary status of king in Babylon (SAA 10 185:5-13, cf. Nissinen 1998b: 158-59).
5) enemies at the king's feet (SAA 9 1.1 i 13-14, 3.2 i 29-30, 4:4, 5:7, cf. van der Toorn 1987: 83; Parpola 1997: 23)
6) promise of destruction of enemies dominates both Psalm 110 and the Assyrian oracles (Laato 1996: 276; 1997: 93)
7) promise of universal dominion (SAA 9 3.2 ii 3-6; 7:12-13)
8) presence of loyal supporters (implied in covenant ritual of SAA 9 3.4, cf. Laato 1996: 276; 1997: 93)
9) divine promise accompanied by a denial of lying (SAA 9 1.6 iii 32)
10) affirmation of priestly responsibility (SAA 9 2.3 ii 24-27, 3.5 iii 27-37, cf. Laato 1996: 276; 1997: 93-94)[10]
11) eternality of royal prerogatives (SAA 9 1.6 iii 11-14; 19-22; iv 15-17)
12) deity at the king's right hand affirms security (cf. Ps 16:8, SAA 9 1.4 ii 24 and 5:6, cf. Gunkel 1926: 481)

Thus, on the basis of stylistic and ideological similarities between Psalm 110 and Assyrian prophecies, the introduction of the psalm as a prophetic oracle accurately reflects its characteristic speech throughout.

3.2.2 Formal Unity of the Psalm as a Prophetic Oracle

Psalm 110:1 displays the introductory formula, נאם יהוה, implying that the entire poem should be regarded as a divine oracle. However, Weiser (1962: 693; 1987: 476) suggests that the oracles of a court prophet form only the "nucleus" of the song. Allen (1983: 86) similarly argues that a court poet has enlarged upon an original prophetic revelation. Kraus (1978b: 928-29, 935; 1989: 346, 351) questions how far the actual oracle extends,

---

[10] The high priesthood of the Assyrian king is common in the sources. Because of the association between Ištar and Esarhaddon in the prophecies, a noteworthy example is the claim, "Ištar who loves my priesthood" (Nin A i 74, Borger 1967: 44). The word "priesthood", šangûtu, is frequently used for the high priesthood of the Assyrian king (cf. CAD 17.1: 383-84).

preferring only three oracular statements in the first-person divine speech (vv. 1, 3 [variant reading], 4) while viewing the switch to third person as the prophetic singer's wishes for the king. Tournay (1960: 30; 1991: 209) would place the limits of the oracle at vv. 1-4, with vv. 5-7 constituting interpretation. Gerstenberger (2001: 263) also accepts only the statements voiced in the first person as divine speech whereas the remainder of the psalm is interpretation (cf. Jacquet 1979: 218, 225). Regarding verse 2, he writes, "Yahweh is mentioned only in the third person, so he can no longer be the speaker" (Gerstenberger 2001: 265). The remark, "he will not withdraw it" (v. 4) is, in Gerstenberger's words, "obviously a spokesman's comment" (Gerstenberger 2001: 265), illustrating how the whole oracle has been worked over by the mediator (whether prophet, priest, Levite, or leader of worship). However, he does maintain that the address to the king in second person which follows are divine words because of structural parallelism with the first half of the psalm, even though first-person divine speech is not expressed explicitly.

These views are apparently based on the form-critical expectation for prophetic speech that a switch from first to third person necessarily signals a change in speaker. However, a shift between first-person divine speech and third-person reference of the deity is not unusual in OT prophetic style (e.g., Isa 3:1-4; Hos 5:1-7[11]; Amos 3:1-7; Mic 1:3-7). The Assyrian oracles also display a rapid shift between persons within the same relatively short oracle (see above). In the Assyrian prophecies the entire speech was conceived as the word of the deity. The human prophet was merely the mediator of the whole oracle. Therefore, the shift in person is insufficient reason to divide Psalm 110 between the original divine speech and secondary poetic commentary. Furthermore, the second part of the oracle in Psalm 110, introduced by the phrase, "Yahweh has sworn" (v. 4), has not been interrupted by an editorial insertion as Gerstenberger maintains. First, the phrase, נשבע יהוה, is a standard formula to introduce prophetic speech.[12] Since, in prophetic texts, the

---

11 See de Regt (2000: 237, 241).
12 Amos 6:8 offers the best example where the expression functions as an introductory formula but is nevertheless formally part of the prophetic speech

words following this expression are part of the prophetic speech, there is no reason to regard ולא ינחם as a non-prophetic editorial insertion. It is formally part of the prophetic speech. Second, the phrase, נשבע יהוה, when used as an introductory formula to prophetic speech, is frequently reinforced with a supplemental expression. The expression, "Yahweh has sworn by X", is found in Isa 62:8; Jer 51:14; Amos 4:2; 6:8; and 8:7 (cf. Ps 89:36). A very close parallel to ולא ינחם in Ps 110:4 is found in Ps 132:11 where the same style of oracular speech appears, as well as in SAA 9 1.6 iii 31-32, which utilises the first-person form. Therefore, the whole of Psalm 110 has integrity as a unified prophetic oracle, and the components of the psalm should not be differentiated in terms of Yahweh's words in distinction from the prophet's words.

3.2.3 Cultic Setting of Psalm 110

Mowinckel (1923: 88 92) and Gunkel (1926: 481, 483) argued that Psalm 110 was spoken by a prophet (for Gunkel, "inspired singer") in the cult on the occasion of the anointing of the newly enthroned king.[13] While the identification of Psalm 110 as a prophetic oracle has strong support, it is less clear whether the psalm originated in the cult or was first delivered in the court and subsequently brought into use in worship (cf. Allen 1983: 85; Booij 1994: 302-303). However, it is probable that the setting in which the oracle was first delivered and subsequently used is a cultic enthronement ritual of the king. This has support from two directions: 1) references within Psalm 110 suggest an association with cultic enthronement ritual, and 2) the psalm likely mirrors aspects of Egyptian coronation ritual and is simi-

---

(note the parallelism with "oracle of Yahweh" [נאם יהוה]). At times it introduces a subunit within a larger prophetic discourse (Isa 14:24; 62:8; Jer 51:14; Amos 4:2; 8:7). In Jer 22:5 and 49:13, the first-person form, נשבעתי ("I swore"), is coupled with "oracle of Yahweh" (נאם יהוה).

13 Rowley (1950) proposed that Psalm 110 was written for the occasion when David was recognised as master of Jerusalem and Zadok confirmed as priest. However, the second part of the psalm regarding priesthood is introduced by the oath formula and contains themes alluding to the Davidic dynastic tradition (Day 1998: 73).

lar to Assyrian cultic prophecies performed at the king's enthronement.

3.2.3.1 OT Cultic Enthronement Ritual

Von Rad (1947; 1966b) summarised what can be surmised of the enthronement ritual in the OT. The initial phase of enthronement involved legitimation of the king at the shrine (1 Kgs 1:39; 2 Kgs 11:14). Subsequently, the newly crowned king proceeded to the palace to take his place on the throne (1 Kgs 1:40, 46; 2 Kgs 11:19). If Psalm 110 had a cultic setting, then its performance was intended for the shrine where this initial phase of divine legitimation would have taken place. The observation that it is "from Zion" (the location of the cultic shrine, Ps 20:3) that Yahweh extends the king's sceptre (Ps 110:2) reinforces this presumption. The pronouncement of divine relationship in Ps 110:1 ("sit at my right hand") might imply a cultic setting. It has been suggested that reference to Yahweh's "right hand" is more than metaphorical, alluding to a special ceremonial place of the king in the temple (cf. 2 Kgs 11:14; 23:3, denoted as "his pillar/place" in 2 Chr 34:31).[14] While this is an attractive idea, the evidence is insufficient to make the connection with Ps 110:1. The same might be said for interpreting Ps 110:7 as an allusion to a sacred fountain at the shrine (1 Kgs 1:38, 45, Weiser 1962: 697; 1987: 479). But the designation "priest" is most appropriate if conferred in the context of the cult over which the king exercised considerable responsibility (cf. Kraus 1978b: 934; 1989: 351).

3.2.3.2 Ancient Near Eastern Counterparts

The association of Psalm 110 with cultic enthronement ritual is strengthened by similarities between Psalm 110 and aspects of cultic enthronement in Egypt, and more significantly, cultic prophecy in Assyrian enthronement ritual. The similarity be-

---

14 Cf. Weiser (1962: 694; 1987: 477) and von Rad (1947: cols. 212-13; 1966b: 223-24).

tween OT descriptions of enthronement and Egyptian custom has been noted by numerous scholars (e.g., von Rad 1947: cols. 213-14; 1966b: 224-30; Herrmann 1986: 129). In particular, the coronation rituals of Hatshepsut and Horemheb illustrate a process similar to that outlined in the OT: election by divine decree in the temple followed by enthronement in the palace.[15] Bell (1985: 270, 280) argues that the coronation rituals undertaken by Hatshepsut and Horemheb at the Luxor temple served successive Egyptian kings from the New Kingdom onwards, the importance of which was recognised even at the time of Alexander the Great. Baines (1995: 35) suggests that by the Third Intermediate Period "kingship and succession may have been more directly dependent on gods and oracles" for legitimation.[16] This was likely reflected in some manner in temple rituals. With specific reference to Psalm 110, Keel illustrates several expressions using iconographic images from Egypt.[17] Of particular interest is the fact that Horus (at whose right side Horemheb is seated in Keel's illus. 353) is described in Horemheb's coronation inscription as bringing Horemheb under his embrace before Amun for coronation.[18] In the same coronation inscription is the declaration that "The Nine Bows (i.e., the king's enemies) are beneath his feet" (cf. Keel, illus. 342a).[19] Another important parallel is that of the high priesthood, established at Egyptian coronations and conferred upon the Davidic king in Ps 110:4. Although no explicit declaration of this appears in the extant Egyptian coronation texts, the role of the Egyptian king as high priest is stressed in iconography, which portrays the king as the sole priestly functionary.[20] In Horemheb's coronation inscription, his duty upon receiving the crown is the restoration of temples and

---

15 For a description, see Kemp (1991: 206-208) and O'Connor (1995: 277-78).
16 Apart from descriptions of the deity's binary response to oracular questions during festival processions, the means by which the divine words were communicated in the Egyptian context are unknown. The more extensive, non-binary, divine address recorded in coronation inscriptions must have been communicated through some human agency (cf. McDowell 1990: 109-110). In the OT and Mesopotamian context, divine words are known to have been conveyed through prophetic agency.
17 Keel (1978: 253-56 [enemies as a footstool], 263 ["sit at my right hand"]).
18 Breasted (1906b: 16) and Murnane and Meltzer (1995: 231).
19 Breasted (1906b: 18) and Murnane and Meltzer (1995: 232).
20 Kemp (1991: 190) and Baines (1998: 28).

installation of priests, implying the investiture of high priesthood at his coronation.[21] Starbuck (1999: 143-58, 152) summarises other similarities between Egyptian royal ideology and the language of Psalm 110; but as he observes, expression of royal ideology is not necessarily language restricted to enthronement ritual.

The similar royal ideology expressed in Assyrian prophetic texts and Psalm 110 has been noted above. But one collection of Assyrian oracles is most likely linked to enthronement. Parpola (1997: LXIV, LXX) argues that SAA 9 3 was read at the coronation celebration of Esarhaddon conducted at the Aššur temple (note the temple name, "Ešarra", in SAA 9 3.1 i 14) and publicly delivered by the prophet (cf. Nissinen 2000c: 251-53). Especially noteworthy in this oracle collection is the forging of a covenant between the deities, the king and the people, and the reading of the covenant in the king's presence, which parallels Israelite custom as well (SAA 9 3.3 and 3.4; 2 Kgs 11:12, 17).[22] Laato (1996: 276; 1997: 88-95) associates the coronation ritual reflected in SAA 9 3 with Psalm 110: 1) legitimation of kingship; 2) destruction of enemies; 3) presence of loyal supporters; and 4) priesthood of the king. Further illustrating a connection between divine oracle, cult and enthronement in Mesopotamia is the re-investiture of kingship during the Late Babylonian Akitu Festival, which involved priestly declaration of a salvation oracle legitimising the king's rule with removal and re-investiture of royal symbols.[23] The Egyptian enthronement was likewise celebrated annually.[24] If the commemoration was cultic, it is likely that the original act was too. In sum, based on affinities to both practices described in the OT and broader ancient Near Eastern custom, it is likely that Psalm 110 was a prophetic oracle originating and subsequently used in conjunction with cultic celebration of the king's enthronement.[25]

---

21 Breasted (1906b: 18) and Murnane and Meltzer (1995: 232-33).
22 Ishida (1977: 116), van der Toorn (1987: 92-93) and Laato (1996: 277; 1997: 92).
23 Van der Toorn (1987: 93; 1991: 333-34); Lambert (1998: 64-65).
24 Hoffmeier (1997: 32-33); Kemp (1991: 206).
25 On the basis of the anonymous nature of the royal psalms, Starbuck (1999: 104, 206-208) questions the common view that royal psalms had their *Sitz im Leben* in the royal cult and were reused repeatedly as an integral part of

3.2.4 Date of the Psalm

It was once common for many scholars to place Psalm 110 confidently in a post-exilic context (e.g., Duhm 1899: 254-56), a position against which Gunkel and Mowinckel argued at length (Mowinckel 1923: 88-89; Gunkel 1926: 484). Subsequent scholarship has tended to date the psalm in the early monarchy; however, proponents of a post-exilic date remain.

Gerstenberger (2001: 265) states that the question of a "priest-king" is not a matter of "if" but "when" the merger between the political and sacred took place. He concludes that the universal outlook, world government from Zion and eschatological battle against the nations are incompatible with preexilic Judean theology; rather the psalm emerged with post-exilic messianic expectation using veiled language to avoid arousing the attention of Persian officials (Gerstenberger 2001: 266-67). Tournay (1960: 26; 1991: 211-12; 1998: 330-31) argues that Psalm 110 cannot date earlier than the fourth or third centuries because of its dependence on the narrative about Abraham and Melchizedek, which must be dated in the post-exilic period.

The Assyrian evidence does not constitute a decisive argument regarding the date of Psalm 110. Therefore, before considering the implication of the Assyrian sources, the arguments for a post-exilic date merit some discussion. The most important observation with respect to the date of Psalm 110 is the reference to "my lord" (Ps 110:1), which necessitates a present royal addressee and therefore a pre-exilic context.[26] The supposed in-

---

Israel's worship. It does not seem to follow necessarily from the anonymity of royal psalms that their setting is not the royal cult. Anonymity could arise from the distinctly (Davidic) dynastic nature of royal ideology in Judah in which oracular liturgy such as Psalms 2 and 110 is not concerned with David, *per se*, but with all succeeding Davidic kings (cf. Psalms 89 and 132). In this regard, Starbuck (1999: 99, 207) correctly notes that biblical psalms are concerned for the *institution* of kingship over against the promulgation of ideological claims of individual kings.

26 In spite of his recognition that "lord" can be used in royal contexts (he cites 1 Sam 25:25 and 2 Sam 1:10; a better example is 1 Sam. 22:12), Tournay (1960: 6-7, 39; cf. Treves 1965: 86) regards the absence of such words as "king", "royal", "anointing", "throne" to be a significant problem for the view that Psalm 110 addresses a monarch. The Assyrian oracles offer a parallel in this regard. SAA 9 1.4 is an exception to the other oracles in that the word "king" is absent. Nevertheless, it is a royal prophecy. Even if Esarhad-

compatibility of universal dominion with pre-exilic national realities has been adequately explained by reference to ancient Near Eastern royal ideology, which tended toward the hyperbolic, particularly as an expression of optimism for a newly enthroned monarch.[27] Seybold (1996: 439) notes that Melchizedek's association with the Creator God confers universal dominion upon the Creator's representative, in this case the Melchizedekian Davidic king. Regarding the use of veiled language, the psalm could not be more clear in supporting military conquest on the part of a ruling Judean monarch in spite of the difficulties in text and interpretation of imagery. If post-exilic, Psalm 110 would easily have roused the concern of Persian authorities. Furthermore, the militaristic language of Psalm 110 is not "eschatological" and therefore offers no basis for dating by comparison with a theorised chronological development of Israel's view of the future.[28] Gunkel (1926: 484) specifically addressed the problem of a monarchic period merger of royal and priestly titles. Among his other arguments in support of the possibility of a pre-exilic date, he notes that the theology of the post-exilic community (reflected in 2 Chr 26:16) was no less cautious about such a merger than the pre-exilic community. Likewise, Rooke (1998: 206-208) argues that the Jewish community was ambivalent toward Hasmonaean pretensions to royalty: A king might function as priest by virtue of sacral responsibilities, but a priest (i.e. the Aaronic Hasmonaeans) was not an acceptable substitute for the expected *Davidic* monarch. Day (1998: 74) has argued that "the most natural time for the Israelite royal ideology to have been fused with that of the Canaanite

---

don's name were not attached to the oracle, its royal nature might be surmised on the basis of divine legitimation metaphors (DN your right side; DN at your left; SAA 9 1.4 ii 20-26). Similarly, Psalm 110 can be identified as a royal psalm on the basis of the numerous metaphors which support the royal connotation of "lord".

27 See the discussion by Gunkel on Psalm 2 (Gunkel 1926: 8-9 cf. Gunkel and Begrich 1933: 147-49; 1998: 104-105). See also the discussion on the date of Psalm 2, in particular regarding Egyptian execration texts which symbolised the Egyptian king's dominion over nations outside of Egyptian jurisdiction.

28 Such militaristic language is common in ancient Near Eastern royal texts (e.g., the comparative Assyrian oracles in SAA 9) and frequent in the psalms as well (Pss 2:8-11; 18:48-50; 21:9-13; 72:8-11; 118:10-12).

Melchizedek is soon after David's conquest of Jerusalem".[29] Thus, in his view, Psalm 110 preserves authentic traditions concerning the royal priesthood of Jebusite Jerusalem. Against proposals for a post-exilic fusion, he notes that post-exilic theology sought to enhance the standing of the Aaronite priesthood, making the origin of a Melchizedek tradition unlikely at this time.[30]

While not decisive evidence, the Assyrian oracles are relevant to the question of the date of Psalm 110, offering an external parallel to the biblical sources. All of the Assyrian prophecies in SAA 9 originated during the reigns of Esarhaddon and Assurbanipal and concern royal affairs. Since Psalm 110 conforms to a pattern used in the real monarchic situation of seventh century Assyria, it is reasonable to place the psalm in a similar monarchic setting, thus supporting the other arguments adduced for a pre-exilic date.

3.2.5 Conclusion

Assyrian prophecies testify to the existence of cultic, royal prophecy in the seventh century in a society rather near to Israel and Judah. With respect to Psalm 110, they offer comparable stylistic and form-critical features which bear on the questions of the nature, form, setting and date of the psalm. On the basis of these similarities, Psalm 110 should be classified as a unified cultic enthronement prophecy dating to the monarchic period.

---

29 Cf. Day (2004: 226-27, esp. n. 1).
30 Cf. Gunkel (1926: 485). See also the more extensive discussion of Emerton (1971: 414-19), who posits an early monarchy date for the Melchidezek tradition and specifically argues against a proposed post-exilic date.

3.3 Psalm 2

3.3.1 Authenticity of Prophetic Speech in Psalm 2

Several stylistic features of Psalm 2 are similar to prophetic literature, such as rhetorical question (v. 1)[31], report of hostile intent and musing of the nations (vv. 1-3),[32] first-person divine speech (vv. 6-8), admonition and threat to foreign kings (vv. 10-12).[33] This has led some commentators to conclude that Psalm 2 is of prophetic origin. Mowinckel (1923: 88) maintained that on the occasion of a new king's enthronement either a cult prophet spoke these legitimising words of Yahweh or perhaps the king himself was seized with the spirit of inspiration at the time of his anointing. Anderson (1972: 63-64) regards Psalm 2 as coming from a cult (or possibly court) prophet. Kraus (1978a: 146; 1988: 126) speaks of the "prophetic power" of Psalm 2 and leans toward authorship from a court prophet. But the prophetic flavour is explained differently by others. In spite of appreciation for the prophetic style of Psalm 2, Gunkel (1904: 9-10; 1926: 5) argued that the psalm is only a fictive, poetic imitation of prophetic speech. Craigie (1983: 64-65) suggests that the psalm might be a poetic liturgy in which the opening words were spoken by priestly or prophetic leaders, or the congregation, after which the king uttered divine words from the covenant between God and the Davidic dynasty. Others, such as Weiser (1962: 109; 1987: 74), are reticent about prophetic authorship and speak only in terms of a "court poet" who perhaps wrote words recited by the Davidic king. Indeed, a major difficulty in assigning prophetic origin to Psalm 2 is that the stylistic devices being compared are not exclusive to prophetic speech. For example, Gunkel (1926: 5, citing Pss 3:2, 8:2, 10:1, 13:2, 15:1) shows that the use of rhetorical questions is not unusual in poetry. Gerstenberger (1988: 45) traces the plaintive "Why?" to forensic

---

31 Gunkel (1926: 5-6) notes the opening rhetorical question and compares it with Isa 22:1; 63:1; and Jer 46:7 (cf. למה: Isa 40:27; Jer 44:7; Amos 5:18; Mic 4:9).
32 E.g., Mic 4:11-12; Hab 2:18-19 (report of speech following rhetorical question).
33 Gunkel (1904: 15-16) compares this with Jer 27:1-11.

speech.³⁴ He also notes that the citation of the words of enemy nations appears elsewhere in psalms of national complaint (e.g., Ps 83:3-5). The first-person divine speech can be understood as a secondary citation, possibly from covenant formulas. This type of approach removes the necessity of a prophetic origin for the psalm.

Assyrian cultic prophecies share numerous features in common with Psalm 2, which supports the similarities pointed out from OT prophetic texts and strengthens the case for the prophetic character of the psalm. In addition, the probable setting in which the Assyrian oracles and Psalm 2 functioned is inseparable from the content and strengthens the comparison (Ringgren 1983: 91). While the question of setting is discussed in the next section, the similarities in form and content can be summarised as follows:

1) rhetorical questions (SAA 9 1.1 i 6-7; 1.2 ii 2-3; 1.4 ii 34-36; 2.4 iii 16).
2) the wavering of vassals is a central concern in both Psalm 2 and Assyrian prophetic exhortations (SAA 9 2.4 ii 29; SAA 9 7:3-13).
3) citation of the words of foreign peoples and kings (SAA 9 2.4 iii 7-10 [words of rebellion]; SAA 9 7:8-11 [words of allegiance³⁵]; perhaps 3.4 iii 7-8 if this includes the words of vassals mirrored in the words of their deities).
4) the reference to royal protocol, חק (von Rad 1947: cols. 213-15; de Vaux 1961: 1:103; 1966b: 225-27). Laato (1997: 92) relates this term to reading the covenant in the Assyrian enthronement ceremony (SAA 9 3.3 ii 27). The term *adê* in the Assyrian oracle is cognate with biblical Hebrew עדות, which is used similarly with covenant implications in Israelite kingship (2 Kgs 11:12, 17; Ps 132:12). The covenant implications of חק are seen most clearly in conjunction with עדות in Ps 81:5-6 and with ברית in Ps 105:10.³⁶

---

34 Compare Ps 79:10 with Ps 2:1-3.
35 While presenting a contrasting posture on the part of vassals, both texts exhibit the theme of foreign conspiracy. See below for more detailed discussion.
36 Jones (1965) argues for an emphasis on the demand aspect of חק, which in the context of enthronement consists of Yahweh's institution of Davidic

5) installation to kingship (SAA 9 1.2 i 33-35; 1.6 iii 19-22[37]; 1.8 v 22-23[38]). It is difficult to distinguish between these passages, which probably anticipate the actual installation to kingship, and those that merely affirm security of kingship (e.g., SAA 9 1.6 iv 33; 1.7 v 8-9; 1.10 vi 19-30; 2.3 ii 1-14). According to Parpola's reconstruction of the historical background, the oracles collected in SAA 9 1 precede the actual accession of Esarhaddon whereas those in SAA 9 2 refer to the consolidation of his power (Parpola 1997: LXVIII-LXXI).[39] Particularly relevant is SAA 9 7, which promises to Assurbanipal his installation as king and dominance over foreign kings whose words of allegiance are cited (Ringgren 1983). As discussed below, SAA 9 3 probably played a part in the coronation celebration (and perhaps renewal of kingship).
6) declaration of divine sonship (SAA 9 1.6 iv 6, 20-21; 1.9 iii 29; 2.5 iii 26-27, iv 20; 7 r. 6-10). Parpola (1997: XXXVI-XLII) has discussed this theme at length and noted the comparison with OT royal ideology. However, against Parpola's opinion that the Assyrian king was portrayed in a semi-divine fashion, Weippert (1985: 72-73; 2002: 24-28) argues that the relationship between deity and king in Assyrian ideology was functional rather than ontological (cf. Cooper 2000: 440). A functional interpretation of "divine election to kingship" is also followed by Oded (1992: 22) and Nissinen (1993: 234, 246-47). In any case, in Ps 2:7 the idea of divine kingship is excluded by the use of "today" (Gunkel 1926: 7; Seybold 1996: 32).
7) promise of universal dominion (SAA 9 3.2 i 28-34; ii 3-6).
8) subjugation of rebels paying tribute at the king's feet and destruction of enemies (SAA 9 1.1 i 8-10, 1.2 i 31-32, ii

---

kingship with its implications for submission by all people. The Assyrian oracle SAA 9 3 contributes to this discussion in that it contains installation to kingship with promises of sovereignty, a call to Assyrians and vassals to submit, and a demand on the king to fulfil cultic responsibilities.

37 The present tense in lines iii 14 and iv 17 *anticipate* Esarhaddon's rule.
38 As Parpola (1997: LXVIII) notes, oracle 1.8 is addressed to the queen mother anticipating the enthronement of her son, Esarhaddon.
39 He differentiates between the original historical context in which the oracles were delivered and the later time when the oracles were edited into collections (Parpola 1997: LXXVII-LXXVIII).

4-7, 2.3 ii 15-16, 2.4 ii 31-33, 2.5 iii 23-25, 3.2 i 29-30, 4:4, 5:7, esp. 7:9-13, cf. van der Toorn 1987: 80; Laato 1996: 276; 1997: 93).

9) exhortation to subjects of the king (SAA 9 3.2 i 27 is comparable to the call to the king's vassals in Psalm 2)

10) invitation to be joined in covenant with the newly enthroned king—includes deities and their vassals by proxy (SAA 9 3.4 ii 35-36).

These formal characteristics demonstrate that Psalm 2 is similar in many ways to the content and rhetorical thrust of Assyrian prophecy. As Ringgren (1983) observed, SAA 9 7 and Psalm 2 share several features in common.[40]

However, the following summary sets forth the parallels in a more detailed manner:

SAA 9 7	Psalm 2
Prophetic title	The king himself speaks prophetically at the ritual, not needing introduction (?)
Divine speech formula (2; *abat DN*)[41]	Introduction of divine speech (4-5; יְדַבֵּר)
Promise of Enthronement (3-7)	Performance of Enthronement (6-7) (allusion to covenant; "today")

---

40   Ringgren outlines the contents of the respective texts as follows:

          SAA 9 7   Psalm 2
1. World dominion   1. Rebellion of the princes (vv. 1-3)
2. Allusions to coronation   2. Allusions to coronation (v. 6)
3. Rebellion of the princes   3. Sonship (v. 7)
4. Promise of victory   4. World dominion (v. 8)
5. Sonship   5. Promise of victory (v. 9)
6. Protection

41   Weippert (1981: 77) argued that the phrase *abat* LUGAL in SAA 9 7:2 is borrowed from technical legal literature referring to the judicial decision of the king in response to a royal appeal; rejecting the possibility that the logogram LUGAL can be translated "Queen". However, Parpola's translation (word of Queen [Mullissu]) appears satisfactory on the basis of the syllabically written parallel (*abat šarrati* [Mullissu]) in SAA 9 2.4 ii 30 to which Parpola appeals, a view Weippert (2002: 48) now accepts.

Vassals speak of allegiance (8-11)[42]	Vassals speak of rebellion (1-3)
Promise of Suzerainty (12-r. 5) (2nd person address to king)	Promise of Suzerainty (8-9) (2nd person address to king)
Affirmation of Sonship (r. 6-11) (promise of protection-"fear not")	Affirmation of Sonship (7) (followed in Psalm 2 with promise of suzerainty)
	Warning to foreign kings and blessing (10-12)

Several striking differences also merit comment. First, none of the Assyrian oracles, including SAA 9 7, are spoken by the king. However, *Assurbanipal's Hymn to the Ištars of Nineveh and Arbela* (SAA 3 3) is in first-person speech of the king with several themes corresponding to those in the Assyrian oracles and Psalm 2 (affirmation of sonship, reference to Ištar's words for enthronement, promise of suzerainty and fear of rebellious vassals who kiss the king's feet). While direct first-person divine speech does not appear, divine speech is referred to with con-

---

42 According to Ringgren's (1983: 93) interpretation, lines 8-11 constitute words of rebellion. Parpola subsequently translated this section in SAA 9 7 as an acknowledgement of Ashurbanipal's suzerainty. The difficulty appears to stem from the understanding of the preposition *ina*. Ringgren interprets it in an adversative manner ("against"), drawing upon the context of rebellion in the second half of the oracle for support. However, his translation of line 11, "Let [his might?] among us be dissolved", is not possible in view of the G precative *liprus*, which must be active, not passive. In addition, Ringgren's translation of *ina* (line 8) as an adversative preposition has no other lexical support. Parpola's interpretation appears to be grounded in the acquiescence of the vassals to Assurbanipal's judgment in line 11. For understanding the preposition *ina* in an unusual directive sense, he cites three texts in his notes where the phrase *alāku ina muḫḫi* means "to go to see". There is some evidence for a merger between *ina* and *ana* in Neo-Assyrian (cf. SAAS 13, p. 69-70). Weippert's translation (2002: 50-51) agrees with Parpola's on this point, although he differs in other minor matters in reconstructing the text. In Ringgren's (1983: 93) view, this section of SAA 9 7 refers to the rebellion of Egyptian vassals against Assurbanipal recorded in his annals. However, the date of SAA 9 7 before the Egyptian rebellion renders a direct connection unlikely (cf. Otto 2002: 48-49 n. 65). On the other hand, Otto's dismissal of Ringgren's argument for a parallel between Psalm 2 and SAA 9 7 is too hasty (Otto 2002: 48-49 n. 66).

tents that are conceptually similar to Psalm 2. If it were not for the first-person divine speech in Psalm 2 on the one hand, and the declarations of praise in *Assurbanipal's Hymn* on the other, SAA 3 3 might be considered a close parallel to Psalm 2.

A second important difference between Psalm 2 and SAA 9 7 is the absence in Psalm 2 of the "fear not" formula, which appears so frequently in Assyrian and OT salvation oracles. However, this formula is also conspicuously absent in the Assyrian oracle collection SAA 9 3. Perhaps the special use of the oracles in SAA 9 3 as part of an enthronement document resulted in a variance in form from the salvation oracles of collections 1 and 2. After all, the Assyrian king is not in a state of distress or anxiety in the coronation setting of SAA 9 3 as he is in the background to the other oracles. The use of prophetic oracles in royal psalms such as Psalms 2 and 110 might be comparable. Because the setting of these royal psalms is not one of distress for the king, the "fear not" formula is inappropriate. The variation of form can be illustrated elsewhere in psalms. While in OT and Assyrian salvation oracles the "fear not" formula frequently appears in conjunction with the divine self-presentation formula, where the self-presentation formula appears in Psalms 50 and 81, the "fear not" formula is absent. This is understandable in that the tone of warning in these psalms does not lend itself to the inclusion of "fear not" in the message.

Third, Psalm 2 concludes with a warning, or perhaps invitation, to foreign kings and a promise of blessing for submission. One associates the blessing formula (אשרי) at the end of Psalm 2 with wisdom literature. This has contributed to the conclusion of some commentators that Ps 2:10-12 is a redactional addition in order to merge Psalm 2 with Psalm 1.[43] However, wisdom themes and blessing formulas are not foreign to Assyrian coronation texts. Assurbanipal's coronation hymn (SAA 3 11 r. 3) ends with instructions for a priestly "blessing" (*karābu*). This dual blessing contains wishes of "happiness" and effective rule for Assurbanipal (the "circumspect man", *māliku*, an advisor, counsellor) and a warning of curses on those disloyal to the king. Therefore, similar themes in the concluding section of Psalm 2 are also appropriate to the psalm's content and prob-

---

43 E.g., Zenger (Hossfeld and Zenger 1993: 49); Seybold (1996: 31).

able setting. The fact that Psalm 2 urges submission to Yahweh can be understood as an example of Israelite piety in the mouth of the king (cf. loyalty to Ištar = loyalty to Esarhaddon in SAA 9 3.4).

3.3.2 Cultic Setting

Gunkel (1926: 5; 1933: 144-45; 1998: 102) and Mowinckel (1923: 80-88), followed by most modern commentators, place Psalm 2 in the context of an enthronement ceremony.[44] While the psalm is frequently assigned to a cultic setting, the consensus on this is less well formed. Craigie remarks, "it is . . . uncertain whether the psalm may reflect the coronation liturgy of the temple or a later ceremony in the palace" (Craigie 1983: 65).[45] However, the likelihood of the psalm's use in cultic enthronement ritual receives support similar to that adduced for Psalm 110: 1) references within the psalm itself suggest an association with the sanctuary; 2) the psalm likely mirrors aspects of Egyptian coronation ritual in the temple and is similar to Assyrian cultic prophecies performed at the king's enthronement.

---

[44] E.g., Weiser (1962: 109, 112; 1987: 74, 76); Anderson (1972: 64); Kraus (1978a: 145; 1988: 126). Seybold (1996: 31) associates Ps 2:7-9 with enthronement ritual but the royal psalm as a whole (Ps 2:1-11a) with a national crisis. Loretz (2002: 41-43) accepts Ps 2:6-9 as part of pre-exilic coronation ritual even though he regards the greater part of the psalm as Hellenistic.

[45] Willis (1990) argues against an enthronement setting altogether, in part out of concern that this interpretation necessitates a mythic drama, thereby excluding a historical setting. He theorises that the psalm was performed prior to the king engaging the enemy in combat. However, mythic drama is not concomitant with an enthronement interpretation and in any event would not preclude real historical circumstances; and the similarity in language between pre-combat contexts and enthronement is not surprising, since the military invulnerability of the king was a predominant theme of enthronement ceremonies in the ancient Near East.

3.3.2.1 OT Cultic Enthronement Ritual

As in the case of Psalm 110, Psalm 2 corresponds to the divine legitimation phase of the enthronement ritual, which took place at the sanctuary. In Ps 2:6, Yahweh's affirmation that he installs his king "on Zion", specifically, his "holy mountain", connects the royal ideology of the psalm with the sanctuary.[46] The employment of the word, "today", in Ps 2:7, with the performative (or recent) perfect indicates that the announcement of the oracle in verses 7b-9 took place in the same context as royal adoption, i.e., during the enthronement festival.[47]

3.3.2.2 Ancient Near Eastern Counterparts

The general correspondence between Egyptian custom and the OT has been discussed above. However, with specific reference to Psalm 2, attention has often been drawn to the decree of divine sonship.[48] This is well attested in Egyptian coronation rituals, the coronation texts of Hatshepsut being the model.[49] The declaration of sonship was spoken by the deities themselves, and such divine statements were accompanied by promises of triumph over rebellious vassals. Hatshepsut's father commands

---

46 "Zion" and "holy mountain" are identified with the sanctuary in Pss 20:3; 3:5 and 15:1 respectively.
47 For examples of the performative perfect, see Joüon (1996: 362). The perfect tense, ילדתיך, if not performative (Wagner 2002: 76-77), refers to the recent past. Waltke and O'Connor (1990: 487) cite along with Ps 2:7 a similar construction employing the word היום in Deut 5:21. They may be correct to view the action in Ps 2:7 not as instantaneous in the speech-act but as merely recent. In this case, a sufficient time lag could be imagined to allow for movement from the temple to another location such as the palace. However, even in this case, the utterance would have occurred at the temple before secondary recitation by the king. Consequently, a prophetic cultic context still emerges at least for Ps 2:7b-9.
48 Cf. Keel (1978: 248-49) and more recently Koch (2002: 7-8, 11-15) and Otto (2002: 34-38).
49 See Breasted (1906a: 89, 91-92). Note as well the coronation inscription of Horemheb in the Luxor Temple in which Amun-Re says: "You are my son, my heir, who issued from my body" (Murnane and Meltzer 1995: 233).

the court to pay homage to the new king under penalty of death.⁵⁰

In addition to the Egyptian parallels, the comparison with Assyrian sources can be added in support. The similar royal ideology and speech form expressed in both Assyrian prophetic texts and Psalm 2 have been noted above, and SAA 9 3 is explicitly linked to enthronement. Laato (1996: 275-76; 1997: 92-93) associates the coronation ritual reflected in SAA 9 3 with Psalm 2 in the following ways: 1) the legitimation of the king's reign through affirmation of sonship; 2) this affirmation is part of a covenant (חק/*adê*); and 3) the demand for loyalty and assurance of destruction of enemies. Like Psalm 110, Psalm 2 comports with enthronement festivals in both Egypt and Mesopotamia, and it is likely that Psalm 2 was used in conjunction with cultic celebration of the king's enthronement.

It is still possible that Psalm 2 is a poem written in prophetic style for recitation by the king in an enthronement ritual, or it could be a coronation hymn that happens to cite one excerpt from an oracle (Ps 2:6-9). In the latter case, the presence of the prophetic speech would be a secondary citation and the psalm as a whole would not necessarily be associated with cultic

---

50 See Breasted (1906a: 98). Otto (2002: 38-40, 47) and Koch (2002: 10-11) attribute the origin of divine sonship imagery in Psalm 2 to the Egyptian New Kingdom which influenced Judean kingship ideology through Late Bronze contacts between Egypt and Jebusite Jerusalem. They maintain that loss of Egyptian hegemony over Palestine during the Third Intermediate Period as well as dilution of divine birth imagery at this time among the Egyptians themselves (even at Thebes) makes an Iron I derivation historically impossible. As Koch suggests, Herodotus 2:142 supports their contention that the idea of a god-man eventually became lost. However, Otto and Koch's chronological constraint on the time of borrowing fails to account for the continued celebration of the Opet Festival in the Third Intermediate Period, which featured New Kingdom divine birth ideology for royal legitimation (cf. Bell 1985: 270, 280). Kings of the 21st Dynasty (10th c. at Tanis) still looked to Amun at Thebes for legitimation (in general, contact remained close), and the 22nd Dynasty (10th-8th c. Libyans at Tanis) was legitimised by an oracle of Amun at Thebes regarding Shoshenq, its probable founder (cf. Baines 1995: 35). Therefore, Egyptian sonship imagery could have passed directly from Egypt to Judaea during the early Davidic monarchy. In any event, both Otto and Koch trace the derivation of the imagery in Psalm 2:7-8 to Egyptian coronation ritual, while at the same time stressing the uniqueness of the OT concept of sonship as a performative, legal act (Koch 2002: 12, 14-15; Otto 2002: 38, 43-44).

prophecy. However, the reference to "today" stresses a special ritual in which there is an affirmation of the king's adoptive relationship to Yahweh, which is particularly suited for enthronement. If the psalm as a whole is not set in an enthronement context, the section of the psalm citing divine speech (Ps 2:6-9) most likely originated on such an occasion of cultic enthronement. Even then the themes of the whole psalm may well reflect, in the light of the Assyrian parallels, fuller oracles that were spoken in an earlier ceremony.

3.3.3 Date of the Psalm

Gerstenberger (1988: 48) argues that the ideology of world domination does not fit any historical context and therefore Psalm 2 is best seen as a post-exilic messianic hymn. He acknowledges the similarities with ancient Near Eastern royal ideologies, but views the psalm as an Israelite reinterpretation of them (Gerstenberger 1988: 46). Zenger (Hossfeld and Zenger 1993: 50) argues from the presence of Aramaisms and the theology of world revolt against Yahweh that the psalm is post-exilic. In his view, the royal imagery, which he acknowledges is similar to that in Egypt and Assyria (but also Greece), was brought into the service of a renewed kingship ideology. Against Ptolemaic pretence of divine claims, Psalm 2 set an aggressive program (c. 300 B.C.); a hopeful vision of an endangered minority who held fast to their God and his promises (Hossfeld and Zenger 1993: 50-51). Tournay (1991: 218), as well, sees Psalm 2 as a rekindling of messianic hope based on old traditions of Davidic promises. He argues that the theme of religious rebellion is a forerunner of apocalyptic texts, the word pair "nations/peoples" is a post-exilic idiom, and themes reminiscent of Chronicles (Mt. Zion and the ruler-messiah belong to Yahweh, the celestial ruler) point to a post-exilic date.

The theme of Yahweh's universal sovereignty is not to be confined to the post-exilic period, which is a necessary supposition for Gerstenberger's argument. First, even in the midst of national disaster, the pious affirmed the cosmic rule of Yahweh (Ps 89:6-19). If this is the case when suffering from foreign oppression, one expects that Yahweh's universal sovereignty over the nations would be affirmed during times of relative national strength (such as in the context of an enthronement celebration in the early monarchy). There is no incompatibility in such affirmations when the Judean king, Yahweh's vice-gerent, did not actually rule over a geographically extensive kingdom. First, this theme of the king subduing the nations is not limited to psalms of enthronement (cf. Pss 18:48-51; 72:8-11; 118:10-12). Second, Yahweh is viewed as Lord of the nations in Pss 7:7, 9; 56:8; and 59:6, 9 (cf. Gunkel and Begrich 1933: 147-48, 160). In these psalms of individual complaint, the psalmist's call for Yahweh's justice is dependent on his role as cosmic judge. This theme therefore is not dependent on royal or messianic expectations of a universal theocratic kingdom purported to have developed in the post-exilic period. Rather, the appeal to Yahweh as cosmic judge is found in deuteronomistic passages such as 1 Kgs 8:27-32. Third, ancient Near Eastern ideology of a king's universal rule is not conditioned upon the reality of such a kingdom. For example, Middle Kingdom Egyptian execration texts affirmed the domination of the king over peoples of the Levant, accompanied by symbolic destruction of the pottery (cf. Ps 2:9), even though Egypt did not engage in efforts to dominate these city-states militarily or politically at the time.[51] Redford (1992: 89) notes

---

[51] Otto (2002: 45-48) maintains that this motif is derived from 8th-7th century Assyrian texts (following Becking 1990) and that composite iron sceptres are attested only in Iron II Syria and Assyria but not Egypt (following Lemaire 1986). Thus, he posits that divine birth imagery adapted from Late Bronze Egyptian/Jebusite custom (Ps 2:7-8) was framed with language borrowed from eighth-century Assyrian royal texts (Ps 2:1-3-conspiracy, and v. 9-iron sceptre) and supplemented with Judean theological commentary (Ps 2:4-5) to form a unified literary composite (Otto 2002: 50-51). However, Lemaire (1986: 25) acknowledges the possible find of an iron mace by Petrie in an Iron I Egyptian tomb at a site near Gaza. But even if iron sceptres were not used in Egypt, the royal ideology regarding the use of the sceptre to break pottery might derive from Egypt, even if the specific *type* of sceptre corresponds to Palestinian custom. The term "iron" was used metaphorically in texts as early as Middle Bronze Age for hardness and strength (cf. Millard 1988: 489-91), so the reference in Ps 2:9 could be construed accordingly. Also, the general motif of breaking enemies like pottery is, as Becking (1990: 78-79) acknowledges, a widespread image throughout the ancient Near East well before Iron II, even if not specifically applied to *foreign conquest*. In any case, the point of comparison here between Egyptian execration texts and Psalm 2 is that royal claims to universal dominion in the ancient Near East need not have a corresponding reality.

that these rituals are used in cases when direct action against a potential rebel is impossible because he is out of Pharaoh's jurisdiction. Byblos is a good case in point, since Middle Egyptian kings maintained friendly partnership with the king of Byblos. Thus, actual control over an "enemy" is not necessary for expression of an ideology that boasted such domination. Gerstenberger and Zenger both admit that such ideology is common in the ancient Near East and are forced to argue a Jewish *reinterpretation* of such themes in the post-exilic context. But with such ideas common in ancient Egypt and Mesopotamia, it is better to accept that they existed as well in contemporary (i.e., pre-exilic) Israel than to limit the origin to renewed kingship ideology in the post-exilic period borrowed from more ancient patterns. Jacquet's (1975: 221) observation remains correct, that the degree of triumphalism expressed in Ps 2:4-9 would mean little after the ruin of Jerusalem and the first temple.

As Gunkel (Gunkel 1926: 10) notes, the claim that Aramaic terms are used in Psalm 2 proves nothing. The appearance of בר, in Ps 2:12, is textually questionable. The term רגש in Ps 2:1 occurs in Arabic as well as Old Babylonian, therefore it is not so exclusive to Aramaic as to suppose it must be a loan word in biblical Hebrew. The word, רעע, in Ps 2:9, while probably the correct reading, is found in Jer 11:16 and 15:12. If it is a loan word, its entrance into biblical Hebrew is not post-exilic. Tournay's claim that the word pair, "nations/peoples", is post-exilic idiom can be questioned by its use in Gen 25:23, which is likely to be pre-exilic.[52] Perhaps the most important observation bearing on the date of Psalm 2 is the presence of a king of whom Yahweh speaks "today". The improbability that post-exilic high priests regarded themselves as kingly figures has already been discussed under Psalm 110. Psalm 2 envisions a monarch acting in an enthronement ritual and therefore must be pre-exilic. Reconstructions of a post-exilic background have not adequately taken this observation into account. As in the case of Psalm 110, since Psalm 2 conforms to a pattern used in the real monarchic situation of seventh century Assyria, it is reasonable to

---

52 Commentators describe Isaiah 34 as a theological unfolding of the destiny oracle in Genesis 25.

place the psalm in a similar monarchic setting, thus supporting a pre-exilic date.

3.3.4 Conclusion

Psalm 2 shares numerous form-critical features with Egyptian royal oracles and seventh-century Assyrian royal prophecy that originated in a cultic context. This supports the position that Psalm 2 contains cultic enthronement prophecy dating to the monarchic period.

3.4 Psalm 132

3.4.1 Authenticity of Prophetic Speech

Gunkel (1926: 565) identified the first half of Psalm 132 as a prayer, with parallel petitions in verses 1 and 10 forming an inclusio. The second half of the psalm (vv. 11-18) concerns how God answers this prayer, taking the form of divine speech, similar in structure to Psalm 20 and numerous communal laments (Gunkel 1926: 567).[53] In contrast to Psalm 20, however, in

---

53 Fretheim (1967) stresses the parallelism between verses 1 and 10 as the respective opening petitions for two halves of the psalm. However, his division fails to take adequate account of the oracular nature of verses 11-18 as the controlling organisational feature for the second half of the psalm. In criticising Fretheim's structural conclusions, Laato (1992: 50 n. 5) notes the lexical parallelism between verses 9 and 16 (clothing of priesthood) and verses 10 and 17 (anointed one). This groups verses 9-10 together in the petitionary section of the psalm, receiving Yahweh's answer in verses 16-17. It also maintains the unity of verses 17-18 with the preceding verses rather than making them a separate, concluding section in the psalm. In addition to Laato's observations, Fretheim's analysis passes too easily over the structural differences between verses 1 and 2 on the one hand and verses 10 and 11 on the other (Fretheim 1967: 292). In verse 1, there is a specific referent of the petition, David (זכור . . . לדוד), followed in verse 2 by a relative clause modifying this referent (cf. Exod 32:13). In contrast, there is no corresponding syntactical link between verses 10 and 11; rather, verse 11 offers a significant disjunct from verse 10 in the change from petition to Yahweh in the second person in verse 10 to an introductory oath formula of prophetic speech referring to Yahweh in the third person in verse 11. Tournay (1991: 208) divides the psalm in the same way as Fretheim, but he stresses the

Psalm 132 God speaks in the first person. Gunkel regards Psalm 132 as an example of a prophetic liturgy performed in the Jerusalem temple, contrasting with other psalms that only offer examples of *imitations of prophetic liturgies*, such as Ps 12:6 or 85:5-8 (Gunkel and Begrich 1933: 138). Evidently Gunkel thought of Psalm 132 as genuine prophetic speech uttered in worship, albeit possibly from the mouth of a priest or "other representative of God". Mowinckel (1923: 32) presumed "without doubt" that the psalm preserved the cultic action of an officiating prophet. Several commentators follow this view that Ps 132:11-18 reflects divine speech from a priest or cultic prophet (e.g., Weiser 1962: 781; Anderson 1972: 883; 1987: 539-40). Others offer a variation of the cultic prophecy interpretation. Allen (1983: 205, 210) views Ps 132:11-12 not as a spontaneous answer to the prayer cited in Ps 132:1-10 but as the words of an older oracle; nevertheless, he maintains that the original oracle came from a cultic prophet. Similarly, Booij (1978: 156-57) conjectures that verses 11-18 are a repetition of previous prophetic speech, because the two halves of the psalm are textually interlocked thereby suggesting composition of the whole prior to performance. It is thus prophetic speech only in a "liturgically derived sense" (Booij 1978: 157). Kraus (1978b: 1064; 1989: 481) interprets the first bicolon in Ps 132:11 ("Yahweh swore . . . ") as the poet's introduction formula to his own adaptation of Nathan's original oracle; however, he regards this section of the psalm as cultic prophecy typical of monarchic Jerusalem.

Assyrian sources support the authenticity of Psalm 132:11-18 as prophetic speech. Laato (1996: 277; 1997: 88-92) draws attention to the relevance of SAA 9 3 to understanding royal covenant ideology in Psalm 132. Even as the enthronement of the Assyrian king, Esarhaddon, was authorised by a divine covenant document of Aššur (*tuppi adê*; SAA 9 3.3 ii 27), so too Psalm 132:12 (ברית, עדות) emphasises the covenantal foundation of the Davidic dynasty. Within the Assyrian ritual there is an

---

similar alternation between second and third person referring to God in verses 1-2 and 10-11. This comparison is superficial, since the syntactical link between the verses in each case is very different, and God is the grammatical object in verse 2 but the grammatical subject in verse 11. Therefore the parallelism in alternating grammatical persons is not the same. These dissimilarities weaken the force of Tournay's observation.

admonition to the king to maintain the cult of the deity, Ištar, who mediates the covenant (SAA 9 3.5 iii 25-37). Similarly, Psalm 132 is concerned with the role of the king in establishing Yahweh's cult. While Laato uses the Assyrian text to emphasise the similar royal ideology, it is important to note in the context of this discussion that the Assyrian document originated from cultic prophets. Even though these oracles are used secondarily in a collection, both their original and their secondary function were cultic (serving as part of an enthronement ceremony in the temple of Aššur [SAA 9 3.1 i 14]). This does not mean that Psalm 132 was necessarily part of an enthronement celebration, either of the king or, as Mowinckel supposed, of Yahweh. But Psalm 132:11-18 does contain divine speech and, as will be argued below, functioned in a cultic context, thereby offering an analogy to the Assyrian oracles.

3.4.2 Cultic Prophecy in Psalm 132

Several other comparisons between Assyrian cultic prophecy and Psalm 132 support the supposition that Ps 132:11-18 originated as cultic prophecy. First, because kingship and cult were closely related in the social system, dynastic succession was not only the concern of court officials but especially engaged the attention of officials in the cult, including prophets. The historical context out of which the Assyrian prophecies emerged was internal political turmoil surrounding the succession of Esarhaddon and Assurbanipal. The Assyrian prophecies concerned the establishment of the throne for the succeeding king:
- SAA 9 1.2 i 33-36 (safety in the Palace of Succession)
- SAA 9 1.6 iii 19-22 (throne established for long days and everlasting years)
- SAA 9 1.6 iv 6 (rightful heir of the deity)
- SAA 9 1.8 v 22 (the kingdom is Esarhaddon's)
- SAA 9 2.3 ii 11 (safety in the palace)
- SAA 9 2.6 iv 27 (putting the kingdom in order)
- SAA 9 7:6 (security in the Palace of Succession)
- SAA 3 3:6-12 (endurance of throne spoken by the goddess Ištar)

The Assyrian prophecies also addressed the succession of the king's heirs:
- SAA 9 1.10 vi 27-30 [son and grandson shall rule as kings)
- SAA 9 2.3 ii 13-14 (son and grandson shall rule)

Parpola (SAA 9 1.6 iii 25, footnote) draws attention to the "lamp" set by the goddess before Esarhaddon as a comparison to Ps 132:17; but the metaphor is different. In Ps 132:17, "lamp" (נר) denotes the dynasty itself, perhaps connoting duration of that which shall not be extinguished (cf. 1 Kgs 11:36). However, in the Assyrian oracle, "lamp" (*nūru*) denotes the goddess' heavenly sight of the king's life, connoting her protective watchfulness.[54] Therefore, this parallel is not helpful. However, the theme of victory over the king's enemies found in Ps 132:18, which is related to the stability of the throne, is common in Assyrian prophecies. Ps 132:18 speaks of the shame (בשׁת) that will come upon the enemy, while in SAA 9 1.6 iv 2 the king is promised protection from shame (*bâšu*).

Laato (1997: 22-23) and Gakuru (2000: 57-77) have compared the dynastic succession in the Assyrian prophecies and that of Nathan's oracle in 2 Samuel 7, which stands in the background to the oracle in Psalm 132. Laato maintains that eternal dynastic succession was implicit in a Davidic Covenant established by Nathan's oracle at the outset. Gakuru asserts that the notion of eternal succession did not develop until the exilic period. In his view, Psalms 132 and 89 are later covenant interpretations (Psalm 132 as conditional; and later Psalm 89 as unconditional) of the original dynastic oracle in 2 Samuel 7 which granted promises only to David and his son.[55] In either

---

54 Parpola (1997: 7) points to a cross reference in SAA 3 39:32 that indicates this is a lamp in heaven. The parallel expressions in SAA 9 1.6 iii 23-29 suggest that the imagery is one of clear vision by which the goddess protects Esarhaddon.

55 Elements of both conditionality and unconditionality are compatible in ancient Near Eastern treaties and wills, with wording similar to that of 2 Samuel 7 and Psalms 89 and 132 (Weinfeld 1970: 189-94). Weinfeld (1970: 196) notes that in some texts one or the other might be the dominant theme, such as conditionality in Psalm 132. Knoppers (1997) correctly points out that the form of royal grants is more complicated than Weinfeld proposed and, therefore, that the close form-critical parallel between them and the Davidic covenant has been misconstrued. However, what remains intact

case, security of the throne and some degree of dynastic succession is explicit in Nathan's oracle and Ps 132:12, similar to the Assyrian prophecies.

Second, the establishment of the throne is closely associated with the well-being of the city (and cultic life) in which the throne and the deity's shrine are found. In SAA 9 3.1 i 9-12, the well-being of the king's rule is linked with the well-being of Aššur's temple.[56] Assurbanipal reports that his effort to rebuild Ištar's temples was ordered through prophetic messages (Assurbanipal Prism T ii 7-24; SAAS 7 2.2); and in his *Hymn to the Ištars of Nineveh and Arbela* (SAA 3 3:4-12), he attributes the stability of his throne to the word of these goddesses to whose rebuilt temples he traces his own birth. It might be implied in this hymn that Assurbanipal thought of the endurance of his kingship as a reward for his pious deeds. A similar theology is implied in Psalm 132, linking David's efforts toward securing a stable shrine for Yahweh with Yahweh's commitment to the endurance of both David's throne and the city of his kingship.[57] In summary, the words of Ps 132:11-18 are very consistent with what might be expected of a prophet whose concern is to relate the stability of the Davidic throne with the well-being of Zion.

3.4.3 Limits and Unity of the Oracle

The second half of the psalm begins with an oath formula of Yahweh.[58] As noted above, Kraus (1978b: 1064; 1989: 481) interprets the first bicolon in Ps 132:11 ("Yahweh swore . . . ") as the poet's introduction formula to his own adaptation of Nathan's original oracle. The phrase "Yahweh swore" (נשבע יהוה) can be used in narrative context to refer to a temporally antecedent

---

from Weinfeld's observations is the fact that conditional and unconditional elements are not incompatible in the same document.
56 Royal palace and temple complexes were frequently adjacent in city plans throughout the ancient Near East, so the welfare of the one was integrally linked to the welfare of the other.
57 The privileged position of David's dynasty and Zion are mutually supportive. Not only does the stability of the city contribute to the security of the dynasty, but as van der Toorn (1987: 94-95) observes, the destiny of city and dynasty are bound together in the special protection afforded the latter.
58 Cf. note 53.

oracle, such as in 2 Sam 3:9 or the references to the land grant in Deuteronomy (e.g., Deut 1:8).[59] However, in the context of direct divine speech, such as is found in Psalm 132 and demonstrated for Ps 110:4, the oath formula should be regarded as part of the prophetic speech and not an editorial remark of the poet introducing a secondary use of an oracle. Another feature of Ps 132:11 is the extension of the oath formula with the parallel colon: "Yahweh has sworn an oath to David/a truth he will not turn from", an identical construction to Ps 110:4 and similar to extensions found in prophetic speech. Since these features have parallels in prophetic literature it is most likely that the oracle in Psalm 132 begins formally with the words of verse 11.

This evidence addresses the argument of Gerstenberger, who comments in the context of Psalm 132 that cultic prophecy is inadequate to explain divine speech in the psalms. In view of prose passages that use a divine "I", even with oath formulas (e.g., Num 14:20-25, 26-35), he maintains that "kerygmatic types of divine speech in the Bible . . . probably reflect discourse patterns used and perused in the early Jewish parish assemblies" (Gerstenberger 2001: 368). The implication for Psalm 132 is that it is similar to narrative representations of divine speech in early Judaism and is not a product of prophetic speakers in the cultic context. However, Ps 132:11-18 is not parallel to the narrative genre, rather it agrees in style with formal prophetic speech. In addition, the narrative patterns reflect what people expected of divine intermediaries, suggesting that these individuals existed in real community (including cultic) life. His case is weakened further by the fact that his examples of such early Jewish "sermons" are taken from biblical texts that feature normally expected functionaries, such as Levites and prophets (cf. Gerstenberger 1997: 234). Therefore, Gerstenberger's difficulty with cult prophets as a source for divine speech in the psalms is not well founded.

Seybold (1996: 497) argues for a three-stage development of the psalm. First, there was a dramatic poem consisting of a midrash on 2 Samuel 6-7 (Ps 132:2-5, 6-9, 11, 17-18). Second,

---

59 In Deuteronomy, this is so formulaic that it should not be considered part of a citation of a divine oracle; rather, it constitutes an interpretive expression found throughout the book.

the poem was reframed by addition of a second layer (verses 1, 10, and 12) which transformed it into a royal psalm with prayer and prophecy for the anointed (Ps 132:1-5; 6-10; 11-12, 17-18). The close relationship of this layer to Psalm 89 means it is of exilic provenance. Third, the psalm was adapted as a pilgrim psalm through the inclusion of verses 13-16, thus transforming it into a Psalm of Zion. The theological substructure to this redaction, the election of the Zion sanctuary, suggests a post-exilic outlook. The composition must have been completed before insertion into 2 Chr 6:41-42.

This analysis rests heavily on the different "theological substructures" assigned by Seybold to the pre-exilic and post-exilic periods. There is good reason to suppose that Zion-election theology existed in the pre-exilic period, and therefore, proposing a post-exilic addition on this basis is unwarranted.[60] For example, the election of Zion is implied in Exod 15:17, Ps 2:6 places the king's enthronement on Zion, and Ps 78:67-72 combines the same two themes as Psalm 132 (election of David / election of Zion) in what is probably an anti-northern polemic from as early as the time of Rehoboam. Seow (1989: 185 and 187-88) notes that the psalmist rejects Shiloh, not Samaria in Ps 78:60 (cf. Ps 47:5 for another pre-exilic reference to Zion theology in the Psalms).[61] Psalm 20, which presupposes an active king and therefore a pre-exilic context, refers to Yahweh's sanctuary at Zion in an appeal for the king's protection, similar to the coupling of these two themes in Psalm 132. It seems unlikely that a text such as Psalm 48, which promises the inviolability of Zion, would have arisen after the destruction of the temple. The eighth-century prophet, Micah, attacks such complacent thinking (Mic. 3:10-11). Indeed, resistance to the message of Jeremiah was due in part to the entrenchment of Zion theology in the minds of pre-exilic Jerusalemites (Jeremiah 26). So the idea of Yahweh electing Zion should not even raise the question of a post-exilic date.

Seybold's layering is also dependent on the assumption of a post-deuteronomic redaction that resulted in the addition of

---

60 Cf. Laato (1996: 267-71).
61 Seybold (1996: 308) gives an exilic date for Psalm 78, which still undermines his argument for the necessity of a post-exilic date for Ps 132:13-16.

conditional elements to the tradition of the Davidic covenant (Seybold 1996: 498). A number of studies have argued that Psalm 132 does not depend on a deuteronomic source (Seow 1989: 185-90; Laato 1992; 1997: 84-85; Gakuru 2000: 110-111). Laato (1992) maintains that the conditional element of the covenant found in Psalm 132 is early as well. Even if deuteronomic theology did influence Psalm 132, such a process need not presuppose the exilic period, for a Hezekian or Josianic reform could account for deuteronomic ideas, and as noted above, an element of conditionality is not necessarily incompatible with the original theological structure of the covenant.

There are also structural reasons for questioning Seybold's suggested composition history for the psalm. Fretheim (1967) has shown numerous ways in which Psalm 132 is unified, although he maintains that interruptions in the psalm suggest temporal breaks in the setting that may reflect liturgical parts (Fretheim 1967: 299). These breaks, however, are not necessarily those suggested by Seybold's analysis. One example is the beginning of verses 13-16, Seybold's post-exilic layer. The conjunction כי provides the logical connection between the stability of David's dynasty and the bringing of the ark to Jerusalem. Kings needed divine authorisation for cultic undertakings (cf. Nissinen 1998b: 35-42, esp. 38), and Ps 132:13-16 legitimises David's cultic initiative to which the stability of his throne is inseparably linked. It is difficult to understand in Seybold's reconstruction how verse 2 might ever have existed independently of verse 1. The petition in verse 10, also ascribed to the second layer, is coupled with the corresponding oracular answer in verse 17 which Seybold ascribes to the original composition. Given the numerous coupling of themes between the prayer section and the oracular section of the psalm, it is most likely that verse 10 was original. In conclusion, Seybold's suggested composition history appears unlikely; and, as most commentators note, Psalm 132 exhibits a unified compositional structure reflecting a prayer section (vv. 1-10) with oracular response (vv. 11-18).

3.4.4 Specific Cultic Setting

Mowinckel (1922: 111-18; 1923: 32) argued that Psalm 132 accompanied a dramatic ark procession at an annual Yahweh enthronement festival, a re-enactment of the first such occasion when David brought the ark to its resting place. Mowinckel's theory of an annual enthronement festival, at which Yahweh's cosmic victory over chaos was ritually re-enacted, has fallen into disfavour among most contemporary scholars. This is due primarily to the lack of evidence for a dramatised reading of *Enūma eliš* at the Mesopotamian Akitu Festival, a cultic use of the Baal cycle at Ugarit or reference to any such ritual in the OT itself (van der Toorn 1991; Petersen 1998). However, apart from the element of a dramatised cosmic battle, other parallels between an OT autumn festival and the Akitu Festival remain. Van der Toorn (1991: 339-43) summarises four points of correspondence: 1) an agrarian feast celebrated in the autumn, although Akitu was celebrated at least one other time in the year as well; 2) the central rite was the procession of the deity (2 Samuel 6; 1 Kings 8; Psalm 132); 3) annual purification of the shrine (1 Kgs 8:64) and enthronement of the god as king (Psalm 47); 4) religious legitimation of the king. On this last point, van der Toorn (1991: 342) writes, "the divine mandate of the ruler is celebrated in oracles, some of which have been incorporated in the processional psalms as 'frozen prophecies' (Ps. cxxxii 11-18; cf. Ps. lxviii 23-4; 1 Kgs viii 15-16, 20-1; see also Hag. ii 1-9 for a prophecy delivered at the Festival)". Probably Mowinckel's intuition was turned in the right direction even if his central thesis, an enthronement celebration through dramatic re-enactment of the cosmic battle, finds no support. While Gunkel was cautious about speculating on the details of such a festive procession, he proposed that Psalm 132 celebrated the founding of the royal house and its sanctuary (Gunkel 1926: 568; Gunkel and Begrich 1933: 141-42; 1998: 100). He thought that the change in voices in the psalm (esp. v. 6) lends colour to the performance, bringing the past vividly into the present ("let us go", v. 7). Anderson (1972: 879) associates Psalm 132 with an autumn festival of temple dedication, noting that the psalm is placed in such a context in the biblical tradition (1 Kgs 8:2, 2 Chr 5:3, 6:41-42, cf. Weiser 1962: 779; 1987: 538).

Kraus (1978b: 1057; 1989: 475), on the other hand, is dissatisfied with Gunkel's proposal because there is no allusion to a *temple dedication* ceremony in the psalm itself. The basic subject of Psalm 132 is not temple dedication but the election of Mt. Zion and the Davidic dynasty. He poses the question, is there a real cultic act behind 1 Kgs 8:16 to which Psalm 132 refers, or is it simply a theological statement? After assessing the relationship between Psalm 132 and 2 Samuel 6 and 7, Kraus (1978b: 1059; 1989: 477) concludes that there is a primary cultic and factual connection between the election of Zion (transfer of the ark) and the election of David. First, the central role of the king to cultic life in the ancient Near East attests to the authenticity of the report in 2 Samuel 6, recalled in Psalm 132. Second, cultic initiatives demanded divine authorisation, an issue which 2 Samuel 7 and Psalm 132 address (Kraus 1978b: 1060; 1989: 478). It is in this context that the prophetic address in Psalm 132 makes sense. As an alternative to Mowinckel's Yahweh enthronement festival and Gunkel's temple dedication festival, Kraus (1978b: 1061; 1989: 478) proposes a "royal festival of Zion" at which time Psalm 132 accompanied a cultic demonstration of the joint election of David and Zion. Whether one adopts Kraus's theory or not, his argument supports a cultic background for Psalm 132.

In spite of Kraus's critique, Gunkel's case merits review. First, Gunkel's argument in favour of a cultic background is helpful. Because of the speech form, the second half of the psalm would have been viewed by the original audience as a prophetic *response* to the prayer of verses 1-10, not simply poetic reflections on Nathan's oracle that underscore the hope for the Davidic throne. Prayer followed by prophetic response suggests liturgical action. In addition, the psalm recalls the Davidic foundation for the Jerusalem shrine and, as Gunkel observed, presents it in such a vivid, dramatic fashion that some sort of celebration of cultic foundations is in view (note the volitive mood of the verbs in verses 7 and 8 as well as the cultic invocation, "Arise Yahweh . . . you and the ark", cf. Num 10:35).[62] Ger-

---

[62] Hillers (1968) argues that Ps 132:8 should be translated "Arise, Yahweh, from your resting place", a call for Yahweh to act on David's behalf, rather than a cultic call for Yahweh to move with the ark in procession (ל on

stenberger (2001: 365) argues that the call to cultic acts portrays present action, not past actions of the Davidic host, meaning "we are witnessing parts of a 'live' worship, not simply historical remembrances". Gerstenberger (2001: 366) is reluctant to admit that the reference to the ark is significant (he calls the appearance of the ark in v. 8 "curious" and "isolated"); and therefore, he discounts the importance of dramatic rehearsal of the past for understanding the psalm.[63] The fact remains, however, that the ark is central to the cultic call in Ps 132:8, a guide to understanding a historical portrayal, and critical to understanding the connection between the two halves of the psalm (Yahweh's oath in response to David's).[64] In spite of the weakness in Gerstenberger's denial of real cultic actions, his judgment regarding the cultic vividness of the psalm is similar to Gunkel's. Second, in response to Kraus's critiques that Psalm 132 preserves no trace of temple dedication (Gunkel) or enthronement of Yahweh (Mowinckel), the following might be observed. Psalm 132 is only one psalm among many that would have had a part in a festival, and therefore, all themes celebrated at the festival need not be encapsulated in this one psalm. Kraus correctly points out that Psalm 132 stresses two themes: 1) the transfer of the ark = Yahweh's election of Zion, and 2) the promises to David = Yahweh's election of David's dynasty. The association of this psalm with temple dedication (cf. 2 Chr 6:41-42) is consistent with the idea that the procession of a deity into his sanctuary (i.e., palace) is tacit acknowledgment of the deity's kingship (cf. Psalm 24). Therefore, the ark procession is not far removed from celebration of Yahweh's enthronement.

למנוחתך in the sense of "from"). However, in spite of his objections, understanding the ל as directive is possible and better fits the immediate context of actions on the part of cultic officials to fetch the ark rather than the broader context of a prayer for intervention.
63 Gerstenberger's dismisses the possibility that the feminine pronouns in v. 6 could refer to the ark (usually masculine). He comments that appeal to passages in which the ark is feminine (e.g., 1 Sam 4:17; 2 Chr 8:11) is "a result not of insight but of despair" (Gerstenberger 2001: 365).
64 Kraus (1978b: 1057; 1989: 475) argues that the transfer of the ark emphatically recalls events from David's time and gives meaning to the claim of v. 13: 'Yahweh has chosen Zion.".

In summary, Psalm 132 is more than a mere theological statement. The psalm with its prophetic speech likely originated as liturgical accompaniment to cultic action, recapitulating in oral liturgy (if not accompanied by re-dramatising in a physical way) the historic transfer of the ark.

3.4.5 Date of the Psalm

A pre-exilic provenance for Psalm 132 is most commonly accepted. The range of dates varies: Solomonic (Weiser 1962: 779; 1987: 538; Laato 1992: 65; 1997: 84); pre-deuteronomic, perhaps as early as Rehoboam (Seow 1989: 149; Gakuru 2000: 112-13); generally pre-exilic (Gunkel 1926: 568; Anderson 1972: 889; Kraus 1978b: 1061; Allen 1983: 207; 1989: 479).[65] Seybold, as we have seen, spreads the composition of the psalm from the pre-exilic to post-exilic periods. Others have argued for a post-exilic date (Duhm 1899: 280; Tournay 1991: 208-209; Gerstenberger 2001: 368-69).

Tournay (1991: 209) states, "Psalm 132 fits naturally into the Psalms of Ascents and forms part of the liturgy of pilgrims to Jerusalem during the Second Temple period. It bears witness to the intense messianic hope in Israel in the Persian period, expressed so precisely in Pss. 130:7 and 131:3". However, the fact that Psalm 132 found its final place among the Psalms of Ascent does not serve as evidence for a post-exilic composition. It only implies that the theology it reflects was meaningful for the pilgrims of the post-exilic community.

Tournay utilises the date of certain phrases to support his argument for a post-exilic date. He maintains that the phrase "for evermore" (עדי־עד v. 12) is post-exilic, citing the other occurrences in Biblical Hebrew (Isa 26:4; 65:18; Pss 83:18; 92:8). Not only is this a very small lexical sampling from which to draw diachronic conclusions, but it is doubtful that several of the passages cited can be firmly dated in the post-exilic period.

---

[65] Seow (1989: 147 n. 10) aligns Gunkel with a Davidic date for the psalm; however, Gunkel argued only for a late monarchic date (Gunkel 1926: 568). Similarly, Cross (1973: 97) seems only to argue that the psalm preserves material from David's time reworked in the later royal cult. This nonetheless argues for a pre-exilic date.

While the consensus is that Isaiah 26 is post-exilic, Sweeney (1996: 312) notes that some place its origin in the exile. Psalm 83, which lists Assyria but not Babylon as an arch-enemy of Israel, is more likely pre-exilic. Tournay claims that the term, ציד ("provisions"), came into use after the exile, citing Ps 78:25; Josh 9:5, 14; Job 38:41; and Neh 13:15. There are several problems with this evidence. First, it would appear that the use of the noun and denominative verb in Josh 9:5, 12 and 14, more likely a pre-exilic text, undermines his argument. Second, Psalm 78:25 is doubtfully post-exilic and may even be one of the more securely dated pre-exilic psalms (it expresses a theology for subsuming the remnant of the northern kingdom under Davidic rule). But also significant is the fact that the Ps 78:25 citation draws in the feminine form of this root which further weakens the diachronic distinctive of ציד (II). If Tournay cites Ps 78:25, then texts such as Judg 7:8 and 1 Sam 22:10 must also be taken into account, neither of which are post-exilic. Third, his lexical sample is restricted to instances of ציד (II). As far as I can tell, this separation of roots is based primarily on a semantic distinction between food obtained in a hunter-gatherer context (ציד [I]; e.g., Gen 25:28; 27:7) and that associated with an urban context (ציד [II]; Neh 13:15; Ps 132:15). Apart from further evidence, which I cannot discern here, one root would be adequate to account for the semantic range of both roots.[66] This question is pressed by the use of ציד (II) in Job 38:31. Is not the food for the raven more akin to raw game (ציד [I]) than general domestic provisions (cf. Job 38:39)? The related Akkadian words, ṣadûm ("receive sustenance", "make provision for") and ṣidītum ("travel provisions"), suggest that the word ציד (II) ("provision") might have been present very early in the language and that only accidental sampling in the Hebrew Bible leads to the impression that the term is post-exilic. Of course, as noted above, the root does not appear to be restricted to post-exilic Hebrew at all.[67] The relevance for this discussion is that inclusion of ציד (I) weakens the diachronic argument further. One must argue that

---

[66] This lack of clarity regarding the number of roots is also raised by Oeming (1989: col. 931), who suggests both could go back to a common meaning "to provide nourishment".

[67] The lexical base may also occur in a personal name on Arad ostracon No. 52 (Lemaire 1977: 212).

only in the post-exilic period did the root come to refer to urban food provisions in addition to wild game. The early cognate use casts doubt on this premise. In sum, Tournay's argument based on the entrance of a new root into the language in the post-exilic period is lost.

Gerstenberger (2001: 369) thinks that "preexilic 'royal ideology' hardly plays a role in this psalm"; rather, "traces of late community organization and of messianic hopes for a restoration of the Davidic monarchy make it necessary to think of early Jewish congregational activities as the matrix". However, Psalm 132 expresses pre-exilic royal ideology as strongly as any passage in the OT. Gunkel (1926: 568) notes that there is no trace in the psalm that at any time Yahweh had vacated Zion or that the Davidic throne was vacant. Gerstenberger's opinion that the ark is "loosely connected with Psalm 132" contributes in part to his dissociation of the psalm from early royal ideology (Gerstenberger 2001: 369). But as discussed above, his opinion is poorly substantiated. Laato (1992: 55) notes that attention to the ark in Psalm 132 as an important cult object is evidence of a pre-exilic date.[68]

In summary, several lines of evidence point to a pre-exilic date for Psalm 132. First, the royal ideology in Psalm 132 is consistent with that expressed in other early texts. Second, the psalm appears rooted in Israel's own traditions about the foundation of the First Temple. Third, the psalm presupposes the existence of the monarchy. Fourth, as argued at the outset of this section, the psalm is very analogous to royal ideology expressed in seventh-century Assyrian cultic prophecy.

3.4.6 Conclusion

Psalm 132 originated in the context of a pre-exilic cultic celebration at which a prophetic functionary gave oracular response to prayers offered on behalf of the ruling monarch. In the background to the psalm is remembrance of David's transport of the ark to Jerusalem, thereby making Zion the political and religious centre of the kingdom. The prophetic response legitimated

---

68 Cf. Day (2004: 231-32).

the king's sanctuary initiative and his kingship. This appears to be the primary focus of the psalm. In addition, the theory that the psalm corresponded with an autumn celebration of royal order, both human and divine, has support.

3.5 Psalm 89

3.5.1 Authenticity of Prophetic Material

Regardless of the theory of composition history espoused, Psalm 89 is generally recognised to preserve genuine prophetic material in verses 3-4 and 20-38, or at least an interpretive expansion of prophetic tradition.[69] The fact that Ps 89:20-38 was viewed as a report of prophetic speech by the psalmist himself is evident from the introductory phrase, "Once you spoke in a vision" (חזון, v. 20). Whether or not this material *originated* in a cultic context will be discussed in the next section.

Of interest here is the similarity between prophetic expressions in Psalm 89 and Assyrian prophetic oracles. Some of these parallels have been observed by several scholars (cf. Nissinen 1993: 233; Parpola 1997, footnotes to relevant lines in SAA 9). Most recently Steymans (2002) has made an extensive comparison, particularly with respect to Psalm 89 and SAA 9 1.6.

1) divine sonship and chosen heir of the deity (Ps 89:4, 27-28; SAA 9 1.6 iv 6, 20-21; 1.9 iii 29; 2.5 iii 26-27, iv 20; 7:6-10)(cf. Ishida 1977: 91; van der Toorn 1987: 88; Nissinen 1993: 233).
2) throne established for long days and everlasting years (Ps 89:5, 30, 37, SAA 9 1.6 iii 19-22, cf. SAA 3 3:6-12, cf. Steymans 2002: 194-95).
3) descendants rule (Ps 89:5, 30, 37; SAA 9 1.10 vi 27-30; 2.3 ii 13-14). Gakuru (2000: 39) maintains that the Assyrian prophets extend the promise only into the near future (a few generations), whereas the Davidic dynasty is presented as eternal in Psalm 89. While this contrast may be true, it doubtful that Gakuru (2000: 47) is correct

---

69 Tate (1990: 413-18) offers perhaps the most complete summary of views, all of which agree on the limits of oracular material in the psalm.

that linear projection into the distant future was not imaginable in pre-exilic Israel. In addition, the comparable idea of an enduring rule/throne in Assyrian oracles probably implied dynastic succession.

4) divine love for the king (Ps 89:25, 29, 34 [חסד]; SAA 9 1.6; 9 4 [*râmu*])(cf. Steymans 2002: 196-97).
5) rule from sea to rivers (Ps 89:26) as a merism comparable to "sunset to sunrise" (SAA 9 2.5 iii 35-36, 3.2 i 31-34, ii 4-5, cf. Ishida 1977: 91).
6) royal covenant ideology espoused by prophets (Ps 89:4, 27, 35 [ברית]; SAA 9 3.3 ii 27 and iii 11 [*adê*])(cf. Ishida 1977: 116; Steymans 2002: 194).
7) subjugation of enemies (Ps 89:23-24; a dominant theme in Assyrian oracles)
8) divine promise accompanied by denial of lying (Ps 89:36, SAA 9 1.6 iii 32, cf. Ishida 1977: 92; Steymans 2002: 195)
9) Unlike the Davidic covenant, which provides for the divine discipline of a rebellious vassal-king (Ps 89:31-33), the Assyrian oracles never threaten the rule of the king but merely chastise him for failure to perform cultic duties (SAA 9 2.3 ii 21; 3.5 iii 25). Nissinen (1993: 250) observes that this is a basic difference between prophetic rebuke in the OT and that found in Assyrian prophecy.[70]

Steymans (2002: 192-93, 197) makes the important observation that not only are there numerous semantic links between Psalm 89 and SAA 9 1.6 but that combinations of terms occur in a similar form. A summary of the most valid points of his form-critical comparison is as follows:

SAA 9 1.6	Psalm 89
Naming of king: Esarhaddon my king (iii 7-11; second person)	Naming of king: David my servant (4, third person)

---

[70] While this observation is true regarding the extant prophetic oracles, Steymans (2002: 209-10, 230-31) notes that the possibility of divine punishment of a king occurs in other Mesopotamian sources (cf. SAA 3 33; SAA 3 44:7-10; Mari text A.1968).

long days and years, throne made firm (iii 11-12, 19-21)	eternality of dynasty and throne (5)
denial of lying (iii 30-32)	denial of lying (34-36)
rightful heir, son (iv 5-6, 20-21)	firstborn son (27-28)
protection against enemies (iv 8-10, 19)	protection against enemies (23-24)
remembrance, great love (iv 22-25)	faithfulness, loyal love (25)
I hold you (iv 28)	my hand established with him (22)

This Assyrian evidence highlights the authenticity of Ps 89:3-4, 20-38 as prophetic speech intended for support of the royal dynasty.

3.5.2 Relationship of Oracular Material to the Literary Context and Cultic Setting

There is no consensus regarding the historical setting for this psalm. Mowinckel (1923: 37) proposed that it was part of a pre-exilic public lament used on the occasion of military defeat of the king.[71] Kraus (1978b: 783-84; 1989: 202-203) thinks it "can hardly be doubted" that the person praying is the king; therefore, the "explanation that the song belongs to post-exilic time is not appropriate".[72] On the other hand, others argue for a setting after the Babylonian invasions, judging that only the complete loss of the monarchy could account for the intensity of language in Psalm 89 (Booij 1994: 83; Heim 1998: 297-98). Gunkel (1926: 396) preferred a post-exilic origin, since the absence of prayer

---
71 Cf. Weiser (1962: 591; 1987: 402) and Sarna (1953: 44-45).
72 Cf. Ward (1961: 337-38) and Booij (1978: 79) Contrary to Kraus' confidence, it is uncertain whether the speaker in Ps 89:47-52 is the king or some other official representing the community, such as a priest or a prophet. Floyd (1992: 450-51) argues that the speaker's reference to "our king" in Ps 89:19 precludes the speaker being the king at the end of the psalm. On the other hand, this same reference might imply a present monarch, even if the speaker of the psalm is a non-royal individual.

for restoration from exile might preclude a date during the exile.[73] Similarly, Tate (1990: 417) thinks the psalm reflects a situation in which the temple had been restored but not the monarchy. An exilic date, however, should not be ruled out. A worship setting of lament might be suggested for the exilic period in the community remaining in and around Jerusalem. Favouring this setting for Psalm 89, Floyd (1992: 456 n. 22) observes that continuing worship at the former temple site is presupposed in Jer 41:5. Additional support is implied in Zechariah 7-8, which records instructions to the post-exilic community around Jerusalem to transform their lament festivals of the past 70 years into celebrations of joy (cf. 2 Kings 25, Ackroyd 1968: 207 n. 122). Even as Psalms 74 and 79 lamented the fall of the city, Psalm 89 lamented the downfall of the monarchy.[74] Thus, one facet of the catastrophe could be remembered in one song while ignoring other related themes commemorated in other songs. Psalm 89 has relatively little, if anything, to say about the destruction of the city (Ps 89:41-42 could refer to destruction of other key cities in Judah). On the other hand, Psalms 74 and 79 do not address the loss of the king. Therefore, exclusion of Jerusalem's demise in Psalm 89 does not preclude an exilic setting simply because it does not address this important theme.[75] Aside from the question of date, however, there is a consensus that the psalm arose in the context of community lament.[76]

---

[73] However, he places the origin of the hymnic portion in the north before the fall to Assyria (Gunkel and Begrich 1933: 416, 419; 1998: 319, 321-22)

[74] Tournay (1991: 202), following Veijola (1982: 176-77, 209-210), places the origin of these psalms at this time but located at a northern site such as Bethel or Mizpah. Seybold (1996: 350) similarly traces the hymnic portion to a northern pre-exilic provenance and posits the early exile for the royal aspect of the psalm and the later exile for the lament. On the other hand, Gakuru (2000: 130) dates the psalm as a whole to the exile but dates the *oracular* portions to late monarchy.

[75] Contrary to the view of some commentators (e.g., Weiser 1962: 591; e.g., Sarna 1963: 43; 1987: 402).

[76] The view that the psalm accompanied ritual humiliation of the king (cf. Johnson 1955: 103-104; Eaton 1976: 131-22) is not likely, primarily because it depends upon a questionable imitation of the Babylonian Akitu Festival and lacks any support from the OT that such a ritual was practised. Steymans (2002: 225, 243-45) doubts that a specific historical catastrophe necessarily stands in the background to Psalm 89. Rather, it may have been part of the standard lament ritual following the death of a king, which an-

Even if Psalm 89 was a cultic song of community lament, the prophetic speech sections are possibly only secondary citations not derived from the original setting of the psalm. This supposition is based primarily on the introduction formula in Ps 89:20 and the syntactical relationship between the citation of divine speech in Ps 89:4-5 and verse 6 which follows. Such secondary citation casts doubt concerning the cultic origin of the oracular material itself. It could be only a poetic adaptation of prophetic material.

The extensive oracular address in Ps 89:20-38 is introduced with the phrase:

"Once you spoke in a vision/to your faithful ones you said"

Two features of this verse suggest that the citation is a secondary incorporation of prophetic tradition, not spontaneous prophetic speech in a cultic setting. First, the particle אז ("then," "once") with the perfect (דברת), as well as the preterite with *waw*-consecutive (ותאמר), reflect *back* in time to the original utterance(s).[77] Second, the plural form (לחסידיך) might suggest multiple sources from the prophetic tradition, i.e., the succeeding generations of prophets from which the psalmist draws to create a composite citation (Anderson 1972: 639; Kraus 1978b: 790; 1989: 208; Floyd 1992: 453).[78] Veijola (1982: 60-69, 117-18)

---

ticipated a confirmation by divine oracle (specifically Psalm 2) when the new Davidic king was enthroned. However, the references to destruction of the king's cities (Ps 89:41-42) does not fit well with this proposed setting.

77 Booij (1994: 89) insists that אז should not be translated "once", referring to the more distant past; rather, it is an emphatic reference to the cultic situation described in the immediately preceding verses (16-19). However, Ps 89:16-19 does not report a past situation to which verse 20 could be in narrative sequence, as is the case for the other contexts he cites for this use of the particle (Booij 1994: 98 n. 52).

78 A number of Hebrew manuscripts support a singular instead of plural suffix, referring to Nathan or perhaps David. However, the plural reading is more difficult, since the text was likely changed to singular in consideration of 2 Samuel 7. The plural reading also has the support of the Old Greek and 4QPs˟ (לבחריכ, "to your chosen ones"; *DJD* XVI, 165). While a different lexeme, referring in the Qumran manuscript to the Davidic line rather than the community, the reading supports the plural sense of the verse. Starbuck (1999: 130) also notes that some LXX manuscripts read plural υἱοῖς. However, Starbuck's suggestion that the plural places the oracle on the lips of the community is not as likely as the idea that the worshipping community was the recipient of the prophetic address. Gerstenberger (2001: 151) states,

argues on the basis of vocabulary and theological themes that Psalm 89 is dependent on the text of 2 Samuel 7 and other deuteronomistic texts. Seybold (1996: 353) suggests the source could be 2 Samuel 7 or other various revelatory material, as in Psalms 110, 132 or 60. Gakuru (2000: 128-29) argues that the psalmist used 2 Sam 23:1-7, in addition to 2 Samuel 7, as one of his sources. Hossfeld (Hossfeld and Zenger 2000: 585; 2002: 487-88) assigns the oracular material in Ps 89:20-35 to an interpretive re-reading of 2 Samuel 7 that also transfers the covenant theology traditions of Sinai and Deuteronomy to the Davidic covenant. He argues on the basis of the oath formula and structural detachment from the other sections of the psalm that Ps 89:4-5 and 36-38 belong to a redaction dependent on traditions behind Pss 110:4 and 132:11 (Hossfeld and Zenger 2000: 582-83; 2002: 486-87).[79]

However, Steymans (2002: 198-216) argues cogently that literary dependence on 2 Samuel 7 or 23 is neither likely nor necessary in view of the literary parallels between Psalm 89 and Assyrian royal texts. The psalmist was clearly aware of the same tradition as that behind 2 Samuel 7 (esp. 2 Sam 7:14-15/Ps 89:33-38); but most linguistic features of Psalm 89 and 2 Samuel 7 are common characteristics of Assyrian royal texts (including oracles), and some of these features common with Assyrian texts are not shared between Psalm 89 and 2 Samuel 7 (Steymans 2002: 207, 215).[80] The dependency on 2 Samuel 23 is similarly called into question by common language shared with Assyrian royal texts (Steymans 2002: 199 n. 47). Hossfeld's reconstruction of compositional history is doubtful not only on the basis of Steymans' conclusions but also on account of the unified structure of the psalm. Specifically, Ps 89:4-5 together with Ps 89:2-3 anticipate in dual fashion the extended praise

---

"The MT plural, however, anachronistically portrays the exilic-postexilic community as the recipient of divine communication". However, the plural reference easily accords with the understanding of a later community looking back to the pre-exilic prophetic origin of the covenant tradition.

79 Mowinckel (1923: 35-36, 38) thought that the shared features with Psalm 132 made a common liturgical origin likely (cf. Ward 1961: 329-30, although his argument that Ps 89:16-19 corresponds to an ark procession setting is not likely).

80 Steymans (2002: 210) illustrates the same phenomenon with Mari texts as well.

and oracular sections which follow, and Ps 89:5 is syntactically linked with Ps 89:6 in an inseparable manner as discussed below. In Steymans' view, 2 Samuel 7 is a redactional use of royal oracular tradition in a narrative context whereas Psalm 89 makes use of the same tradition in a unified poetic lament. Therefore, Ps 89:4-5, 20-38 is a poetic construct of oracular tradition incorporated into the psalm (Steymans 2002: 214). In any event, the important point is that even if the specific textual source behind Psalm 89 cannot be identified, the preservation of the same tradition in other texts supports the notion that the *prophetic* tradition concerning David's dynasty extended beyond Nathan's singular oracle, hence, in the view of some, the plural reference in Ps 89:20.

The link between the divine speech in Ps 89:4-5 and verse 6 also suggests a secondary citation for this oracular material. Ps 89:6 begins with a jussive prefixed with a *waw*, suggesting a logical inference from the previous verse. This is stressed by Tournay (1991: 203); but for the most part, commentators ignore the *waw*.[81] The opening declaration of praise (vv. 2-3) is resumed by a call to praise (ויודו, *waw* plus jussive, v. 6), both motivated by the brief reference to Yahweh's promises to David. The hymnic section (Ps 89:6-19) celebrates the incomparable strength of Yahweh as Creator who can guarantee the eternality of the Davidic covenant (cf. Floyd 1992: 447). If this analysis of the syntax is correct, then the divine speech in verses 3 and 4 would be textually inseparable from the composition of the hymn and therefore unlikely to be spontaneous prophetic speech. Like verses 20-38, it is a secondary citation of prophetic tradition that may have originated in the cult but the presence of which in Psalm 89 cannot serve as evidence for such an origin.

Not only might the original oracle have originated in a setting other than the cult, Psalm 89 has been thought not to preserve an actual oracle at all. Numerous scholars argue that Ps 89:4-5, 20-38 is merely a poetic interpretation (or exegetical adaptation)

---

[81] Tate (1990: 406) correctly translates it as "so" but does not comment on the implications; and Kraus (1978b: 778, 780; 1989: 198, 200), who translates it as "*und*", notes that two manuscripts and the versions omit it (cf. Seybold 1996: 346, "und").

of 2 Samuel 7 composed in unity with the hymnic and lament portions of the psalm.[82] Consequently, Ps 89:20-38 could not be spontaneous prophecy, since its composition is inseparably linked with other sections of the psalm.[83] These observations regarding compositional unity of the whole of Psalm 89 are not affected by Steymans' case against identifying a specific textual *Vorlage*. Whatever model one proposes for the composition of Ps 89:4-5, 20-38 must take into account its unity with the other parts of the psalm. The reference to the past is merely to the oracular tradition presently being interpreted by the poet, not introducing the direct citation of an older oracle.

Mowinckel (1923: 35-36) expressed dissatisfaction with any theory that regards the oracle as poetic fiction. He preferred viewing the oracular portion as drawing on an authentic cultic oracle, similar to Psalm 132. Considering the numerous lexical and thematic links as well as the overall structural unity of the psalm, there is a problem in imagining that the hymnic and oracular portions ever existed as independent compositions.[84] But, as noted above, Gakuru (2000: 130) viewed the hymnic and lament portions of the psalm as composed after and around an existing late pre-exilic oracle. Thus, the oracle may have existed independently before serving as the basis of a larger composition which included hymn and lament.

Another possibility is that the whole psalm be viewed as a unified prophetic composition. Floyd (1992), while accepting a

---

[82] E.g., Gunkel (1926: 392); Ward (1961); Sarna (1963); Clifford (1980); Fishbane (1985: 467); Gerstenberger (2001: 148).

[83] See the table of lexical repetition between segments of the psalm compiled by Ward (1961: 339), who argues on this basis that the psalm must be an originally unified composition: "the poet employed from first to last a conscious repetition of key words to contribute to the formal and substantial unity of his poem" (Ward 1961: 323).

[84] Mowinckel (1923: 36-37) observed that metrical changes between the hymnic and oracular portions suggests some discontinuity in composition. He proposed that a suitable hymn (4+4) was selected to complement the oracle (3+3) sitting before the poet, who then wrote the transitional verses and the lament in 3+3 according to the oracle before him. Ward's criticism of discontinuity is weakened at this point, since he admits that vv. 16-19 are transitional to the oracular section and that the metric change reflects this function (Ward 1961:323). Thus, as Mowinckel argues, the transition could be a redactional composition designed to mesh the oracular and the hymnic sources.

unified composition of the whole, argues that the psalm is a prophetic adaptation of the lament form; hence, the fundamental form of the psalm is a prophetic lament (cf. Hab 2:2-17 and Jer 15:10-18). This is consistent, he argues, with the prophetic content that dominates the psalm. It concerns not just the welfare of the Davidic dynasty, but perhaps more important is the question of the status of the oracular promises (Floyd 1992: 453-54). Particularly important to his theory is the identification of a prophetic speaker in Ps 89:2-5. The declaration of praise (cohortative) in verse 2 is motivated by a self-referential citation in verses 3-5 (כי אמרתי) which includes first-person divine speech (oracle of vv. 4-5). Thus, the speaker might be referring to his own oracular pronouncement.[85] Similarly, Booij (1978: 79) suggests that this self-reference to the singer draws attention to an unannounced speech from God that follows.[86] The prophetic role of bearing responsibility in the face of nations (v. 51) is compatible with the portrait of prophetic ministry elsewhere (e.g., Jer 1:10, Isa 52:15, Floyd 1992: 450-51), as is the role to pray for the king and bless the congregation (vv. 16-19). Even if Ps 89:4-5 is regarded as secondary citation, the observation remains that the character of the whole is strongly prophetic; and the adaptation of earlier oracles or oracular tradition illustrates a type of prophetic exposition (Floyd 1992: 444-45, 453). The important contribution of Steymans is not at odds with this view. In comparison with Assyrian texts, Ps 89:4-5, 20-38 features the style of royal oracles. The fact that earlier oracular tradition lies behind Psalm 89 does not exclude the prophetic authenticity of the message in its current form preserved in the psalm. Thus, it is possible that the psalm as a whole is cultic prophecy, since it constitutes a continuation of the prophetic tradition at the time of the psalm's composition and original performance, even

---

[85] Floyd (1992: 451-52) notes the textual possibility that the verb אמר in verse 3 is second person (LXX) instead of first person (MT). In this case, secondary citation of another's oracle is in view.

[86] Booij describes this as a form of ecstatic singing, associated with the following hymnic praise; but for him it is not an instance of prophetic proclamation. In his later commentary he views the singer as the heir apparent to the throne whose rightful place is thwarted during the exile; and the self-referential phrase in v. 3 only introduces the reflective thought motivating his vow of praise (Booij 1994: 83-84).

though older oracular tradition was adapted homiletically. In the context of royal lament, Assyrian prophecies encouraged the king. Prophetic exposition in Ps 89:4-5, 20-38 functioned in a similar manner. Consequently, the classification of the oracular portions of this psalm as genuine prophetic speech (albeit exposition of earlier material) must remain a viable option.

It is important to note a further observation regarding the cultic origin of the oracular material in Psalm 89. None of the above considerations excludes the possibility that the oracle (or oracle tradition), upon which Ps 89:4-5, 20-38 is based, was originally cultic prophecy.[87] The plural חסידיך ("your faithful ones"), rather than referring to prophets, most likely refers to the worshipping community itself (Pss 30:5; 50:5; 52:9; 145:10; 149:1; and probably also 31:24 and 85:9).[88] The plural of חסיד can refer to God's people in general (Pss 37:28; 79:2; 97:10; 116:15; 148:14). However, even though the nature of the group as the worshipping assembly is not stressed in these verses, it is presupposed that such people comprise the worshipping community when gathered. For example, the referent in Pss 149:5 and 9 is God's people in general, but on the basis of verse 1 of the same psalm, such people are assumed to be part of the worshipping community. Probably, then, the plural of חסיד in Ps 89:20 does not denote prophetic individuals, even if cultic, rather the worshipping community that was audience to cultic prophecy.[89]. Indirectly then, Ps 89:20 would attest to the phenomenon of cultic prophecy even if the citation of the oracle in Ps 89:21-38 is either secondary or a poetic interpretation of the tradition, since the *oracular* testimony of Yahweh's promises to David was delivered to the worshipping community.

---

87   Ward (1961: 329) proposes a public setting for the original Nathan oracle as a possible reference, although he does not expand on the semantic implications of חסיד. Booij's (1994: 89, 98 n. 52) suggestion that the oracle in Ps 89:20-38 is addressed to the worshippers of Ps 89:16-19 would support this understanding of חסיד, however, the historical connection is doubtful.
88   The strong likelihood that the plural is the correct reading has been noted above.
89   Because of the frequency with which the worshipping community is denoted by the word, it is unlikely that חסיד in Ps 132:9 and 16 should be restricted to the priestly officials in the first half of these two verses. The second colon expands the reference from cultic officials to cultic community in general.

Besides affirming the prophetic character of the speech in Ps 89:4-5, 20-38, the Assyrian sources make another important contribution to this discussion. First, the *Dialogue Between Assurbanipal and Nabû* (SAA 3 13) utilises a report of a divine oracle and other affirmations of divine support (possibly textually related to the oracle SAA 9 9) in the context of a royal lament set in the temple. As discussed in Chapter 2, the oracular material in SAA 3 13 is possibly a literary fiction based upon real cult-prophetic tradition illustrated in SAA 9 9. Even if the citation in SAA 3 13 is a secondary use by the poet, it corresponds to genuine cultic prophecy. Such inclusion of oracular material in a royal lament is perhaps analogous to Psalm 89. Second, reference to earlier prophetic material and repetition of stock phrases from the prophetic tradition are also illustrated within the corpus of Assyrian prophecies. Oracles SAA 9 1.1 i 15-17 and 1.10 vi 7-9 refer to previous prophetic promises.[90] While not in any way exhaustive, examples of repeated use of stock expressions include: 1) gods on right and left (SAA 9 1.4 ii 22-26; 2.2 i 21; 5:6); 2) kept safe in the palace (SAA 9 1.2 i 33-34; 1.10 vi 25-26; 2.3 ii 11; 7:6); 3) eternality of royal prerogatives (SAA 9 1.6 iii 11-14; 19-22; iv 15-17); 4) reconciliation with gods (SAA 9 1.4 ii

---

90 Weippert (1997: 152-57) argues that SAA 9 7 incorporates a direct citation of an earlier oracle. According to his interpretation, SAA 9 7:2 should be translated, "An appeal of Mullissu to the king is thus:", which introduces the citation of a previous oracle. However, his reconstruction is based on an unlikely translation of LUGAL in SAA 9 7:2 (cf. note 41). Another example of secondary citation suggested by Weippert is SAA 9 3.3 (Weippert 1997: 157-59). He argues that the verbs in lines ii 16-18 are a promise of future deliverance, necessitating that this section be a secondary citation, since their fulfilment is referred to in past tense in lines ii 19-23. However, his understanding of the verbs is unlikely. The verb *attaqallalla* is most likely an N perfect (so Parpola), not an Nt present (a stem not otherwise attested) as Weippert maintains (Weippert 1997: 158-59; 2002: 45). Gemination of the form need not be due to a present tense (cf. *GAG* 101h). The present tense verb, *tazaz*, in line ii 18 is used here for past time, since there is no stative form of *uzzuzu*, which would otherwise be expected to express a past condition (cf. SAAS 13, p. 99). The precatives in line ii 17 can naturally be understood as indirect volitives stating the intention or result of Aššur's intervention in line ii 16. The correctness of the N perfect interpretation was confirmed to me in personal conversation with J. N. Postgate, whom I also thank for the reference in *GAG* and SAAS 13. Thus, the whole of ii 10-23 is consistent with a past report of intervention, as Parpola's translation indicates.

31; 2.5 iii 20). In SAA 9 9:8-15, the goddess speaks of her own labour on behalf of the king using phrases from the *Epic of Gilgamesh* (Parpola 1997: 41 notes; Nissinen 2000b: 97-98). This illustrates that prophetic re-use of existing tradition was common and that such borrowing need not negate the authenticity or freshness of the oracle presently delivered. Thus, if Floyd's interpretation is correct that Psalm 89 constitutes a prophetic exposition of earlier tradition, then it is still possible that the psalm was received as cultic prophecy even though the psalmist explicitly credited the oracular portions to earlier tradition.

3.5.3   Conclusion

Ps 89:3-4, 20-38 may have originated as cultic prophecy, albeit preserved as a secondary citation or reinterpreted tradition in Psalm 89. There is no argument for the cultic use of the oracular material based on internal textual clues associating the oracular material with liturgical ritual (cf. Ps 110:1, Ps 2:7, or the likely setting implied by Psalm 132). On the contrary, the syntactical and thematic links of the oracular material with the surrounding verses suggest a secondary incorporation of material from outside the immediate compositional setting of the psalm. However, the reference to the worshipping community (חסידיך) as the audience for the original oracular material points indirectly to the existence of cultic prophecy, even if its preservation in Psalm 89 is purely secondary. In addition, it is possible that the older prophetic tradition which was interpreted and incorporated into the unified psalm was performed by a prophetic functionary. The cultic origin, in some sense, of oracular speech in Psalm 89 is supported by the close similarity to cultic prophecy preserved in Psalms 2, 110, and 132, as well as the ideology, expressions, and compositional techniques of Assyrian cultic sources.

3.6 Conclusion

Because of the inclusion of first-person, divine speech in Psalms 110, 2, 132 and 89, as well as the use of introductory speech formulas (Pss 110:1, 4; 2:7; 132:11 and 89:20), these psalms presented to the worshipping community divine words concerning the legitimacy of the king, his royal prerogatives, and the hope for his dynasty and kingdom. Rather than prophetic speech uttered in the context of worship, some have suggested that in each case the poet drew from elements of the prophetic tradition that originated outside the cult. However, two lines of argument suggest that Psalms 110, 2, 132 and 89 witness to prophetic ministry within the cult. First, details within the psalms suggest that prophecy was uttered in the liturgy. The opening announcement of an "oracle" in Ps 110:1 aroused in the congregation the expectation of prophetic speech. Similarly, the performative "today" in Ps 2:7 lends a spontaneity to the divine words of the psalm. Psalm 132 narrates the transfer of the ark (a liturgical event) and offers prayer for the king (a liturgical act), to which the divine words form a response. Psalm 89, as a whole, may be a prophetic lament liturgy; or at least, the report of visionary revelation to the worshipping community in Ps 89:20 attests to prophetic ministry in the cult. Second, both the form and function of comparative sources support the likelihood that these psalms preserve cultic prophecy. Egyptian enthronement ritual, including oracular speech, corresponds in many respects to Psalms 110 and 2. The form and style of Assyrian cultic prophecy is very comparable to the speech of all four psalms and functionally similar in royal legitimation and enthronement as well as in response to petition for the king. The presence of Assyrian cultic prophecy in a seventh-century monarchic context lends support to arguments that prophets served the king in worship in pre-exilic Israel as well. Psalms 110, 2, 132 and 89 very likely preserve elements of this cultic prophecy.

Chapter 4
Asaphite Psalms

4.1 Prophetic Tradition of the Asaphite Psalms

4.1.1 Introduction

The Asaphite psalms (Psalms 50; 73-83) have frequently been characterised as containing prophetic material (in particular, Psalms 50; 75; 81; 82). Delitzsch (1902: 142) considered this to be one of the distinguishing features of the collection, and more recent works on the Asaphite collection continue this line of thought.[1] Even though Illman argued against Delitzsch that no distinctive tradition can be ascribed to the Asaphite collection as a whole, he agreed that prophecy plays an important role in this psalm group and that the function of cultic prophecy was given to the Asaphites, possibly as early as the pre-exilic period (Illman 1976: 58-59, 63-64). Hossfeld (1998: 227) observes that recent monographs on the Asaphite psalms accept cultic prophecy as a key characteristic. However, as the following discussion shows, the issue of whether its origin lies in genuine prophetic speech or in an imitation of prophetic style remains an open question. A common interpretation is that the prophetic features are due to the nature of post-exilic Levitical preaching/singing, which accounts for the origin of these psalms. After a survey of views on the prophetic origin of the Asaphite tradition, closer examination will be given to Psalms 50, 75, 81, 82 and 95 (considered with the Asaphite psalms because of its thematic affinities with Psalms 50 and 81).

---

[1] E.g., Buss (1963: 384, 389-91); Schelling (1985: 141, 246); Nasuti (1988: 158); Goulder (1996: 19-20); Weber (2001: 122-23).

4.1.2 Asaphite Psalms Preserve Genuine Prophetic Speech

4.1.2.1 Jörg Jeremias

Jeremias (1970: 195-97) argues that pre-exilic cult prophets sought to bring restoration to Israel by announcing God's immediate judgment on sinful individuals and groups within Israel. They emphasised the promises of the covenant traditions which assured salvation of the nation as a whole through internal purification in contrast to the classical prophets who announced a wholesale destruction of the nation and the creation of a new Israel. On the basis of similarities to Habakkuk, Jeremias (1970: 111-17) concludes that Psalms 12 and 14 are prophetic lament liturgies in which a cult prophet laments vicariously for God's oppressed people and mediates a divine response. The Asaphite Psalms 75 and 82 also contain a shortened and modified prophetic lament liturgy from late pre-exilic times. However, he regards the great festival psalms (Psalms 50; 81 and 95) as post-exilic priestly sermons, not cultic prophecy (Jeremias 1970: 125-27).

In Psalm 75, the lament proper is absent, being replaced in the course of tradition by communal praise (Ps 75:2). The remainder of the psalm exhibits the following form: the divine answer stating intention to intervene (Ps 75:3-4), a warning to the wicked (Ps 75:5-8), an announcement of judgment (Ps 75:9), and a vow of praise in view of the hearing (Ps 75:10-11). The *waw*-disjunctive at the beginning of this last section presupposes that a lament originally stood in the background (Jeremias 1970: 117-18). As additional evidence that a cult prophet speaks, Jeremias observes: 1) the divine answer revolves around the timing of God's intervention (cf. Hab 2:3), presumably anticipating doubt about Yahweh's promise through the prophet; 2) Yahweh brings together the disruption of cosmic order with the actions of the wicked (cf. Hab 3:17); 3) the issue of an ultimatum (Ps 75:5-8) in view of the hastening judgment (Ps 75:3) is imaginable only in the mouth of a prophet; 4) in form[2] and con-

---

2   Portrayal of the state of affairs; action of Yahweh; consequences for the threatened ones.

tents[3] the announcement of judgment in Ps 75:9 is of prophetic origin; 5) the closing certainty of a hearing (Ps 75:11) corresponds with Hab 3:18-19. In Jeremias's model, this certainty is rooted in the faith of cult prophets that the present distress of the nation stems from the actions of the wicked and that only after their destruction can the guiltless experience salvation (Jeremias 1970: 118-19).

Psalm 82 is close to a prophetic lament liturgy, only it concerns an event in the divine realm. Like Habakkuk 3, it is a prayer (Ps 82:8) for the realisation of the prophetic vision (Jeremias 1970: 120). The form follows the sequence: accusation (v. 2), reproof with ultimatum (vv. 3-4), judgment (v. 5), announcement of penalty (vv. 6-7). Not only does the opening verse parallel other prophetic reports of heavenly visions but the rhetorical question in Ps 82:2 corresponds to other prophetic admonitions. The question particle (עד־מתי, v. 2) also intimates a complaint/lament. Psalm 82 shares other features with prophetic lament liturgies: exhortation and warning (Pss 75:5-8; 82:3-4); the insensibility of the wicked (Ps 14:4; 82:5); the wobbling earth (Hab 3:17; Pss 75:4; 82:5); second person announcement of judgment (Pss 14:6; 82:7); and the word "arise" (Pss 12:6; 82:8) (Jeremias 1970: 121-22).

Jeremias (1970: 125-26) considers Psalms 50, 81 and 95 together and argues that they contrast with Psalms 75 and 82 in a number of important ways. First, all of Israel, not just the wicked, are brought to account. Second, the *Sitz im Leben* for Psalm 50 (together with Psalms 81 and 95) is a great celebration with a correspondingly more extensive Yahweh-speech that is not in response to lament. Third, in Psalms 50 and 81 the divine speech is introduced with the self-identification formula ("I am Yahweh"), which cannot belong to the genre of genuine prophetic speech.[4] Fourth, Jeremias doubts that an extensive didactic sermon concerning right sacrifice is imaginable in the mouth of a cult prophet; rather, the language of Psalm 50 appropriates technical terms more fitting in the mouth of a priest. With this last point, he surveys the theological traditions behind

---

3   E.g., cup in Yahweh's hand; cf. Hab 2:16; Jer 25:15-16.
4   Jeremias depends here on the conclusions of Zimmerli (1953: 204, 207; 1982: 23, 26).

these three psalms. Psalms 81 and 95 reflect the diction and ideas of "Dt", "DtrG" and the "C stratum of Jeremiah"; and most important is the theme of deuteronomic preaching that submission to Yahweh's law is the condition for victory. However, because of deviation in some speech peculiarities, literary dependence on these texts is improbable. Jeremias suggests that the best explanation for these links is Levitical familiarity with the old traditions, such as Massa and Meriba (cf. Deut 33:8) (Jeremias 1970: 127). If Psalms 81 and 95 originated in Levitical circles, then they probably were the earliest speakers of these psalms. Psalm 50, on the other hand, differs at certain points from the Levitical preaching in Psalms 81 and 95. Whereas Psalms 81 and 95 hark back to the lessons of history as a warning to the present generation, which stands in a somewhat neutral position morally, Psalm 50 focuses on the present guilt of the people. But no announcement of punishment follows in Psalm 50, as one would expect in prophetic speech form, only a threat. In addition, Psalm 50 does not exhibit the mood of festive joy present in Psalm 81 and 95. In sum, Jeremias argues that Psalms 50, 81 and 95 belong to the same *Sitz im Leben*, although Psalm 50 portrays a later modification showing how prophetic forms were adapted in psalmody. This, in Jeremias's judgment, is understandable if in post-exilic times prophets had merged into Levitical circles with the result that these festive songs were composed and spoken by Levites, not by cult prophets.

While it is still possible to argue that Psalms 75 and 82 were composed merely in imitation of prophetic style, Jeremias's form-critical and stylistic grounds for accepting them as genuine prophetic speech are impressive. He has also suggested a possible setting (the prophetic lament liturgy) in which such speech might have functioned. However, his treatment of Psalms 50 and 81 is open to several criticisms. Jeremias draws attention to different addressees in these psalms, i.e., the wicked in Psalms 75 and 82 but the whole nation in Psalms 50 and 81. This might indicate, as he suggests, a different setting for the two pairs of psalms. However, excluding Psalms 50 and 81 from the category of prophetic lament liturgy is not evidence against the presence of genuine prophetic speech. Jeremias's basic thesis is that cult prophets did not address the nation as a whole but only the wicked element within the nation.⁵ However, we should not exclude the possibility that at times cult prophets could address the nation as a whole. Jeremias himself notes the criticisms by the prophet Jeremiah that such broader proclamations of judgment should be expected of cult prophets, so that some cult prophets were potentially also doom prophets (Jeremias 1970: 8). This possibility appears to have been lost in his later discussion of the setting of Psalms 50 and 81.

Jeremias relies heavily on the conclusion of Zimmerli that the self-identification formula is incompatible with a genuine prophetic genre. Nasuti (1988: 136-39) has refuted Zimmerli's case on a number of grounds. First, the self-identification formula appears in prophetic texts from Mari and Assyria.⁶ At the time of Nasuti's research the full collection of Assyrian oracles was not easily accessible and his citation of Assyrian evidence is limited to the references in K4310 (=SAA 9 1) listed by Wilson (1980: 117; cf. Nasuti 1988: 138 n. 90). In addition to several more references in K4310 not listed by Wilson, there are numerous other examples of the self-identification formula in the Assyrian oracles, making this one of the most obvious features of Assyrian cultic prophecy.⁷ Zimmerli (1953: 194-95; 1982: 15-16) cites both the Mari text A.1121+A.2731 and the Assyrian oracle SAA 9 1.6 as well as the oracle preserved in SAA 3 13, regarding the Assyrian examples as evidence of *priestly* oracles. However, recognition of their distinctly cult prophetic origin poses a substantial difficulty for Zimmerli's thesis. Thus, a

---

5   His assignment of the term "wicked" in Ps 50:16 to a later addition appears to be without good reason.

6   Nasuti cites one Mari text, A.1121+A.2731 (Lafont 1985) — erroneously numbered A.2925 in Nasuti's source, which was Huffmon (1968) (see Roberts 2002: 160) — in which the deity speaks with an interrogative formula, "Am I not Addu". Two additional Old Babylonian examples are relevant. If the reconstruction *anāku* in line 3 of ARM 26 194 is correct, an example of self-predication can be added. Self-identification in apposition to the first-person pronoun appears in FLP 1674 published by Ellis (1987).

7   SAA 9 1.1 (i 11-12 [twice], 18, 20-21); 1.2 (i 36-37); 1.4 (ii 17, 30, 38); 1.5 (iii 4); 1.6 (iii 7, 15-16); 1.8 (v 12); 1.10 (vi 2); 2.1 (i 5, 8); 2.2 (i 24); 2.3 (i 36); 2.5 (iii 26); 2.6 (iv 8); 3.3 (ii 25); 3.5 (iv 7-8 ["you are Ištar"]). Most cases involve use of a proper name, but several examples are with a divine epithet. The absence of the self-identification formula in the individual oracle reports (in contrast to oracle collections) is curious, but perhaps the absence is accidental due to the broken nature of these tablets.

priestly announcement of law cannot be deduced from the presence of this formula in Psalm 50 and 81; on the contrary, the presence of this phrase is evidence of genuine cultic prophecy. Second, the form of the first-person pronoun in Ps 50:7 and 81:11 (אנכי) is the same as in the Decalogue (Exod 20:2; Deut 5:6) and Ephraimite prophecy (Hos 12:10; 13:4) as well as other non-priestly texts (Gen 31:13; Exod 3:6); whereas nearly all of Zimmerli's examples from priestly texts use the form אני. A similar distinction appears in the use of the second-person pronominal suffix on the word "God". Psalms 50 and 81 align with the Decalogue and Hosea passages in using the singular form, whereas the priestly-Ezekiel material uses the plural form (Nasuti 1988: 139). Nasuti's point is that the affinity of the Asaphite tradition is not with the priestly-Ezekiel material (Nasuti 1988: 138). Thus, the self-identification formula does not provide evidence that the tradition behind Psalm 50 and 81 is necessarily priestly. Third, another distinction between Psalms 50 and 81 and the priestly contexts cited by Zimmerli is the function of the legal citations. The use of the law in these psalms is accusatory, similar to the prophetic function in Hosea, and not simply a mediation of legal instruction implied in Zimmerli's priestly use of the formula. Therefore, "a prophetic role in the actualisation of these psalms is surely not to be dismissed" (Nasuti 1988: 140).

A final weakness in Jeremias's argument is that the use of priestly technical language does not exclude the possibility of cultic prophecy. Jeremias (1970: 110) criticises Mowinckel for refusing to distinguish between priest and prophet, thereby including some psalms within the category of cultic prophecy that may not have originated as such. Conversely, perhaps Jeremias can be criticised for drawing too sharp a distinction between priest and prophet. Because he considers Psalms 50 and 81 to have arisen from a priestly circle, he rules out cultic prophecy. However, a priest could function prophetically, as Mowinckel allows, and cult prophets could be familiar with priestly vocabulary. Assyrian cult prophets used technical language in promoting sacrifice (SAA 9 2.1 ii 25; 3.5 iii 26-27).

4.1.2.2 Pieter Schelling

Schelling (1985: 126-42) argues that the Asaphite psalms are united by their theology of judgment against foreign enemies as a means of liberating Israel. In addition to the tradition in Chronicles concerning the place of Asaphites in worship, the content of the psalms themselves places their common origin in the cult (Schelling 1985: 210-18). Because of their similarity in form and content to the prophetic writings, these psalms "breathe a prophetic spirit" (Schelling 1985: 141). The prophetic reproach of God's own people has the goal of making them obedient, similar to the proposal of Jeremias (Schelling 1985: 142). Psalm 50 is no mere imitation of prophetic speech, but it was spoken through a priest, cult prophet, or singer (Schelling 1985: 126, 211). The core of Psalm 75 stems from a cult prophet (Schelling 1985: 214). The divine speech in Psalm 81 evidences the emergence of a priest or cult prophet during the worship (Schelling 1985: 136-37, 218). Psalm 82 exhibits prophetic language and form characteristic of the community of cult prophets (Schelling 1985: 140, 218). He places the ministry of the Asaphites after the exile, as the content and form of all twelve psalms fits the period and is consistent with the portrait of the Asaphites in Chronicles. The psalms presumably originated in Judah, although they show an interest in northern traditions, reflecting a longing for a total Israel. Consequently Schelling dates all twelve psalms from shortly after the destruction of Jerusalem to around 400 B.C. (Schelling 1985: 219-30). However, as argued below, this conclusion about date is questionable.

4.1.2.3 Harry P. Nasuti

Nasuti (1988) explores characteristics of the Asaphite tradition at length, including the role and nature of prophecy. Against Illman, Nasuti argues that the Asaphite psalms exhibit common elements that help define the content and function of the Asaphite tradition.[8] These include rare or unique words and

---

8   Against the possibility that the superscription is due to the random attribution of individual psalms to Asaph composed by a number of unconnected

phrases (e.g., זיד, Pss 50:11; 80:14; "Joseph", Pss 77:16; 78:67; 80:2; 81:6; and 105:17 [also "Asaphite" according to Nasuti on the basis of 1 Chronicles 16]), a theological tendency associated by some scholars with the northern Ephraimite tradition[9], and similar form-critical characteristics.[10] While not all features are displayed by all the Asaphite psalms, the concentration of features is significant and ties together the various psalms of the collection (Nasuti 1988: 115-16). The Asaphite psalms show a particular concern for prophecy (Ps 74:9, Nasuti 1988: 70) and four of the psalms (Psalms 50; 75; 81 and 82) display a prophetic form (Nasuti 1988: 127, 158).[11] Nasuti (1988: 117) notes that the forms of the Asaphite psalms are shared with the rest of the Psalter and therefore are not proof of a tradition exclusive to this group; but if the existence of a tradition group is assumed, the formal aspects can be used to describe the functional character of the group and the institutional settings in which the group was active. Thus, on the basis of form, he characterises the Asaphite tradition as communal and prophetic (i.e., cult

---

authors and later grouped by some editor, Nasuti (1988: 56) observes that we are dealing with a relatively small collection ascribed to a rather peripheral figure (in contrast to the Davidic collections). The process envisaged is unlikely and leaves the common superscription without an adequate explanation. The existence of an Asaphite group attested outside the psalter (1 Chr 25:1-2) places the burden of proof on those who would deny this *traditio*.

9 Weber (2001) accepts the northern provenance of the circle behind the Asaphite psalms; however, rather than Jerusalemite redactions of northern psalms, he sees the psalms composed by northerners who fled south to the Jerusalem sanctuary and whose compositions served to ground the hope of the Israelites in restoration through the Davidic/Judean kingdom. Many of the theological tendencies suggested by Nasuti are not necessarily exclusive to a theorised Ephraimite tradition. Nevertheless, regardless of the origin of the theological tendencies within the Asaphite psalms, they share numerous common threads.

10 The attention to concrete linguistic data and forms is an important methodological shift in Nasuti's work. As Nasuti indicates, earlier studies are rightly criticised for cataloguing abstract themes resulting in a subjective criterion for distinguishing these psalms from the rest of the Psalter. He focuses his more objective criteria on defining the content of the tradition rather than using it to prove its existence (Nasuti 1988: 44-58); however, a common content renders its existence more probable (Nasuti 1988: 116).

11 Judging from his later discussion, Nasuti's listing of Psalm 83 in this group on page 127 must be construed as a typographical error for Psalm 82.

prophets within the group, Nasuti 1988: 157-59).[12] An interest in cultic prophecy among the Asaphites is portrayed in Chronicles as well (1 Chr 25:1-2, 6; 2 Chr 29:30), which in his view preserves reliable information regarding the pre-exilic association of Asaphites and temple prophecy (Nasuti 1988: 179, 188).

Of particular importance in Nasuti's discussion is 2 Chronicles 20, which narrates the cultic prophecy of an Asaphite. As evidence of authenticity of a pre-exilic tradition here, Nasuti (1988: 182-86) appeals to several converging themes: a royal spokesman for the community; a foreign military threat (i.e., pre-Persian); and the oracular form ("fear not") associated with the ark and holy war (in Nasuti's view, Ephraimite traditions). Noting Miller's (1970) discussion of the pre-exilic cultic status of the Korahites, as witnessed in an inscription from Arad, Nasuti (1988: 186) argues that this lends further credence to the existence of a distinct Asaphite group in the pre-exilic cult.[13]

Nasuti supports his characterisation of the Asaphite group on form-critical grounds. In the absence of a quotation formula in psalms (such as כה אמר יהוה), the use of first-person divine speech may indicate the prophetic status of a speaker (Nasuti 1988: 127-28). In his view, the latter is an indication of possession type prophecy, in contrast to non-possession type. In this distinction he depends on Wilson's (1980: 144-46) definition of

---

12 Nasuti (1988: 119-23) suggests that the emphasis on communal lament within the Asaphite psalms (Psalms 74; 79; 80; 83) might also be connected with cultic prophecy. Given that communal lament was at times coupled with a divine response (e.g., 2 Kgs 19:8-37), Nasuti proposes that it was the role of the Asaphites not only to participate in lament but also to provide the oracular answer (e.g., 2 Chr 20:14-17). Since none of the Asaphite communal laments contains an element of divine response, he suggests that perhaps the Asaphite prophetic psalms functioned as answer to these laments proper (Nasuti 1988: 123). As additional support Nasuti (1988: 121 n. 14, 144) cites the Zakkur inscription and the Neo-Assyrian oracle collection as discussed in Wilson (1980: 111-19, 130-32). A weakness in this use of Assyrian sources is that none of the oracles are in response to *communal* lament; however, they do testify to the dynamic of prophetic response to lament generally, which supports Nasuti's suggestion.
13 The inscription, Ostracon 49, is a ration list including the name "sons of Korah". For more recent commentary, see Renz (1995: 153-55), who holds that the people with names on Ostracon 49 occupied public offices, possibly as priestly servants. The discovery of the ostracon near the Arad temple strengthens the possibility that the sons of Korah had a cultic role.

possession in which the deity takes control of the prophet's physical being in order to speak, customarily in the first person. This differs from prophetic speech in which the intermediary reports divine words with third-person reference to the deity. In this latter case, the mediation may be a result of technical divination, although Nasuti recognises that this form is found among prophets as well. His point is that first-person speech is evidence of a particular form of prophecy (i.e., possession) involving a real encounter with the divine presence, a form utilised in the Asaphite psalms. An exception to this, Nasuti (1988: 128-30) argues, is where introduction formulas appear in psalms (e.g., Pss 2:7-9; 60:8-10; 68:23-24; 108:8-10; 110:4; 132:11-18; and possibly 89:3-5 and 12:6). In these cases, one is not dealing with a present divine encounter but rather a report of a past encounter, even though first-person divine speech may appear. In contrast to these quotation type examples, Nasuti (1988: 130-31) points to Pss 46:11; 87:4; 91:14 and 95:7 where the transition into first-person divine speech in the psalm is abrupt, without introductory formulas. In these cases there is the implication of a "present encounter with the Deity" or "cultic reality" (Nasuti 1988: 130). With these non-quotation examples he groups the Asaphite psalms, the implication being that they emerged in situations of divine presence as a cultic reality (Nasuti 1988: 131-32).

Nasuti may be correct that the prophetic speech in the Asaphite psalms corresponds to a "cultic reality"; however, it is doubtful that this can be concluded on the basis of his form-critical argument. First, one cannot distinguish between possession and non-possession prophecy by observing the presence or absence of first-person divine speech. For example, the incident in 2 Kings 3 is a description of Ephraimite possession prophecy (the hand of the Lord comes upon the northern prophet whose speech is induced by musical accompaniment)[14]; yet, the reference to Yahweh is in the third person as well as the first (2 Kgs 3:18). Nasuti (1988: 128 n. 45) admits that there are occasional exceptions to the dominant pattern of first-person divine speech, but such a clear narrative description like 2 Kings 3 casts seri-

---

14 This is a primary example in Wilson's citations of Ephraimite possession prophecy (Wilson 1980: 145).

ous doubt upon his definition. As discussed with respect to first- and third-person divine speech in Psalm 110, such changes are characteristic of prophetic speech in general and characteristic of Assyrian cultic prophecy. The person of speech should not be used to determine a particular type of mediation (possessive versus non-possessive). While a "cultic reality" may be implied where possession type prophecy occurs, this type of mediation cannot be proven for the Asaphite psalms.

Second, the absence of an introductory formula does not indicate a more "real" cultic setting, as Nasuti maintains. He argues that the *absence* of an introductory formula is possible only because "it is the expectations of the original cultic audience which allow such a transition [without a formula] to be meaningful. Only the setting makes sense of the text" (Nasuti 1988: 130).[15] However, one might wonder, how does the *repeated* use of a psalm *without* an introductory formula indicate a "real" divine encounter on every subsequent occasion in which the psalm is used, unless perhaps every performance of a psalm with first-person divine speech required a prophetically recognized functionary? Conversely, Psalms 2, 110, and 132 utilise introductory formulas; but the prophetic speech was likely viewed as a real divine encounter by the original audience. Secondary performances of these psalms might have been thought as mere recitation of an original cult-prophetic oracle; or perhaps in the case of coronation rituals such as Psalms 2 and 110, they were viewed as a fresh prophetic affirmation of divine legitimation for the king. In any event, these examples establish the point: the reality of divine encounter in prophetic speech cannot be dependent upon the absence or presence of introductory formulas. Indeed, the presence of a quotation formula is characteristic of the Ephraimite, possession type of prophecy (cf. 2 Kgs 3:17, Wilson 1980:145). Conversely, Meier (1992: 222) observes that prophets do not always formally introduce citation of divine speech, and he parallels this phenomenon with the Asaphite psalms. Miller (1996: 225-26) makes the same point that

---

15 Gerstenberger (2001: 82) maintains that the appearance of a Levitical preacher, instead of a prophet, would provide the same effect upon the audience. His view will be addressed in discussions relative to Psalm 75 below.

in prophetic speech the divine words might be unframed (e.g., 1 Kgs 21:21-22). Similarly, the Assyrian oracles use first-person divine speech, sometimes introduced with quotation formulas (e.g., SAA 9 2.4; 5; 7) and at other times not (e.g., SAA 9 1; 2.1-3, 2.5-6; 3.2-3; 9)[16]; nevertheless, they originate from a similar cultic setting with an implied real divine encounter

Third, Nasuti (1988: 132-33) observes that the non-quotation prophetic psalms are almost always of a communal genre, never lament and rarely individual. In contrast, the quotation type psalms tend to be individual. He concludes, "If, as suggested above, the non-quotation first person divine speech is a reliable sign of a present encounter with the Deity in the cult, the latter would seem to have been especially at home in those ceremonies of a communal nature in which hymns played a role" (Nasuti 1988: 133). It may be that the Asaphite psalms are communal, but his categorisation of psalms by genre and the contrast between individual and communal is problematic and says little about the life setting in which prophetic elements are used. For example, he classifies Psalms 2, 110 and 132 (quotation type) as individual royal; yet, all three of these psalms should be set in a context of corporate celebration. Nasuti (1988: 133) acknowledges that these royal psalms are "in a certain sense communal" and that Psalms 12 and 60 are collective. This constitutes a substantial number of psalms that render his distinction in setting insignificant. There is further evidence of overlap in the Assyrian prophecies, which are all individual[17] yet arise from a real cultic encounter with the deity. In conclusion, the form-critical *contrasts* to which Nasuti appeals provide no basis for inferring the "cultic reality" of the divine speech. His judgment regarding the prophetic nature of the Asaphite psalms may be correct, and his arguments derived from the character of the Asaphite tradition portrayed in Chronicles support his conclusion, but his form-critical arguments are not cogent.

---

16 In some of these cases, divine self-identification or use of "Fear not!" accompany first-person divine speech.
17 SAA 9 3 may be an exception since the community is addressed (SAA 9 3.2 i 27).

4.1.2.4 Michael Goulder

Following the observations of Franz Delitzsch, Goulder (1996: 15-36) judges the Asaphite psalms to be a unified collection of northern provenance (he suggests in the vicinity of Bethel).[18] In this regard his view is close to that of Nasuti and Seybold (see below). However, for him, the evidence is also sufficiently strong to postulate an origin for all psalms in the collection in the decade 732-722 B.C. He interprets those portions of the Asaphite psalms that show an interest in Judah/Zion (e.g., Pss 50:2; 74:2) as evidence of a post-722 B.C. redaction in Jerusalem and maintains that the references to cultic catastrophe (e.g. Ps 74:7) were originally composed for a northern incident and later applied to the disaster of 586. As a matter of style, he appears on the one hand to attribute divine speech in the Asaphite psalms to a genuine prophetic voice (Goulder 1996: 19-20) and maintains that the author of Psalm 50 is rightly called a "prophet" (Goulder 1996: 49-50). However, he argues against a cult prophet theory for Psalm 81, preferring to describe the performer as a "preacher" (Goulder 1996: 153-54, 157), assigns the whole of Psalm 75 to a royal voice without divine speech (Goulder 1996: 20, 82-85), and expresses some dissatisfaction with classifying Psalm 82 as prophetic liturgy or oracle (Goulder 1996: 162). Therefore, his perspective on cult prophecy in the Asaphite psalms as a whole is difficult to ascertain.

---

18 He is convinced by 1) the distribution of divine names relatively unique to these psalms; 2) the prophetic speeches of judgment against the nations presented as a hope for Israel's deliverance; 3) the emphasis on Israel's history, especially the "northern" perspective of the exodus, covenant and wilderness traditions that are somewhat different from that which is presented in the (southerly produced) Pentateuchal traditions; 4) the interest in northern geography and proper names; 5) common vocabulary, including several unique words; and 6) the relation to deuteronomic theology, although he proposes that the influence was from the Asaphites to deuteronomic thought in the south, not vice versa, because the psalms do not evidence the loss of national sovereignty and accept worship at local shrines (e.g. Ps 74:8).

4.1.2.5 Beat Weber

Weber (2001: 122, 124) acknowledges the prophetic character of the Asaphite collection and appears to presuppose an authentic prophetic voice for Psalms 50, 75, 81, 82 and possibly Psalm 78 (Yahweh speaking in the voice of the wise teacher in Ps 78:1-2). He views the Asaphites as consciously perpetuating the traditions of Moses, not only in the transmission of early (Moses) historical traditions but also as successors to Moses' ministry of prophetic intermediation after the manner of Deut 18:15 and 18 (Weber 2001: 126, 139-40). Weber's main point is that a post-720 B.C. historical context and theological function best accounts for the unusual northern interest and unified themes of Asaphite psalms. A circle of refugees fleeing to Jerusalem in the aftermath of the Assyrian devastation expressed their lament and sought to encourage Israelites who must now look to the Davidic kingdom for any hope of repatriation and reconstruction in the north. Psalm 78 is the centrepiece of the collection and provides the hermeneutical key (historically and theologically) to understand the movement from lament over northern losses to hope in new leadership in the south.

Given this historical setting, Weber (2001: 129-31, 133) dates all of the Asaphite communal lament psalms, except Psalm 79, to the seventh century (i.e., Psalms 74; 76; 77; 78; 80; 83). Psalm 79 was added to the Asaphite collection during the exile in order to make the lessons of the north applicable to the south after its downfall (Weber 2001: 137). Even Psalm 74 is assigned to the pre-exilic period on the basis of the plurality of sanctuaries (Ps 74:8), which Weber maintains would not have existed subsequent to Josiah's reforms and therefore could not refer to the destruction of Judean cultic sites (Weber 2001: 128).

The dating of the judgment (i.e., prophetic) psalms is, in Weber's assessment, more problematic because fewer internal references exist relevant to dating (Weber 2001: 131). Psalm 81 shows northern interests[19] and Psalm 50 is frequently coupled

---

19 E.g., "Joseph", Ps 81:6; wilderness traditions; cultic setting at Feast of Tabernacles.

with Psalm 81.[20] Therefore, Weber (2001: 131-32) places these two psalms in the same pre-exilic historical context as the communal laments.[21] Because of intertextual links between Psalm 75 and 76, he places Psalm 75 in context with the communal laments as well. Just as Psalm 50 is brought into this pre-exilic context through association with Psalm 81, so Psalm 82 is placed in the pre-exilic context by its similarity to Psalm 75 (Weber 2001: 132). Thus, on the basis of tradition history, Weber assigns all Asaphite psalms to the pre-exilic period with the exception of Psalm 79, which is exilic.[22] This supposition is supported by the absence from the Asaphite collection of what he regards as deutero-Asaphite Psalms 105 and 106, since it would appear that this collection had been closed before post-exilic times (Weber 2001: 132-33).

Weber's thesis offers a reasonable explanation for the dual, and potentially contradictory, northern/Jerusalemite interest shown in these psalms.[23] It also demonstrates that the origin of many of the Asaphite psalms is compatible with a pre-exilic setting, although Weber's dating of Psalm 74 remains questionable in my estimation. At the least, a *post*-exilic date cannot be assumed. However, the explanation that the psalms originated from a northern group is not the only solution compatible with the theological thrust of the psalms. It could also be that these psalms were sponsored by southern royal interests in order to draw the fragmented northern remnant into the orbit of Judean leadership. Therefore, themes most familiar to the northerners would naturally have been used to re-orient the refugees theologically and politically. The same message would also have

---

20 E.g., similar festival context; allusions to Decalogue; divine self-identification formula and calling the nation to attention in Pss 50:7 and 81:9, 11.
21 Weber (2001: 132) disagrees with Hossfeld and Spieckermann who place these two psalms in the post-exilic period, but he agrees with Hossfeld over against Spieckermann that Psalm 81 is earlier than Psalm 50.
22 Psalm 73 presupposes an intact sanctuary, and on the basis of its association with the Asaphite collection he prefers a pre-exilic instead of a post-exilic date (Weber 2001: 132).
23 It is therefore preferable to Goulder and Seybold's proposals. Goulder cannot account for the Jerusalem focus without a radical redaction. Seybold argues for an exilic context, but his view has difficulty accounting for the confident hope in a Davidically controlled and apparently intact Zion.

served to interpret the catastrophic events for the Judean population who witnessed and to a large degree suffered themselves from the Assyrian invasion.

4.1.3 Asaphite Psalms Imitate Prophetic Style

4.1.3.1 Hermann Spieckermann

In contrast to the view that the prophetic Asaphite psalms arose from actual prophetic speech in the cult, others maintain that the speech forms are due to poetic adaptation of prophetic style. Spieckermann (1994: 157-58) affirms that individual royal psalms may preserve remembrance of pre-exilic cultic prophecy. But, in his view, communal psalms composed in the aftermath of 587 B.C. draw on deuteronomic theological traditions and express it by imitation of a prophetic form reminiscent of the pre-exilic prophets (Spieckermann 1994: 158-59).[24] For support Spieckermann relies on the conclusions of Gunkel and Tournay that Psalms 50 and 81 were composed by imitation of prophetic speech. But, aside from the weaknesses of Gunkel and Tournay (discussed below under the respective psalms), one might ask why a psalmist's reliance on a particular theological tradition, such as Spieckermann proposes, should be incompatible with actual prophetic ministry in the cult. Dependence and even expansion on a particular theological tradition does not preclude authentic prophetic speech.

4.1.3.2 Klaus Seybold

Seybold (1994: 145) argues that a distinct social dimension must explain the fact that nearly all community lament psalms are found in the Asaphite collection. He proposes that a refugee community from the downfallen Davidic state located themselves north of Jerusalem (possibly at Shiloh, but more likely Bethel) during the exile. The references to the catastrophe of 587 (Psalms 74; 79; 80) point to the exilic period (Seybold 1994: 145-

---

24 See the discussion of Spieckermann in Chapter One.

46); at the same time some of the psalms express the perception that Jerusalem is spatially distant from the community. In Ps 76:4 (שׁמה), Zion is perceived from a distant vantage point. In Psalm 83, the enemy nations inscribe a circle around middle Palestine, leaving Judah/Jerusalem out of the imagined area; and the situation that allowed for such raiding must be the political vacuum of the Babylonian period. The three tribes named in Ps 80:3 encircle this region. Regarding Ps 81:1-3, he argues that a "lay" community is called upon to take over actions handled up to that time only by professional cultic officials. Thus, he proposes that behind the psalms a religious community of laity exists without state or cultic institutionalisation (Seybold 1994: 146-48).

This last conclusion has important implications regarding the issue of cultic prophecy in the Asaphite psalms. While the Asaphite psalms display a broad knowledge of (pre-canonical?) textual tradition, the prophetic corpus is conspicuously absent (Seybold 1994: 149-50). Yet, the Asaphite psalms display, alongside the oracular royal psalms, a distinctly prophetic character which, in the absence of actual citations or textual allusions, represents an inheritance from the prophetic tradition. While kingship ritual can explain the connection between royal psalms and oracles in the cult, there is, in Seybold's opinion, no corresponding satisfactory explanation for the appearance of first-person divine speech without transitional or introductory formulas in the Asaphite psalms. Seybold states, "I know so far of no clearer explanation for the phenomenon than the assumption that for the praying community, which stands behind these psalms, a new type of liturgical dialogue was found and developed" (Seybold 1994: 150). While Seybold follows the discussion of Tournay (1991) in pointing out the unique prophetic emphasis of the Asaphite psalms, he finds even Tournay's explanation of a form of cultic prophecy somewhat dubious (Seybold 1994: 150).

There are several weaknesses in Seybold's proposal. First, he largely assumes an exilic setting for most of the Asaphite psalms, a conclusion that is not supported by the evidence. His primary dating criterion, the catastrophe of 587, applies with certainty only to Psalm 79 and probably Psalm 74. Psalm 73 presumes an intact sanctuary; and the references to offerings in

Pss 50:14 and 76:12 are probably best understood in the context of a functioning cult at Jerusalem.[25] Similarly, Yahweh can hardly be thought of as "enthroned upon the cherubim" (Ps 80:2) during the exile. The theological thrust of Ps 78:67-72 makes little sense in an exilic or post-exilic context, since the destruction of the Jerusalem sanctuary and downfall of the Davidic monarchy would imply divine rejection like that suffered by northern establishments described in the psalm. According to Weber (2001: 137), it was just this struggle that led to the subsequent appending of Psalm 79 during the exile. If an exilic setting cannot be sustained for the bulk of the Asaphite psalms, then the *Sitz im Leben* suggested by Seybold is unlikely.

The psalms do convey a unique interest in the north and may have originated from circles steeped in northern traditions. However, Seybold's argument that Jerusalem is viewed from a distant perspective in the psalms and therefore that they originate from a community residing outside Jerusalem is not cogent. First, the "distant perspective" on Jerusalem expressed in Ps 76:4 is natural in poetic descriptions of Jerusalem or divine interventions on its behalf (e.g., Pss 48:7, 13-14; 122:4[26]). Second, the use of names associated with the north to describe God's people merely shows a northern (or perhaps pan-Israel) concern and does not necessarily imply that the psalms originated with a community residing outside Jerusalem at the time of composition. Even those psalms or psalm parts that might have been composed in a northern setting were not necessarily composed by post-587 refugees to the north. Weber and Goulder, for example, trace the same psalms to refugees who fled to

---

25 Seybold (1994: 153) suggests that Ps 76:12 orders offerings to be taken to Jerusalem, possibly after the destruction of Bethel. However, the date of destruction at Bethel is very uncertain. Kelso (1993: 194) places it in the early Persian period, but Dever (1971: 468-69) criticises the clarity of the pottery evidence upon which sixth-century occupation at Bethel is suggested. I am indebted to Jules Gomes for the references regarding Bethel.

26 This example is particularly helpful, since the vantage point of the psalmist is stated to be in Jerusalem (Ps 122:2), yet he speaks of Jerusalem as from a distance ("there the tribes go up"—Qumran and Peshitta have שמה, the identical construction to Ps 76:4). In the Akkadian *Hymn to the City of Arbela* (SAA 3 8:19-20), the city is perceived at a distance—"Into its midst enters tribute from the lands, Ištar dwells (there)".

Jerusalem from the north, the exact opposite of Seybold's proposal.

Seybold's puzzlement concerning the source of oracular speech in the Asaphite psalms is difficult to understand. Even if, as Seybold stresses, the Asaphite psalms exhibit a new form of liturgical dialogue that involves divine speech without introductory formulas, this need not present a problem, unless he is uncomfortable with a new liturgical form arising in the midst of a lay community that is dissociated from an institutionalised cult. However, in the light of the above criticisms, his proposed community setting for the origin of the Asaphite psalms is doubtful. The psalms did not arise primarily in an exilic setting nor in one led by lay refugees detached from a cultic institution. Even if his model for a refugee community at Bethel is granted, there is no reason to think of a cultic setting completely free of cultic officials. The prophetic Asaphite psalms could easily have arisen in a context with recognised, prophetically gifted individuals (priests or "lay" cult prophets).

4.1.3.3 Frank-Lothar Hossfeld

Hossfeld (1998: 225) suggests that newer trends in psalms studies are moving away from cult-prophecy theories in favour of literary formation. In his view, the case for a priestly/prophetic salvation oracle in connection with the "certainty of a hearing" can no longer be accepted, which shifts the search for an explanation of prophetic speech in the psalms to an examination of the divine speech itself (Hossfeld 1998: 226). Since the Asaphite psalms are a uniquely developed theological tradition that differs in character from divine speech found in the earlier Davidic Psalters, the divine speech of the Asaphite psalms is a special phenomenon, not a witness to a general practice of actual prophetic speech in the cult (Hossfeld 1998: 229, 242-43).

Hossfeld draws upon Nasuti (1988) and Seybold (1994) to stress the uniqueness of prophetic expression in the Asaphite psalms. As discussed above, Nasuti accepts genuine, prophetic expression in the Asaphite psalms as part of the Ephraimite tradition; but he argues that the Asaphites also exerted themselves in new ways in the post-exilic period, becoming a "singer only" group in the early post-exilic period whose songs bore a more hymnic and less hortatory flavour (Nasuti 1988). Hossfeld seizes the idea of a changing function during the course of history and argues that the Asaphites are not an example of cultic prophecy at all, rather the post-exilic Asaphites merely asserted their particular theological message in the cult in imitation of earlier traditions (Hossfeld 1998: 227-28). In a similar way, Hossfeld utilises Seybold's view that the Asaphites were part of a lay-community that was geographically detached from the Jerusalem cult during the exile. In this new setting they developed a new type of liturgical dialogue in which divine speech was introduced without introductory formulas (Hossfeld 1998: 228-29). In his view, then, the Asaphite psalms display a new form of expression that is detached from the institution of the cult and earlier cultic prophecy.

It is difficult to understand how Nasuti and Seybold's models support Hossfeld's thesis. Nasuti's argument for change in the Asaphite tradition cannot be separated from his view that a genuine prophetic function characterised the Asaphite psalms. Nasuti argues that only in Chronicles and in the hymnic forms of the Asaphite psalms (in his view Psalm 105) does the post-exilic tradition betray a loss of prophetic status for the Asaphites. The prophetic psalms themselves reflect actual prophetic activity (Nasuti 1988: 188-90). Seybold's model is that an exilic lay community gathered at Bethel and Shiloh. Since both of these sites are old cult centres, one can hardly detach the developing traditions of this community from cultic institutions. This is a fundamental weakness of Seybold's position. Therefore detachment from the old Jerusalem shrine in itself does not explain a newly emerging form of divine word preserved in the psalms under consideration.

The primary evidence for Hossfeld's case rests on his comparison between the divine speech found in the first two Davidic Psalters and that of the Asaphite psalms. With respect to divine speech in the first Davidic Psalter (Pss 12:6; 14:4; 27:8; 32:8-11; 35:3) only Pss 12:6 and 14:4 show connection with actual prophetic speech, but due to their brief nature they are not the product of institutionalised cultic prophecy (Hossfeld 1998: 234). In the second Davidic Psalter (Pss 53:5; 60:8-10; 68:12-14), the oracular material in Psalms 60 and 68 is more detailed than in those in the first Davidic Psalter; but they are merely citation of traditional sayings (Hossfeld 1998: 238). In contrast, the Asaphite psalms (and Psalm 95) demonstrate more expanded and comprehensive use of divine speech (Hossfeld 1998: 238). The themes of warning or rebuke bind them together in contrast to the use of divine speech in the Davidic Psalters for the purpose of encouragement (Hossfeld 1998: 239). However, Assyrian cultic prophecy is of comparable length to the Asaphite prophetic psalms. Even if Hossfeld is correct that short oracles in the Davidic Psalter developed into longer passages in the Asaphite psalms, this does not imply that the latter are inauthentic prophecies.

Hossfeld utilises Nasuti's contrast between quotation type prophecy and non-quotation type prophecy but with the opposite conclusion. Rather than depending upon a cultic prophecy hypothesis, Hossfeld prefers to explain the unique, expansive divine speeches in the Asaphite psalms, which are not introduced in the psalms by a quotation formula, as a product of the special theological interest of the Asaphites. In view of their concern over the absence of prophecy (Ps 74:9; 77:9; 83:2), Hossfeld maintains that the Asaphites turned from the older, lost form of divine certitude (cultic prophecy) to newer ways of assuring the presence of God's word, namely, a reactualisation of the older tradition of the word of God theology (Hossfeld 1998: 242-43). However, the theme of prophetic silence depends on only one example, Ps 74:9. Hossfeld's other two examples (Pss 77:9 and 83:2) are more likely references to God's failure to intervene on behalf of his people. More significantly, Ps 74:9 need only express the anxious experience of the community at the time of the psalm (possibly early exilic period). By late exilic and early post-exilic times there was no lack of prophetic word regarding the restoration of the people from exile. Therefore, it is difficult to imagine an absence of prophetic speech as motivation for the creation of a completely new form of expression for the divine word in the cult.[27]

---

27 In view of the continuing ministry of prophets like Ezekiel and Jeremiah in the early exile, Ps 74:9 must be understood as the absence of a particular kind of prophetic ministry, perhaps the cult prophet amply attested by Jeremiah's rebukes but decimated (and discredited) at the fall of Jerusalem (Lam 2:9, 20; 2:14; 4:13). Psalm 74:9 would lament a *relative* loss of the

Furthermore, Hossfeld's argument depends on the emergence of the non-quotation type of prophecy in the composition of Psalms 50, 75 and 82. He observes that in Ps 81:6 there is an indication that the mode of communication is divine speech, which sets this psalm apart from the other Asaphite prophetic psalms and in his view suggests an earlier date from the rest (Hossfeld 1998: 242).[28] This is problematic in view of the similarity between Psalm 81 and Psalm 95 (which he classifies as deutero-Asaphite). Since Psalm 95 exhibits non-quotation type prophecy but likely originated in a similar cultic setting to Psalm 81, his form-critical distinction between genuine cultic prophecy and imitation based on the presence of such formulas is weakened. As already noted in criticisms of Nasuti's view, presence or absence of introductory speech formulas cannot differentiate between various types of prophecy since admittedly genuine prophetic speeches utilise both forms.

4.1.4 Conclusion

While the prophetic character of the Asaphite tradition and their psalms is unquestioned, two different explanations have been offered for the origin of prophetic speech in the Asaphite psalms. On the one hand there is cultic prophecy; on the other hand there is literary formation that merely imitates prophetic style. Nasuti uses his distinction between quotation and non-quotation type prophecy in order to underscore the cultic reality of divine speech in the psalms. Hossfeld, appealing to the same distinction, concludes the opposite. Neither of their respective form-critical arguments are convincing. The various models of tradition history (e.g., Jeremias, Seybold, Goulder, Weber,

---

prophetic word; but it does not reflect circumstances that would give rise to an entirely new genre of psalm.

28 Whether or not this is actually an introductory formula for prophetic speech is addressed below. Hossfeld's conclusion regarding its nature is granted here for the sake of analysing his argument. Nasuti (1988: 131 n. 54, 135) regards this as possibly expressing the transition of the psalmist/prophet into a trance state, not a formal introduction. This, in his view, can only be explained if one presupposes a cultic reality to the prophetic speech of Psalm 81.

Spieckermann) help describe developments in theological tradition but cannot adjudicate between the competing models of the origin of divine speeches. After a review of the history of research on prophecy in the Asaphite psalms, Hossfeld (1998: 226) correctly points to the need to shift the emphasis of study from tradition history to the data from the Asaphite psalms themselves. The next section examines Psalms 50, 75, 81, 82 and 95 more closely, both with respect to form and setting and in the light of Assyrian prophetic sources.

4.2 The Asaphite Psalms in the Light of Assyrian Prophetic Sources

4.2.1 Introduction

Four Asaphite psalms are commonly regarded as prophetic (Psalms 50; 75; 81; 82), with which Psalm 95 is frequently grouped on the basis of its formal and thematic similarity. The discussion begins with Psalm 81 because it potentially preserves a statement proclaiming prophetic inspiration (Ps 81:6).[29] Psalm 50 is formally and thematically similar to Psalm 81, so discussion of it follows. Next is treatment of Psalms 75 and 82, which share several features. Examination of Psalm 95 is last.

4.2.2 Psalm 81

4.2.2.1 Psalm 81 as Cultic Prophecy

The structure of Psalm 81 is generally conceived in two parts: a hymnic introduction with festival instructions (vv. 2-4/or 5) followed by a prophetic admonition (vv. 5/6-17).[30] However, the

---

29 Cf. Hossfeld (Hossfeld and Zenger 2000: 478; 2002: 458) who gives it first place for this reason.
30 E.g., Mowinckel (1923: 38); Gunkel (1926: 356); Anderson (1972: 586); Kraus (1978b: 727; 1989: 146); Weiser (1962: 553; 1987: 376); Tate (1990: 322); Tournay (1991: 173); Gerstenberger (2001: 107-108); Hossfeld (Hossfeld and Zenger 2000: 469; 2002: 457).

setting of the psalm and nature of the prophetic speech have been variously interpreted. Mowinckel (1923: 38) places the psalm in the context of an annual enthronement festival at which time the covenant between Yahweh and Israel was renewed after the fashion of the Sinai tradition. He envisions a short reverential pause at the end of the hymnic introduction, after which the silence was dramatically broken by a cult prophet who spoke the conditions of covenant renewal in the second part of the psalm (Mowinckel 1923: 38-39) Although he interprets Ps 81:6 as a report of inspiration, he considers it to be the introduction of a prophetic address arranged in advance for performance at this point in the liturgy rather than the result of spontaneous free inspiration (Mowinckel 1923: 40).

Weiser (1962: 553; 1987: 376) likewise envisions an autumn festival as backdrop, but sets the psalm in the pre-exilic north. In response to a threat from enemies, a prophet or priest utters a divine word, introduced in 6b, which Weiser translates, "I hear a voice which I do not know". The oracle applies the salvation traditions celebrated in the festival to the present distress; the reality of God's past acts of salvation for the present community is conveyed through a shift to the prefix conjugation (vv. 6-8), which Weiser interprets as present tense ("I answer you", אֶעֶנְךָ, "I test you", אֶבְחָנְךָ, v. 8) (1962: 553-54; Weiser 1987: 376-77). The demand of Yahweh for covenant renewal is then voiced in terms reminiscent of the Sinai tradition (vv. 9-11), together with an admonition based on past failure (Ps 81:12-13). But the oracle also offers hope for the possibility of deliverance (Ps 81:14-15); and on that basis, the speaker himself underscores the potential blessing for the congregation in the last two lines of the psalm, vv. 16-17 (1962: 554-56; Weiser 1987: 377-78).

4.2.2.2 Psalm 81 as Prophetic Imitation or Sermon

Gunkel (1926: 357) considers either an autumn festival of Tabernacles or the beginning of the civic calendar at Passover (cf. exodus tradition in the psalm) to be possible settings for Psalm 81. Because of the reference to "Joseph", he favours a northern provenance. Similar to Mowinckel's liturgical model, he imagines that the worship leader allowed the voice of an individual singer to sound an admonition at a time when the choir grew silent. However, in spite of what he understands to be an introduction to divine speech in Ps 81:6, he considers the form and content to be an imitation of prophetic speech by a Levitical singer (Gunkel 1926: 356-57). Gunkel's treatment is somewhat confusing because he does use the term "prophet" once and describes the event as receiving revelation. However, his extended description of the psalm as "imitation" under the influence of the prophets suggests more strongly that he does not regard the singer as a cult prophet. Gunkel argues that Ps 81:11c originally followed verse 6c as part of the introductory formula.[31] He compares the unfamiliar voice of God in the ear of a prophet with Samuel's experience (1 Sam 3:7) and the metaphor of filling the prophet's mouth with Jeremiah (Jer 15:16). Kraus (1978b: 729; 1989: 149) adopts the autumn festival for the setting of the psalm, but he interprets the reference to "Joseph" as a name for "all Israel" in view of the exodus tradition rather than an indication of northern provenance. He maintains that the form of prophetic address (reason for judgment; threat; promise) is closer to a deuteronomistic sermon (preaching history and judgment) than to familiar OT prophetic forms; and in this regard he accepts the argument of Jeremias (1970: 125-27) that the psalm is a type of post-exilic Levitical sermon (Kraus 1978b: 727-28, 731; 1989: 147, 150-51).[32] The speaker is a prophet only to the extent that post-exilic Levitical preachers saw themselves as prox-

---

[31] Cf. Kraus (1978b: 726-27; 1989: 145-47) and Anderson (1972: 590). Seybold (1996: 323) thinks that originally verse 6b was part of verse 8 referring to the Egyptian experience, but now it functions to introduce a word of revelation, having been transposed from its original order. In view of the speculative nature of all these reconstructions, it is preferable to retain the text as received, which is not necessarily problematic. Tate (1990: 322-23) regards both Ps 81:6c and 11c as oracular formulas, but he prefers to maintain the verses in their present positions as a frame to the oracle in vv. 7-11b, with Ps 81:11c also forming an introductory bridge to the second part of the oracle in vv. 12-17.

[32] Following Jeremias and Kraus, Tate (1990: 321-22) regards the oracle as post-exilic Levitical preaching that continues the prophetic tradition; and Seybold (1996: 322) argues that Psalm 81 was composed of an exilic ground text (a rîb speech of a prophet; essentially vv. 6-17) added to a text of calendar instructions for the diaspora community (perhaps proselytes in need of instructions on basic regulations, vv. 2-5), which was subsequently reworked by Asaphites for liturgical use.

ies of the Mosaic office. For Hossfeld (Hossfeld and Zenger 2000: 473; 2002: 458), the divine speech introduction in verse 6 invests the post-exilic Asaphite singer with authority analogous to prophets. The divine speech is an extension of a pre-exilic call to praise, showing typical Asaphite interest in northern exodus traditions and the deuteronomistic movement.

Agreeing with Gunkel and Seybold that pieces of the text appear to have undergone reordering, Gerstenberger (2001: 108) suggests that oracular elements may have served for the sermon's composition; however, in its present form it served as a liturgical text in the preaching tradition of the early Jewish community (Gerstenberger 2001: 108-109). Because he judges that the audition formula of Ps 81:6c does not belong to prophetic traditions, Gerstenberger suggests it originates from sapiential traditions instead (cf. Job 4:12-16, 33:14-18, Gerstenberger 2001: 109, 111). Thus, the formula indicates a cultic manifestation of direct divine communication that differs from prophetic discourse of an earlier era, more of a homiletical convention that introduces an appeal to authoritative tradition.[33]

---

33 In support he cites three texts: 1) Ps 12:6, where he distinguishes the formula "says the Lord" from the formally prophetic "thus said the Lord" (Gerstenberger 1988: 81); 2) Ps 62:12, which he suggests stems from sapiential discourse (Gerstenberger 2001: 10); and 3) Ps 85:9 does not anticipate an oracle. Instead, he insists that cult prophets should be distinguished from messenger prophets, the former being a case of the worship leader looking to Scripture to ascertain the mind of God on a matter (Gerstenberger 2001: 129). Regarding Ps 12:6, his own example from Isa 33:10 should caution against dismissing Ps 12:6 as prophetic speech on the basis of discourse formula; however, one can also add Isa 41:21 and 66:9. Psalm 62:12 is not a relevant parallel. Gerstenberger has suggested a possible alternative to Mowinckel's and Gunkel's interpretation of Ps 85:9; but this passage merely elicits an explanation for such a cultic interrupt, it does not provide evidence for the nature of the anticipated divine response. None of Gerstenberger's examples offer support to his proposal that Ps 81:6 merely introduces a type of homiletical discourse in contrast to prophetic speech. Gerstenberger recognises that homiletical use of first-person divine speech "unashamedly and without fear" is "extraordinary" (Gerstenberger 2001: 111-12). Yet, it appears that his "cultic prophet" is really nothing more than a "Levitical preacher".

154   Asaphite Psalms

4.2.2.3 Evaluation

As the above survey indicates, most commentators view the prophetic admonition in Ps 81:7-17 as a priestly/Levitical sermon. This is in spite of the fact that the same commentators generally regard Ps 81:6 as some sort of introduction formula indicating the reception of inspiration. There are several reasons, however, to question this near consensus on both counts.

It is questionable whether the phrase שפת לא־ידעתי אשמע (Ps 81:6c) is an introduction formula indicating an experience of inspiration, as most commentators maintain. It is even more doubtful that the command to open the mouth for filling in Ps 81:11c is a metaphor for reception of the divine word. Regarding Ps 81:6c, the prefix form, אשמע, might be construed as present tense; however, the prevalent use of the preterite (without the *waw*-consecutive) elsewhere in the psalm (including vv. 7 and 8) and the perfect in Ps 81:6a makes a past tense reference of this verb possible.[34] This past tense understanding flows naturally in the context of retelling the exodus experience, which is abruptly disrupted if the verb is interpreted as present tense and the phrase understood as an inspiration formula. But more problematic for the inspiration interpretation is the meaning of שפה (usually translated "voice" or "Stimme"). By metonymy שפה is frequently used for "speech" or "language" but never "voice".[35] This is not a pedantic distinction, since "voice" presupposes the immediate auditory experience of the psalmist; whereas the rendering "speech" or "language" is more neutral. The translation "speech" or "language" is consistent with the context, which narrates the past experience of the exodus community. The prophet may still be speaking representatively in Ps 81:6c, or better, Yahweh's report of deliverance begins with Ps 81:6c when he

---

34 Cf. תעבֹרנה (v. 7); אענך and אבחנך (v. 8); ילכו (v. 13). As noted above, Weiser renders the prefix verbs in verse 8 as present tense, but this is strained in view of the immediate context of these verbs.

35 The lip, שפה, is regarded as a speech organ (1 Sam 1:13; 2 Kgs 18:20) and therefore by metonymy to denote speech, most often in construct with qualifying noun (singular Ps 120:2 or plural Ps 31:19) or the genitive of a construct (Isa 28:11; 33:19; Ezek 3:5, 6), but occasionally alone (Job 12:20; Prov 10:19). By extension, the word denotes "language" when the context is the speech character of a group (Gen 11:1; Isa 19:18; Zeph 3:9-reversal of Babel?). In contrast, hearing a "voice" is denoted by שמע קול (see next note).

intervened against those who spoke a language foreign to his people. While the translation "speech" would allow reference to *divine* communication, this use of שׂפה is otherwise unattested.[36] Thus, it would be an awkward expression for God's speech if so used in Ps 81:6.[37] On the other hand, in view of the narrative context, a reference to the foreign speech is appropriate (cf. Ps 114:1 where this notion is associated with the exodus experience).[38] In addition, Goulder (1996: 154) correctly notes the difficulty in the idea that a prophet would not know Yahweh's voice. Gunkel (1926: 357) refers to the experience of Samuel (1 Sam 3:7); but the example of a youth like Samuel may not be a good parallel to the case of an established cultic functionary, which one may presuppose for Psalm 81. Regarding Ps 81:11, the command to open the mouth fits the tradition of disobedience in the wilderness to Yahweh's offer of manna, and it also anticipates the promise at the close of the psalm. It is closely linked with the divine address to the people, so no individual prophet can be in view. Since it is doubtful that the clauses under discussion should be understood as a metaphor for prophetic inspiration, the designation of Ps 81:7-17 as genuine cultic prophecy must rest on other grounds.[39]

---

36 One finds דבר coupled with שׁמע (e.g., Job 26:14; Jer 23:18) and קול with שׁמע (e.g., Deut 4:33; 5:24; Isa 6:8; Ps 95:7; cf. Job 4:16) or both (Deut 4:36; Pss 19:4; 103:20), as well as אמר with שׁמע (Num 24:4, 16), but never שׂפה as divine speech. Conversely, whenever שׂפה is coupled with שׁמע it always denotes language (Gen 11:7; Exod 6:30 [possibly inarticulate speech not language]; Isa 33:19; Ezek 3:6). Goulder (1996: 154) opines that "lip" is too crude for anthropomorphism, but שׂפה does occur once in reference to God (Isa 30:27) where it denotes an act of judgment, not a word of revelation. Perhaps relevant to this discussion, but not of decisive importance, is the use of *šaptu* in SAA 9 9:20. Here the goddess reports on her efforts, probably in the divine assembly, to plead on behalf of the king. The metonymy "lips" for "speech" is repeated in line 22 in reference to the king's words of joy.

37 Booij (1984: 468) interprets the "speech" of Ps 81:6c as a formula introducing divine speech and explains the peculiarity of the expression, "a speech I do not know", as due to the dissonant tone of the prophetic oracle with the utterances of joy expressed in the hymnic introduction to the psalm. Thus, Booij acknowledges the difficulty of this interpretation, but his explanation is not adequate.

38 The Masoretic punctuation joins the clause with 6ab, indicating that they linked שׂפה contextually with the Egyptian experience (i.e., "language").

39 If, as most commentators argue, Ps 81:6 is a reference to inspiration, then Psalm 81 preserves cultic prophecy. In this case, the proposed genre "Leviti-

While the expressions in Ps 81:6c and 11c are not likely to be references to prophetic inspiration, the second part of the psalm as a whole should nonetheless be construed as prophetic speech. As summarised above, the majority of commentators understand Ps 81:7-17 as a sermon that imitates prophetic style or perhaps adapts fragments of what was originally prophetic material. The primary argument for denying genuine prophetic speech in Psalm 81 is the claim that it follows the style of deuteronomistic preaching. But this argument is weak.[40] First, the logic that similarity to deuteronomistic themes precludes genuine prophetic speech is not sound. A prophet such as Zephaniah or Jeremiah serving around the time of Josiah's reforms would be expected to reflect deuteronomistic theology and style. Yet such content does not invalidate the genuineness of their prophetic announcements.[41] If a pre-exilic prophet could evidence deuteronomistic thought, then a post-exilic date for "sermonic" material in Psalm 81 must be argued on other grounds; and if some of this language originated by the time of Hezekiah, then the need to posit a post-exilic setting becomes even more problematic. Therefore, even if similarities to deuteronomistic style in Psalm 81 are granted, this need not relegate it to post-exilic preaching.

Koenen (1996: 16-25) argues against a sermonic genre in Psalm 81 because it has not adequately explained the divine speech functioning in a prophetic manner, and sermons are more associated with one-time use whereas these psalms are part of repeated liturgy. Mathias (1984) challenges the validity of a *genre* designation "Levitical sermon" altogether, because no set of form-critical criteria can be consistently applied to the speeches of Chronicles resulting in a collection of "sermons", and certainly not originating from Levitical circles specifically. After careful form-critical re-evaluation of the sermons in Chronicles (and other post-exilic literature), Mason (1990: 257) echoes the conclusions of Mathias. The majority of addresses

---

cal sermon" must bear the burden of proof to place Ps 81:7-17 in a non-prophetic genre.
40 The view of Zimmerli and Jeremias that the self-revelation formula cannot be prophetic has been criticised above.
41 E.g., Deuteronomic curses in Hos 3:2-3; Zeph 1:13, 17; conditional blessing in Amos 3:1-2; Jer 4:1-4.

are in the mouth of kings or prophets and only once from a Levite (Mason 1990: 133-34). Comparing the addresses in Chronicles with prophetic style he writes: "It is difficult, if not impossible, to find satisfactory, objective criteria by which to determine a literary type 'sermon' so as to distinguish it clearly from prophetic oracles in general" (Mason 1990: 257). Even occasional poetic elements appear in the Chronicles addresses, although he concludes that the classical prophetic form is "breaking down" (Mason 1990: 138-42). In spite of this conclusion, the relative poetic/prosaic contrast between the oracular psalms and Chronicles is significant. But another important observation merits comment, following the above cited objection of Koenen. Whenever first-person divine speech occurs in the sermons of Chronicles, it is presented as prophetic speech (1 Chr 22:6-16; 28:2-10; 2 Chr 12:5-8). Other framed prophetic speeches without first-person divine speech are also evident (1 Chr 12:19; 2 Chr 15:1-7; 20:14-17, 37; 21:12-15; 24:20-22; 25:15). There was no confusion in the social setting of the Chronicler about the identity of a functionary who speaks for God. A preacher would not use first-person divine speech without the authorised mantle of a prophet. Even if one argues, as does Mason, that these addresses in Chronicles echo some of the style and thematic content of post-exilic temple preaching, first-person divine speech is a crucial form-critical element that defines the speech as prophetic, not merely human exhortation. The abiding phenomenon of post-exilic prophetic exhortation (Haggai, Zechariah, Malachi), even when based upon "Scriptural" tradition and therefore "preaching" by Mason's criteria, is further evidence that the community continued to recognise the unique authority of prophetic versus mere human preaching. Thus, the use of first-person divine speech cannot be a formal characteristic of post-exilic non-prophetic preaching, and its appearance in psalms should not be so construed.

This leads to a second criticism of the "deuteronomistic sermon" view. Psalm 81, and the Asaphite psalms in general, are not particularly deuteronomistic, even if one accepts a sermonic genre of Levitical preaching. One of Illman's main objections to a thematic unity in the Asaphite collection is his rejection of a distinct concentration of deuteronomistic language in these psalms (except in Psalm 78 and only marginally in Psalm 81 if at all,

Illman 1976: 48, 63). There is also good reason to doubt a distinctively deuteronomistic style in Psalm 81 on the basis of the form of the psalm itself. Booij (1984) has argued that Ps 81:7-12 follows a "pattern of remembrances", which was considered clearly prophetic in certain circles (e.g., Judg 2:1b-2; 6:8b-10; Jer 7:22-25a; 11:7-8; Ezek 20:5-8, 10-13, 18-21). The style of the pattern includes: 1) Yahweh reminds Israel of deliverance from Egypt; 2) Yahweh recalls the commandment given around that time, occasionally using the self-identification formula; 3) Yahweh complains that Israel would not listen (Booij 1984: 466-67). In both the Jeremiah examples as well as 2 Kgs 17:13-15, the oracle of a prophet is the sequel to Yahweh's commands at the time of the exodus. In Jer 7:22-25a, the pattern of remembrances is conveyed through a messenger (either a prophet or Yahweh's angel) who speaks for God and admonishes the people. This pattern is identical to Psalm 81 (Booij 1984: 467-68). While this pattern flourished in the deuteronomistic tradition, he emphasises that some phrases in Psalm 81 are found outside deuteronomistic texts (including Jeremiah C). Since the similarities are few and not very specific, Ps 81:7-17 cannot be regarded as a genuine deuteronomistic text (Booij 1984: 471-72). The remembrance of Egyptian deliverance and Israel's repeated unfaithfulness are joined in older prophetic tradition (Jer 2:4-13; Hos 11:1-2; 13:4-6; Mic 6:1-4; Amos 2:10-12), and the element of Yahweh's command can be seen in Ezekiel 20 (Booij 1984: 472-73). But significantly, unlike Ezekiel 20, Psalm 81 does not reflect on the disaster of the exile. Therefore, it belongs to the pre-exilic period (Booij 1978: 172; 1984: 475; 1994: 9).[42] Because the psalm is a literary unit composed of hymnic and oracular parts, Booij argues that it was created for liturgical citation by a singer and so the divine speech is not from an actual prophet (Booij 1978: 189; 1994: 8).[43] However, the possibility of a prophet utilising a hymnic introduction is not difficult to imag-

---

[42] Booij is also impressed by the manner in which the psalm speaks of Israel's enemies and rebukes Israel for faithlessness. As noted above and argued by Weber and others, the northern interest of Psalm 81 is an argument for a pre-exilic date as well.

[43] "The prophetic message is interpreted liturgically through a temple singer" (Booij 1978: 221).

ine.⁴⁴ Nor does thematic compatibility between the two parts of the psalm deny the possibility of cooperation between liturgists, one of whom is a cult prophet. If Ps 81:7-17 would have been regarded by the congregation as prophetic speech on the basis of the familiar pattern of remembrance, the implication that Psalm 81 preserves genuine prophecy remains intact.⁴⁵

The Assyrian oracles contain nothing comparable to Psalm 81 with regard to rebuke of the people for disobedience. However, in SAA 9 3.5 the king receives a mild reproof for failing in his cultic duties after the goddess has so graciously delivered him. On the basis of fulfilment of past promises of deliverance, the king is admonished for lack of faith in the goddess during a present trial (compare SAA 9 1.1 and 1.4 with 1.10). In addition, while the Assyrian oracles are predominantly addressed to the king, there is one oracle which contains an address to the congregation similar to the prophetic summons in Ps 81:9 (SAA 9 3.2 i 27 "Hear O Assyrians!").⁴⁶ There may also be a form-critical comparison between Psalm 81 and the SAA 9 3 oracle collection as a whole:

---

44 See the comparison below regarding SAA 9 3, which shows a similar thematic composition to Psalm 81 using oracles of the same cult prophet and, in Parpola's opinion, was performed "live" by the prophet at the enthronement ceremony.
45 Tate (1990: 326-27) notes Booij's form-critical observations, but he also fails to acknowledge the implications of this for the authenticity of the prophetic oracle over against a mere sermonic imitation.
46 Parpola's reconstruction, "[*sitam*]*meā*", is reasonable (cf. SAA 9 2.4 ii 35).

Psalm 81	SAA 9 3
Call to Praise (1-4)	Setting of Celebration (3.1)
Report of Divine Deliverance (5-8) (first person divine speech)	Call to Covenant Faithfulness "Hear O Assyrians" (3.2)
Call to Covenant Faithfulness "Hear my people" (9-11)	Report of Divine Deliverance (3.3) (first person divine speech)
[No other gods!]	Call to Covenant Faithfulness "Come gods" (3.4)
Report of Failings (12-13)	Report of Cultic Failings (3.5 iii 16-31)
Divine Entreaty for Obedience with Assurance of Deliverance (14-17)	Divine Command for Cultic Obedience with Assurance of Deliverance (3.5 iii 32-iv 25)[47]

Two factors reinforce the validity of this comparison. First, while all other oracle collections are composed of reports from various prophets, SAA 9 3 is presumably from one prophet named in the colophon at the end of the collection (Parpola 1997: LXIII-LXIV). This strengthens the possibility that the collection is unified form-critically as suggested above.[48] Second, this Assyrian oracle collection is concerned with covenant ratification, probably at the coronation of Esarhaddon. The setting of Psalm 81 cannot be determined with certainty, but the suggestion of several scholars that it relates to covenant renewal at one of the major feasts has merit. Although the Assyrian collection concerns loyalty to the human king in contrast to the divine king in Psalm 81, both share a similar ideology. On the other hand, there are a few differences between SAA 9 3 and Psalm 81 that deserve comment. The "Report of Failings" sections are perhaps only vaguely parallel. In general, the rebukes of Assyrian prophets

---

[47] In these oracles, past action is implicitly a cause for expectation of future action, as is the case here.

[48] De Jong (2001: 14) argues that SAA 9 3 is a written composition based on prophetic oracles but originally two parts (Aššur oracles and Ištar oracles) which are still separated by the double scribal score at the end of SAA 9 3.3. Nevertheless, as Pongratz-Leisten (1999: 78) notes, the oracles are fully integrated as part of a unified covenant ceremony.

are mild in comparison to that of Hebrew prophets and relate only to lapses in cultic responsibility on the part of the king. However, granting this relative difference between the Assyrian and Hebrew ethical-theological systems, the component of failure is nevertheless there. Perhaps the most striking dissimilarity between the two texts is the object of loyalty. In the Assyrian collection, covenant duty is directed toward the king but the cultic failure is on the part of the king toward Ištar. In Psalm 81, both covenant loyalty and failures in obedience are in reference to Yahweh. So the relationships in the Assyrian collection are more complex. Nevertheless, the general function of the two texts, affirming covenant loyalty, is similar; and the goddess speaks to a human partner in broadly similar terms.

4.2.2.4 Conclusion

The cultic setting and prophetic character of Psalm 81 is generally conceded. Whether it preserves the speech of a prophet in the cultic festival or is more akin to a Levitical sermon is debated. The majority of commentators favour the latter option. However, the psalm corresponds form-critically and thematically to genuine prophetic speech and the similarity to deuteronomistic style is not distinct enough to classify the psalm as a Levitical sermon, even if the latter genre exists. The most important contribution of the Assyrian oracles to the discussion is substantiating the genuine prophetic nature of the self-identification formula, which weakens the case for a Levitical sermon. The Assyrian collection SAA 9 3 may also support the prophetic origin of Psalm 81 on the basis of form-critical similarities, both functioning as part of a covenant renewal ceremony. Booij's identification of the "pattern of remembrances" is significant evidence that the psalm was regarded as prophecy. If Booij's argument on form is accepted, a pre-exilic date is favoured, particularly if Psalm 81 is grouped with a general pre-exilic date for many of the Asaphite psalms. In addition, the northern interests strongly imply a pre-exilic setting. Psalm 81, then, should be regarded as preserving cultic prophecy originating from before the exile.

4.2.3 Psalm 50

4.2.3.1 Psalm 50 as Cultic Prophecy

Weiser (1962: 393; 1987: 265-66), followed by Anderson (1972: 381) and Craigie (1983: 363-64), interprets this psalm as the proclamation of a cult prophet during the covenant renewal festival. Craigie (1983: 364) surmises from the use of the divine names "El" and "Elyon" that an early monarchic setting is suggested. Anderson (1972: 381) favours a date around the time of either Hezekiah's or Josiah's reforms but admits the possibility of the Persian period (particularly if, contrary to his preference, the psalm is an imitation of earlier forms of literature).

4.2.3.2 Psalm 50 as Prophetic Imitation or Sermon

As in the case of Psalm 81, most commentators hesitate to affirm a model of genuine cultic prophecy for Psalm 50. Mowinckel himself places this psalm in the mouth of a Levitical temple singer; although he suggests that the poet had a "prophetic self-consciousness" (Mowinckel 1923: 44). Gunkel (1926: 214) views the psalm as a poetic imitation of prophetic thought and speech. He acknowledges strong prophetic elements throughout;[49] however, the absence of an introduction formula such as "thus says Yahweh" indicates the speaker did not experience the divine word personally (Gunkel 1926: 215). Rather, judging from the similar content to the prophetic message, the psalmist risked adopting for himself a speech form that was the prerogative of a prophet (Gunkel 1904: 115-16). The self-identification formula (Ps 50:7) in association with *tôrah* preaching also points to priestly composition (cf. Leviticus 19); and imitation is implied in that Yahweh's appearing is not on Mt. Sinai but on Zion, which is associated in later literature with the source of *tôrah*.

---

[49] Command to listen (Ps 50:7; cf. Isa 1:2, 10; 28:14; 44:1; 48:1, 12; 51:1; Jer 2:4; 10:1; Mic 3:1, 9); rhetorical question "what are you doing" (Ps 50:16; Isa 3:15; 22:1; Ezek 18:2); "lest I tear you up" (Ps 50:22; Hos 5:14; 6:1); God summons heaven and earth (Ps 50:4; Isa 1:2; Deut 32:1) (Gunkel 1926: 215).

Subsequent commentators echo Gunkel's basic outline, which was reinforced by Jeremias's differentiation between prophetic liturgy and Levitical preaching. For example, in spite of the pervasive prophetic character of Psalm 50 and evidence of roots in pre-exilic covenant renewal, Kraus (1978a: 527-30; 1988: 488-91) follows Jeremias's view that Psalm 50 is a post-exilic Levitical sermon. Hossfeld (Hossfeld and Zenger 1993: 309) also views Psalm 50 (together with Psalms 81[50] and 95[51]) as from a covenant renewal celebration, dated on form-critical and linguistic-historical grounds to the post-exilic period. Because of parallels between Psalm 50 and descriptions of Levitical ministry,[52] Hossfeld (Hossfeld and Zenger 1993: 309-310) presumes that Levitical preachers stand behind the psalm. Noting that theophanies frequently introduce an oracle, Tournay states, "This psalm is a good example of how Levitical singers acted as cultic prophets" (Tournay 1991: 144, 170-71). Of course, for Tournay, this role is a late post-exilic imitation by Levitical singers of earlier prophetic tradition. According to Tournay, the spiritualising of the immolation rites in Psalm 50 is a further indication of a Second Temple Jewish setting (Tournay 1991: 171). This is similar to Booij (1978: 210-11, 221-22), who views Psalm 50 as a liturgical variant of original prophetic-like speech but not prophecy in the original sense, since the absence of voice-switching makes the prophetic aspect even less pronounced than in Psalm 81.[53]

Also following Jeremias, Gerstenberger (1988: 207) ascribes Psalm 50 to exilic, or more likely, post-exilic Levitical preachers.

---

50 Summons to people (Ps 50:7a/81:9); self-identification (Ps 50:7b/81:11); proclamation of law at Sinai (Ps 50:18-20/81:6, 10; the rescue event (Ps 50:15/81:8).
51 Less direct, but thematically related is *tôdah*; Yahweh's theophany in Ps 50:1 is roughly equivalent to his kingship above all gods in Ps 95:3; sovereignty expressed in Ps 50:10-12 parallels Ps 95:4-5; exhortation not to forget the "way" in Pss 50:23 and 95:10.
52 I.e., *tôrah* proclamation coupled with the Feast of Tabernacles (Deut 31:9-13; Neh 8:8, 18).
53 Unlike most commentators, Booij prefers a pre-exilic setting, however. Seybold (1996: 205) places the final form of a multi-stage editing process well into the Second Temple period. Beginning with an original *rîb* speech with deuteronomistic influence from the Decalogue at the time of the exile (as Psalm 81), he sets the final editing of the psalm in the first half of the fourth century B.C.

Jewish modifications to an older theophany report in Ps 50:1-6 include the "universal geographic dimension (v. 1b), the fixation on Mount Zion (v. 2a), and a conspicuous use of the communal 'we' in v. 3a". Since the call to worship (v. 5) is direct address but without a citation or messenger formula it must have been a well known liturgical phrase by that time. Another sign of post-exilic theology is the address to the audience as "covenanters" (Gerstenberger 1988: 207-208). Citing Gunkel, Gerstenberger interprets the lack of a messenger formula as an indication of imitation of prophetic speech (Gerstenberger 1988: 208). Conversely, he writes, "The repetitious expansion of the introductory phrase ("I will speak . . . I will witness," v. 7), however, is by no means a prophetic trait. It is motivated in form by wisdom usage (see Prov 7:1-3; Job 32:17-22) and in meaning by authoritative revelation speech (cf. Exod 20:2; 34:10-16; Isa 51:15-16; 61:8)" (Gerstenberger 1988: 208). Consequently, Psalm 50 shows influences of deuteronomistic and deutero- and trito-Isaianic preaching. Gerstenberger cites Zimmerli's conclusion (Zimmerli 1953) that the full use of the self-identification formula is late, and therefore the psalm "must be placed in the context of synagogal reassurance about the presence of the Lord, Torah reading, legitimation of the preacher, and cultic instruction to individuals" (Gerstenberger 1988: 208). The shift from state to personal ritual (i.e., "tôdah"), as well, fits with post-exilic trends wherein the public and private cult became more separated (Gerstenberger 1988: 209).

4.2.3.3 Evaluation

In spite of its prophetic character, most commentators conclude that the psalmist merely adopted prophetic style for a *tôrah* sermon. Three primary reasons for this, all originally voiced by Gunkel, predominate: 1) the absence of prophetic introductory formulas (Gunkel, Hossfeld, Gerstenberger); 2) the use of the self-identification formula (Gunkel, Jeremias, Kraus, Gerstenberger); and 3) the dominant emphasis in the psalm on *tôrah* preaching (Gunkel, et al.). Related to this last point is the listing of themes thought to fit with post-exilic theology such as the spiritualization/privatisation of cultic rites (even Mowinckel), and for Gerstenberger the emphasis on Yahweh's universal sovereignty, the fixation on Zion, and the address to "covenanters".

Both the lack of introductory formulas as well as the use of the self-identification formula have already been discussed above. Introduction formulas are not necessary to frame prophetic speech; however, contrary to the opinion of some commentators, divine speech in Psalm 50 is clearly framed: 1) the opening theophany effectively frames the divine speech which follows, and 2) the second part of the divine address contains the formula אמר אלהים (Ps 50:16). While Psalm 50 does not bear the same general form-critical similarity to SAA 9 3 as Psalm 81, there is nonetheless an important stylistic comparison.[54] Psalm 50 opens with a theophanic advent of Yahweh, before whom proceeds a consuming fire as he calls his people to recognise that "I am God". Similarly, in SAA 9 3.3 Aššur appears in fire from heaven and devours his enemies, after which he calls people to praise him and to recognise that "I am Aššur".

Regarding the issue of *tôrah* preaching, it is also relevant to the discussion that Assyrian cult prophets issued cultic instructions concerning sacrifice and inward piety, even though they were not part of the priesthood. There are striking differences between the theology of Psalm 50 and that expressed in the Assyrian prophecies. The Assyrian oracles do not demand proper ethical behaviour; and in contrast to the theology of Ps 50:9-13, where Yahweh disavows the need for sacrifice, the deities in the Assyrian oracles languish when deprived of sacrificial offerings (SAA 9 2.3 ii 24-27; 3.5 iii 25-31 [cf. 3.4 ii 30?]). But as Mowinckel (1923: 45) has pointed out, the psalmist in Psalm 50 is not completely opposed to external cultic acts but rather encourages that outward cultic duty be balanced with inward faith and correct ethical behaviour (cf. Pss 40:7-9; 51:18-21; 69:32). So the degree to which sacrifices have been spiritualised is a rather subjective judgment. The Assyrian prophets exhort the king to offer the expected sacrifice, but they also admonish a proper inward piety in relationship to the deity (SAA 9 1.1 i 15-17; 1.4 ii 28-29; 1.6 iv 1[?]; 2.3 ii 17-27; 2.6[?]). Like Ps 50:15, where the congregation is told to call on the Lord in order to be

---

54 The report of "salvation history" is a major component lacking from Psalm 50 that sets it apart from Psalm 81 and SAA 9 3.

delivered, the Assyrian king is reproved for lack of faith. The theme of covenant inauguration/renewal in Assyrian prophecies (SAA 9 3) has already been discussed in connection with Psalm 81. Moreover, the fact that Levites preached *tôrah* does not imply anything about the speaker of Psalm 50, since such activity was undertaken by both priests and prophets.

Nasuti's (1988: 137-38) comments regarding the strong association between theophany and law received as direct speech from God are important in appreciating that the original audience would have understood Psalm 50 as prophecy. Gunkel senses the weight of this when he notes the daring of a preacher to adopt this form for his message. But contrary to his conclusion, no preacher would have dared to speak as the psalmist in Psalm 50 without the legitimisation of a genuine prophetic mantle. Gerstenberger's appeal to post-exilic theology of Yahweh's universal sovereignty and Zion-centrism have been addressed in conjunction with royal psalms. Concerning the expansion of the introductory phrase "Hear . . . I will speak"/"I will witness" in Ps 50:7, the style is similar to Isa 1:2-3 (" Hear . . . for Yahweh has spoken", followed by wisdom motifs) and to Mic 6:1 ("Hear what Yahweh is about to say", which introduces the call of witnesses and rhetorical questions). Also, in view of Exodus 24, there appears nothing particularly late about the concept of making covenant by sacrifice (Gerstenberger's "covenanters" in Ps 50:5b).

4.2.3.4 Conclusion

Given the strong prophetic character of the psalm and the failure of arguments that attribute such prophetic style to imitation, Psalm 50 probably preserves genuine cultic prophecy. No firm conclusion can be drawn on the date of composition; however, arguments adduced to set a secure post-exilic date are unconvincing. On the other hand, Weber (see above) makes a reasonable case for an early exilic closure of the Asaphite collection; and Booij (1978: 205) observes that the description of Zion (Ps 50:2) would constitute a mere illusion unless the psalm is set in a pre-exilic context. Therefore, even if uncertain, a pre-exilic date is possible.

4.2.4 Psalm 75

4.2.4.1 Psalm 75 as Cultic Prophecy

Mowinckel (1923: 47-49) described the performance of Psalm 75 as community praise in expectation of Yahweh's salvation (v. 2), which a cult prophet subsequently announces (vv. 3-6) and continues in prophetic exhortation (vv. 7-9). After the prophet falls silent the community choir resumes singing to close the psalm (vv. 10-11).[55] The idea that Psalm 75 preserves a prophetic liturgy is followed by several commentators. Weiser (1962: 522; 1987: 355) and Anderson (1972: 547) suggest that the divine word (vv. 3-5) is uttered either through the mouth of a priest or prophet, who offers interpretation in the verses which follow. Kraus (1978b: 684-85; 1989: 103-104) views the psalm as a liturgy at the centre of which a cult prophet announces a word of judgment with a closing "doxology of judgment" (vv. 10-11). He follows Jeremias (1970: 118) in comparing the prophetic style of Psalm 75 with Hab 2:1-3 and 3:2-19, however, he is reluctant to accept Jeremias's suggestion that the psalm is a prophetic lament (Kraus 1978b: 685; 1989: 104). Tate (1990: 257-58) views the psalm as a prophetic exhortation in worship and assigns it to a cult prophet.[56]

---

[55] Jensen (2001: 422-23, 427), who thinks the divine oracle might have been spoken by a cult prophet, classifies v. 11 as renewed divine speech (cf. Tate 1990: 257). However, in view of the strong disjunctive emphasising the commencement of the psalmist's speech in v. 10, it is best to regard v. 11 as a continuation of this stanza. Vows to cooperate with divine judgment against the wicked are natural for a cultic leader (e.g., Phinehas [Num 25: 7-8]; Elijah [1 Kgs 18:40]) and do not necessitate a royal speaker as proposed by Eaton (1976: 55). Therefore, emendation of the verb אֲגַדֵּעַ to third-person (cf. Kraus 1978b: 684; 1989: 103) is unnecessary.

[56] Seybold (1996: 291) offers a two stage development of the psalm centred around the judgment speech, but he does not commit himself on the source of the divine word. According to Seybold, the psalm originally addressed exilic conflicts over Assyrian-Babylonian astral deities. Seybold interprets הוֹלְלִים (Ps 75:5) as "Morning Star" (derived from הלל [I] "to shine") and sees in the psalm an assertion of Yahweh's judgment over the pagan gods, parallel to Psalm 82. Later, in the post-exilic period, the psalm was reinterpreted in the light of community problems to refer instead to the רְשָׁעִים, a later addition to the text. Seybold's suggestion is interesting but is unlikely to be correct for at least two reasons. First, the cognate verb follows הוֹלְלִים; and, while it is possible that the command "do not shine" could be a metaphor

4.2.4.2 Psalm 75 as Sermonic Adaptation of Prophetic Style

Other commentators interpret the psalm without invoking a cult prophet to explain the oracle. Gunkel (1926: 327) classified the psalm as prophetic liturgy with a divine oracle (vv. 3-4) inserted between a hymnic introduction (v. 2) and a hymnic reply in the mouth of the singer (vv. 5-11).[57] In his commentary, Gunkel does not address the source of the oracle; although one might surmise from his discussion of the origin of oracles in *Einleitung in die Psalmen* (Gunkel and Begrich 1933: 370-72; 1998: 284-86) that he would not regard the oracle in Psalm 75 as *prophetic* speech in the cult. Gerstenberger (2001: 83-84) resists the category of prophetic liturgy altogether, because he thinks that this is based on a heightened sensitivity to changing voices in worship liturgies. The abrupt change in speaker without transition formula is natural in liturgical proceedings, since such changes are audible and visible. In the case of Ps 75:3-4, some human representative vicariously pronounces the divine word after the congregational opening; but he argues that it should not be regarded as a prophecy, which necessitates special framings to identify and legitimise it (Gerstenberger 2001: 82). Similarly, Hossfeld (Hossfeld and Zenger 2000: 377; 2002: 427) describes the psalm as the literary prayer of a theologian rather than the lament liturgy of a cult prophet.

In Gerstenberger's analysis of the setting of Psalm 75, his interpretation of a shift from divine words back to human words in verse 5 is important. He argues that in psalms אמרתי always in-

---

demanding the astral deities to cease their activities, this interpretation seems strained. Second, the parallel, רשעים, by Seybold's own admission, shifts the interpretation of הוללים to "boastful", and since no reason exists to regard this as a later addition other than Seybold's presupposed redaction history (a circular argument), his interpretation is unlikely. Seybold offers numerous other suggestions of altered structure and additions to the text to accompany his proposed change in setting, but it is outside the scope of this thesis to address them.

57 Cf. Booij (1978: 78) who views the speaker in v. 5 as the singer who has combined God's word with praise and is viewed as a "co-worker" with God in the destruction of the wicked (v. 11). Hossfeld (Hossfeld and Zenger 2000: 376; 2002: 426-30) also thinks the "oracle" ends with v. 4, but he includes v. 11 as a resumption of divine speech.

dicates that the psalmist is speaking,[58] and in the case of Psalm 75 it signals an instructional discourse affirming the insights about God found in the divine words in verses 3-4. He concludes that if human theological exhortation is introduced by this form, then "we are witnessing in vv. 3-9 a type of homiletical venture in early Jewish community service. The voice of God, recorded and recited by the leader in worship (vv. 3-4), is being interpreted by the latter" (Gerstenberger 2001: 82-83). As the exhortation genre arose out of thanksgiving services (e.g., Pss 22:23-27; 32:9-12; 66:16-19; 116:14, 18), it became sermonic when there was no specific occasion for celebrating individual salvation. Thus, efforts such as that of Jeremias to see a prophetic liturgical speech in the psalm are reading a model of prophetism into early community worship (Gerstenberger 2001: 84).

4.2.4.3 Evaluation

Psalm 75 is similar to prophetic speech in both form and content, and the worship context is evident from the opening verse. In spite of this, there is disagreement whether the divine speech preserves the words of a prophet in the cult or is an oracle adapted within a sermon. The key issue is the nature of transitions between parts of the psalm: 1) the abrupt break in speakers at verse 2 where first-person divine speech commences without an introductory formula; 2) the implications of אמרתי (v. 5) for the identity of the speaker from verses 5-9; and 3) the disjunctive beginning verse 10.

As discussed above, the absence of an introductory formula was used by Nasuti to argue that a text is more likely to contain authentic prophetic speech, being as it were more "real" in the cult so that an audience has no need of the formal introduction. Gerstenberger makes basically the same point that a congregation can hear and see changes in the course of liturgical performance, but he draws the opposite conclusion from Nasuti re-

---

58 Gerstenberger notes that this form occurs 17 times outside Psalm 75, and he cites the following supportive examples: Pss 30:7; 31:5; 32:5; 38:17; 39:2; 40:11; 41:5; 73:15; 89:3; 116:11; 119:57 (cf. van Uchelen 1977: 260 n. 5).

garding the identity of the speaker. Because of the absence of a special frame to authenticate prophetic speech, the speaker is a non-prophetic functionary. Hossfeld has also used the absence of formulas to argue that Levites must have adapted the style of first-person divine speech to keep alive the lost prophetic tradition.[59]

In this context, Gerstenberger's use of the terms "marked"/"unmarked" speech merits careful discussion (Gerstenberger 2001: 82). By the term "marked", Gerstenberger means the presence of some sort of "transitional formula" in the text introducing divine speech but not necessarily a prophetic quotation formula, such as "thus says Yahweh".[60] Although one psalm in his list of "marked" texts (Ps 12:6) does contain the formula יאמר יהוה, his other examples of "clearly marked texts" do not contain such a phrase (e.g., Pss 50:4-7; 81:6-9; 82:1-2; 95:7-8). Thus, he appears to mean that these texts are "marked" in some manner so as to anticipate divine speech (whether by customary formula or not). Indeed, Ps 50:4-5 anticipates divine speech in Yahweh's "calling" to his people from the theophany; Ps 81:6-9 is viewed by most to contain a description of inspira-

---

[59] In addition to his general discussion on Asaphite Psalms discussed above (Hossfeld 1998), see Hossfeld (Hossfeld and Zenger 2000: 375; 2002: 427-28) where he states that the absence of introductory formulas means that the speaker has minimised his prophetic role, since the Asaphites only take up the inheritance of the prophetic tradition without themselves being prophets, while maintaining a stance of public authority.

[60] In linguistics, "markedness" is a technical term referring to the presence or absence of linguistic features to indicate opposing values such as singular or plural, masculine or feminine (Crystal 1997: 223). In the context of analysing speech discourse (such as here), the correct terms to denote the presence or absence of formulas or other features indicating a direct speech citation are "framed" and "unframed" (cf. O'Connor 1980: 412-14; cf. Miller 1996: 1, 220). In discussion of direct discourse frames, "unmarked" is the standard (i.e., "default") formula (e.g., simple אמר). The "marked" constructions are those which deviate from this default form (e.g., often multiple verb frames or verbs with the complementary לאמר, although lexical semantics play a part as well) (Miller 1996: 309-318). But "markedness" is used by some scholars to discuss the presence or absence of introductory speech formulas. For example, Meier (1992: 1-2) uses the term "marked" for the presence of verbs, nouns or particles that indicate the presence of reported speech. Gerstenberger also uses "marked"/"unmarked" in this way, and so his terminology is used in this discussion, although the terms "framed"/"unframed" are preferable.

tion on the part of the speaker; Ps 82:1-2 anticipates divine speech in the heavenly court scene; and Ps 95:7-8 anticipates divine speech in the warning "if you hear his voice". In contrast, the texts described as "unmarked" (Ps 46:11; 89:4-5; 91:14-16; and 105:15) contain no such introductions. Concerning these latter examples, Gerstenberger remarks,

> "Unmarked change to divine discourse delivered by spokespersons, on the other hand, is quite in order during liturgical proceedings, because the shift becomes audible and visible all by itself . . . But prophetic pronouncements perhaps needed special framings and legitimations to identify a given communication as divine. Discourses of God within worship services go by different rules and must not be confounded with prophetic, not even cult-prophetic, speech" (Gerstenberger 2001: 82).

He must mean by this that in the absence of "special framings and legitimations" the speech is implicitly understood by the audience as coming from the non-prophetic functionary. Gerstenberger is correct that the liturgical context might provide adequate transitions for "unmarked" divine speech. However, he is not correct to assume that the speaker thereby must be non-prophetic or that rules for prophetic speakers, either inside or outside the cult, are different. As one example, the appearance of a recognised prophet at his customary place in the city gate might be all that was necessary to signal to an audience that a prophet was about to speak God's word (then the ensuing first-person divine speech would confirm the heuristic expectation of the audience). In such a case, non-verbal communication by a known prophet introduced the divine speech. Non-verbal liturgical signals or transitions could introduce a prophetic speaker and divine speech in the cult.[61] Gerstenberger is also mistaken to assume that the more subtle means of framing divine speech (e.g., theophany in Psalm 50 or court setting in Psalm 82) are not adequate to frame genuine prophetic speech.[62] SAA 9 1.9,

---

61 Non-verbal liturgical activity is preserved as ritual instruction in Assyrian texts (e.g., SAA 9 3.2 ii 8, 26-32; SAA 3 11:r. 3-4; and even the narrative description of Assurbanipal's liturgical action in SAA 3 13:r. 1 may reflect cultic reality). Psalms do not preserve these ritual instructions but allude to ritual activity.
62 E.g., Ezek 1:28-29 does not specify the speaker, but the theophany clearly frames this as divine speech.

3.2-3 and 9 contain no special frame, not even the divine self-identification or "Fear not!" expressions that characterise Assyrian cultic prophecy. In sum, not only is "special framing" not necessary to introduce genuine prophetic speech but also more subtle means, both verbal and non-verbal, can frame authentic prophetic speech.

Another important consideration in this discussion is the content and relative length of Gerstenberger's "unmarked" examples. With the exception of Ps 91:14-16, his examples are very brief citations of divine speech. How would an audience discern whether prophetic speech has commenced in these "one liners"?[63] The congregation might have recognised these lines as mere citation of traditional sayings (Ps 46:11, "Be still and know that I am God . . ."; Ps 105:15, "Touch not my anointed ones, do my prophets no harm!").[64] Ps 89:4-5 cannot be separated from the liturgical context of the psalm containing a more extended prophetic citation (Ps 89:20-38), although it may have been a traditionally known saying from the Davidic covenant (but see the discussion of Psalm 89). The final example, Ps 91:14-16, does not match the other examples since it is both a longer divine speech and closes the psalm. It may preserve a liturgical response from a prophet (see next chapter). Psalm 75 is not necessarily brief either, if one extends the divine speech to verse 9 (see below). Thus, Gerstenberger's grouping of these "unmarked" examples and his inclusion of Ps 75:3-4 with them is doubtful. Both his classification of Psalm 75 as "unmarked" as well as his argument to restrict the oracle to a short two verses (vv. 3-4) needs reconsideration.

First, Ps 75:3-4 is not completely "unmarked". With a strong *waw*-disjunctive (ואני, Ps 75:10), the speaker clearly differentiates the divine speech from his own words in verse 10, and so by framing his own words he indirectly frames the end of the divine speech. Jeremias correctly observes that this disjunctive is a common form in the lament genre. Whether he is correct that this psalm is a prophetic lament liturgy is uncertain, but

---

63 Ps 12:6 is clearly framed, so it is a different case from these other brief, unframed examples.
64 Hossfeld (1998: 234) also suggests that these one-line citations are probably not "live" prophetic speech in the cultic performance of these psalms.

the form does indicate a transition between the divine and human speech.⁶⁵ Such transitions are absent in Gerstenberger's "unmarked" texts, which continue on, uninterrupted.

Second, this suggestion about the framing in Ps 75:10 presupposes that the prophetic speech continues in Ps 75:5-7 from the oracle in Ps 75:3-4. In spite of the strong prophetic flavour of Ps 75:5-7, Gerstenberger argues that the human speech begins in Ps 75:5 and contains theological exhortation. He maintains that all seventeen uses of אמרתי outside of Psalm 75 refer to human speech and Ps 75:5 should be no exception (Gerstenberger 2001: 82). However, one must question these statistics. Most uses of אמרתי are part of lament or thanksgiving psalms in which the psalmist reports past experience, and so one expects its frequency to be linked to human speech.⁶⁶ So Gerstenberger's conclusion is questionable because of a biased sample. It is also important to consider the aspect of the suffixed form אמרתי. In contrast to the nearly exclusive past tense use, only one example, Ps 31:15⁶⁷, might involve a present aspect (either gnomic or performative) like the use in Ps 75:5.⁶⁸ Recognising this distinction in verbal aspect further dilutes the significance of Gerstenberger's statistical comparison, which is based upon examples with past tense aspect. Finally, Gerstenberger cites only twelve (if one includes Ps 75:5) of the eighteen examples. Ps 82:6 (not included in his list), illustrates the use of אמרתי in divine speech. Therefore, Gerstenberger's analysis based on the uses of this form is not sound.

---

65 Miller (1996: 213-17) observes that closing frames may be used by the narrator of a speech event, although in all but one case these closing frames are supplementary to an opening narrative frame. Strictly speaking, the disjunct in Ps 75:10 does not directly frame the end of the divine speech, rather it frames the beginning of the psalmist's own words. Nevertheless, the transitional effect is the same.

66 Aside from Pss 75:5 and 82:6 it appears that Ps 119:57 is the only exception in terms of genre. Although the prefix form of אמר in Ps 12:6 shows that this verb can introduce divine speech. Hossfeld (Hossfeld and Zenger 2000: 376) observes that the use in Ps 75:5 differs because it introduces an address rather than a monologue; however he identifies the speaker as human not divine.

67 Mistakenly cited as Ps 31:5 in Gerstenberger's commentary.

68 A true perfect aspect is possible in Ps 31:15. Pss 140:7 and 142:6 might also be performative or gnomic, but unlike Ps 31:15, they are more likely true perfects.

4.2.4.4 Conclusion

There are no strong arguments against Jeremias's conclusions about the genuinely prophetic nature of Psalm 75. The exact liturgical process in which it played a part can be debated (i.e., is it prophetic lament liturgy or simply a prophetic thanksgiving?). But the psalm contains first-person divine speech (Ps 75:3-4) coupled with prophetic exhortation (Ps 75:5-9) that is set off from human speech in a concluding doxology (Ps 75:10-11). Nothing can be said conclusively about the date, unless one places it with the rest of the Asaphite collection in a pre-exilic setting.

4.2.5 Psalm 82

4.2.5.1 Psalm 82 as Cultic Prophecy

Mowinckel (1923: 46) regarded this psalm as a prophetic promise of judgment against hostile deities delivered through the mouth of a cultic servant. Weiser (1962: 560; 1987: 381) similarly considers the speaker to be a prophet, and Anderson (1972: 592) prefers a cult prophet as the source over against Gunkel's suggestion that the psalmist imitates prophetic speech.

As noted above, Jeremias (1970: 121-22) argued that this psalm, together with Psalm 75, is a prophetic lament liturgy. It consists of: 1) an opening report of the heavenly council parallel to that found in canonical prophets (Ps 82:1); 2) accusation (Ps 82:2); 3) reproof with ultimatum (Ps 82:3-4); 4) judgment (Ps 82:5); 5) announcement of penalty (Ps 82:6-7); and 6) closing petition (Ps 82:8). In Jeremias's view, the conclusion that the psalm originated from a cult prophet is based not only on its similarity to a prophetic speech form but also because of its closeness to the prophetic lament liturgy. The complaint in Ps 82:2 is introduced by a lament-like question particle; the reproof in Ps 82:3-4 corresponds to Ps 75:5-6 (a prophetic lament liturgy) as well as the common destabilised cosmos theme in Ps 82:5 and Ps 75:4 (cf. Hab 3:17); the insensibility of the guilty (Ps 82:5) parallels Ps 14:4 (another prophetic lament liturgy) as well as the second-person announcement of judgment being similar to Ps 14:6; the call to God to "arise" matches the petition of the lament liturgy in Ps 12:6; and the formulation of the warning uses wisdom terms (various words for the poor) typical of lament liturgies (Jeremias 1970: 122). He argues that judgment of hostile deities is not a theme found in the canonical prophets, since there Israel's leaders are always addressed.[69] But if the idea is in view that the divine realm stands behind human counterparts, then this heavenly act of judgment is the archetypal cult-prophetic announcement of judgment (Jeremias 1970: 122-23). He finds support for this interpretation in the seamless transition in Psalm 58 between accusation against the gods and against wicked men, followed by a request for Yahweh's intervention (Jeremias 1970: 124). Kraus (1978b: 735; 1989: 154) follows the interpretation of Jeremias that the psalm is a cult-prophetic announcement of judgment set within a lament context.[70]

4.2.5.2 Psalm 82 as Prophetic Imitation or "Scribal Prophecy"

Gunkel (1904: 149; 1926: 361) argues that Psalm 82 is dependent on the prophets in both form and content and is therefore an imitation of prophetic speech. This assessment is due in part to the eschatological nature of judgment in this psalm. Unlike the canonical prophets, later psalms mention only the enemies of Israel as objects of judgment, which is the case in Psalm 82 (Gunkel and Begrich 1933: 336-37; 1998: 257). He notes the similar theme of cosmic warfare in Isa 27:1 and 34:5. Psalm 82, then, offers a liturgical expression of the theology of the post-exilic priesthood couched in prophetic form (Gunkel and Begrich 1933: 413-14; 1998: 317). Seybold (1996: 325-26) also views the psalm as stylistically analogous to prophetic speech following the theological trend of Deutero-Isaiah in announcing the end of the polytheistic system, although some statements (vv. 4 and 8)

---

69 This assertion is strange in view of Isa 27:1; 34:4-5; 46:1-2 (cf. Gunkel).
70 Booij (1994: 19) associates the psalm with "prophetic consciousness"; however, he thinks the cult-prophetic view of Kraus and Jeremias is only conceivable but not provable.

were added to suit a post-exilic context (cf. Hossfeld and Zenger 2000: 485, 490; 2002: 462).

Gerstenberger (2001: 113) suggests that Psalm 82 followed Psalm 81 liturgically, since in prophetic discourse denunciation of foreign powers often follows admonitions to Israel herself (cf. Isa 40:1-22; Zephaniah 1-2; Zechariah 12-14). In his view this might account for the brief introduction in Ps 82:1. The last line of petition proves it was set in community worship, not a purely literary creation (Gerstenberger 2001: 114). Like Psalms 50 and 81, Psalm 82 demonstrates "the possibility of having God himself speak in community worship through a liturgist of sorts within a community service" (Gerstenberger 2001: 115). In Psalm 82, this is shown both through first-person divine speech as well as the portrayal of God's actions in the divine council. Whereas Gunkel and Seybold see in Psalm 82 an emerging monotheism, Gerstenberger maintains that the divine pantheon was an acceptable image throughout Israelite history, in spite of "later monotheistic restrictions of any polytheistic models" (Gerstenberger 2001: 115). He argues that, although the heavenly council scene is similar to 1 Kgs 22:19-22, classical prophetic activity should not be envisioned in connection with Psalm 82.

Tate (1990: 332-33) stresses the literary backdrop for the psalm in 1 Kgs 22:19-23; Job 1:6-12; Zech 1:7-17; 3:1-5; Isa 6:1-13; and 40:1-8. The characteristics that shed light on Psalm 82 are: 1) reports of visionary character in which the narrator describes what is seen (1 Kgs 22:19; Isa 6:1; Zech 1:8 and 3:11); 2) there is a direct and immediate style in the narration as of a direct observer (Isa 40:1-8; Zech 1:8); 3) the narrator may be identified (1 Kings 22; Isaiah 6), but in other cases the voices appear at random (e.g., Yahweh's voice in 1 Kings 22 and the following responses), the latter being the case in Psalm 82. Tate (1990: 333) accepts the argument of Seitz (1990: 245-46) that the divine council report in Isaiah 40 represents a new form of prophecy, called "scribal prophecy". Seitz contends that with Second Isaiah there is a major shift in prophetic literature, one in which God speaks (in the divine council) without the need of prophetic agency. This literary style and sociological location is similar to psalms with which Second Isaiah is often compared (Seitz 1990: 246). Tate concludes that since Psalm 82 has the major features of scribal prophecy, it "probably emerged from a similar matrix" (Tate 1990: 333). Therefore, rather than a preexilic prototype of cult-prophetic proclamations (as in Jeremias 1970: 120-25; Kraus 1978b: 735; 1989: 154-55), Tate (1990: 333-34) draws the opposite conclusion, that Psalm 82 is a postexilic literary production dependent on the prophets.

4.2.5.3 Evaluation

Jeremias's proposal that Psalm 82 is a type of prophetic lament liturgy has better support than does his case for Psalm 75, primarily because the psalm does end in a petition for Yahweh to intervene. But, as Gunkel and others have argued, the psalm could still be a matter of imitation of prophetic style; or in the case of Tate, the concept of "scribal prophecy" might provide an explanation. Seitz's case is built on a theoretical model of how the prophetic consciousness (and ministry) might have changed in the exile. But, considering that Ezekiel and post-exilic prophets continued to function during and after the exile, if Second Isaiah does mark the beginning of a new phenomenon, it did not become a universal one. Moreover, some of the sections of the Book of Jeremiah are not far removed from "scribal prophecy", yet they are form-critically indistinguishable from oral prophecy (e.g., Jer 29:4-23; 36:1-4).[71] Thus, more important than the issue of oral versus written composition, it seems the context of delivery and the status of the author in the eyes of the audience is primary. Jeremiah's scribal prophecy, when read aloud by Baruch, was recognised as prophetically inspired, a genuine prophetic word. Therefore, it may be that Tate's category of "scribal prophecy" for Psalm 82 does not escape the implication that it was regarded by the audience as genuine prophetic speech when performed in the liturgical setting. The presence of first-person divine speech, reported to have been uttered in a vision of the divine council, as well as the prayer at the end of the psalm must have primary weight in evaluating the impact of

---

[71] The divine letter SAA 3 47 and the literary production of SAA 3 13 blur the boundaries between oral and scribal prophecy. This may also be the case for FLP 1674 (Pongratz-Leisten 1999: 203-204, 211, 232).

Psalm 82 upon its ancient audience, which would have regarded the psalm as genuine prophetic speech.

Since the content of Psalm 82 is primarily a judgment speech, even though the final verse lends to it an over-arching form of lament, one would not expect much correspondence to the Assyrian cultic prophecies. However, there appear to be three points of contact. First, there is reference within the Assyrian prophecies to the divine council. In SAA 9 1.6, Ištar speaks from the vantage point of her heavenly residence; and in SAA 9 9:6-24, she testifies to her role as intermediary on behalf of the king in the divine assembly. Second, in the covenant ceremony of SAA 9 3.4, Ištar issues what amounts to an ultimatum to the other gods and goddesses, warning them not to forget the covenant. This bears some similarity to Yahweh's address to the other deities portrayed under the rubric of the divine council in Psalm 82. Third, an important theme of the Assyrian prophets is the disruption of the cosmic order associated with the rebellions in Assyrian society. In SAA 9 2, the predominant concern appears to be the restoration of order during Esarhaddon's rise to power (SAA 9 2.1 i 6-7; 2.2 i 31; 2.6 iv 27; cf. SAA 9 1.4 and SAA 9 6:2-3). The most striking statement in this regard is in SAA 9 2.5: Ištar will simultaneously restore order in both Assyria and heaven; the land and the divine realms are linked and the disorder/order of the two realms are parallel (SAA 9 2.5 iii 19-20, 32-34). This reinforces the similarity already observed by commentators between the Psalm 82 and prophetic literature on the theme of cosmic chaos/order. While these similarities with Assyrian cultic prophecy do not determine the character of the prophetic speech in Psalm 82, they support the argument that the proper context in which to understand the psalm is prophetic speech such as 1 Kgs 22:19-23 and Isa 6:1-13, not a "matrix" of imitative or scribal prophecy.

4.2.5.4 Conclusion

Psalm 82 strongly exhibits prophetic style. First-person divine speech with content reflecting prophetic theology is framed by a vision report of the divine council, comparable in some respects to Assyrian prophecy. The closing prayer supports a liturgical setting, so Jeremias's suggestion of a prophetic lament is suitable. Efforts to date the psalm are inconclusive, since the theological content of the psalm upon which they are generally based can be construed as compatible with either pre-exilic or post-exilic views of the divine assembly.

4.2.6 Psalm 95

Even though Psalm 95 is not associated with the Asaphite psalms by superscription, it is often grouped with Psalms 81 and 50 because of the similar form, themes and possible cultic setting.[72] Therefore, without judging the question of what tradition stands behind Psalm 95 (i.e., whether or not Psalm 95 is "deutero-Asaphite"), it has been included here with the Asaphite psalms for discussion of its prophetic character. The psalm falls into two parts: the first half is a hymnic summons to worship, reflecting a communal and cultic setting with a mood of jubilation; in contrast the second half is characterised by a prophetic (or prophetic-like) warning (Mowinckel 1923: 38; Gunkel 1926: 417).[73]

4.2.6.1 Psalm 95 as Cultic Prophecy

Mowinckel (1923: 38) suggests that Psalm 95, like Psalm 81, was set in the autumn covenant renewal festival. As Yahweh spoke at Sinai, he again speaks through the mouth of a prophet. However, the prophetic intrusion into the liturgy is not an instance of spontaneous inspiration. Similar to his description of the setting for Psalm 81, Mowinckel argues that prophetic speech occurs at a point in the liturgy where the agenda must have been set in advance for the appearance of a prophet. (Mowinckel 1923: 40). Weiser (1962: 626-27; 1937: 429) and

---

72 E.g., Mowinckel (1923: 38, 40); Gunkel (1926: 418); Jeremias (1970: 125-27); Kraus (1978b: 728; 1989: 147); Hossfeld (Hossfeld and Zenger 1993: 309; Hossfeld 1994: 30; 1998: 238-39; Hossfeld and Zenger 2002: 513).
73 In spite of this contrast in mood, commentators generally argue that the psalm was originally a unified whole, for which see Hossfeld (1994: 31-32) and Zenger (Hossfeld and Zenger 2000: 660-62).

Anderson (1972: 679) also hold that the divine utterance was probably spoken by a priest or cult prophet.

4.2.6.2 Psalm 95 as Prophetic Imitation or Sermon

Gunkel (1904: 176; 1926: 419) interprets the prophetic half of the psalm as composed in the form and spirit of doom prophets like Amos, Isaiah and Jeremiah; however, the psalmist merely takes the prerogative of the prophet to speak in the name of Yahweh. To him it is striking that the psalm contains little detail of what Yahweh specifically demands on this occasion; rather, the psalmist speaks of general obedience, presupposing that the content of the law and prophets are by now well known. Because of the similarities between Psalm 81 and 95, Booij (1978: 91-96; 1994: 148, 151 n. 2) also thinks Psalm 95 originated from Levites singing in prophetic style and role, citing Gunkel's notion of "imitation" (cf. Kraus 1978b: 829; 1989: 246). Contrary to Mowinckel's suggestion, Tate (1990: 499) maintains that there is little or no direct evidence from the psalm itself to support a covenant renewal setting.[74] While the psalm may have had its original setting at the central sanctuary in Jerusalem, he follows Gerstenberger's suggestion that it may also have been used in family or small communal groups (Tate 1990: 499-500). In his opinion, Psalm 95, as well as Psalms 50 and 81, have lost the sharpness of original prophetic speech forms, similar to the reports of prophetic speech in Chronicles. This corresponds to the pattern evident in Isa 42:18-43:7 and 43:25-28; and so, with Gerstenberger, he favours the exilic or post-exilic period as the most likely setting for the psalm (Tate 1990: 503). Gerstenberger (2001: 184) argues that in the case of divine discourses such as Psalms 50, 81, 82, 91 and 95 one cannot take the "divine oratory at face value". Psalm 95 is a good case in point because it exhibits clear indications that the speaker is delivering a sermon on the stories of Massah and Meribah.

---

[74] Although Kraus (1978b: 831; 1989: 247) observes that Ps 95:7 contains a covenant formula similar to Jer 31:33.

4.2.6.3 Evaluation

To a large extent, commentators rely on arguments from Psalms 50 and 81 to categorise Psalm 95 as post-exilic Levitical preaching; although a late exilic or post-exilic date is also argued on the basis of the psalm's relationship with creation theology and deuteronomistic prophetic language (cf. Hossfeld 1994: 39). However, the grouping of these three psalms can lead to the opposite conclusion for Psalm 95. If, as argued above, Psalms 50 and 81 are accepted as examples of cultic prophecy, then the possibility remains that Psalm 95 originated from cultic prophecy as well. It is important to bear in mind, however, that Psalm 95 is not as closely linked to Psalms 50 and 81 as these latter psalms are to one another. Hossfeld's (Hossfeld and Zenger 1993: 309) comparison between these psalms shows that the connection of Psalm 95 is "less direct".[75] It is the "direct" features that Psalms 50 and 81 share in common that also associate them with the style of Assyrian cultic prophecy.[76] It is not surprising, then, that Psalm 95 does not exhibit the same degree of similarity to Assyrian prophecy as Psalm 50 and 81. Therefore, judgment regarding the prophetic nature of Psalm 95 (whether genuine or imitation) cannot depend on comparisons between these psalms nor with the Assyrian oracles. Nevertheless, the first-person divine speech in Psalm 95 remains to be explained.

One important similarity that does exist between Psalm 95 and Psalms 50 and 81 is the framing of the divine speech, discussed with respect to Psalm 75. This suggests that the same phenomenon behind Psalms 81, 50, 82, and to a lesser extent Psalm 75, might account for the origin of divine speech in Psalm 95 as well:

Psalm 81 - allusion to Sinai theophany and pattern of remembrance
Psalm 50 - theophany out of which God speaks
Psalm 82 - heavenly court sets the scene for divine speech
Psalm 75 - divine speech contrasted with psalmist's vow

---

75 See note 51.
76 Summons to the people; self-identification formula; theophany; divine intervention to rescue.

Psalm 95 - "today, oh that you would hear his voice:"

The similarity of the oracular introduction in Ps 95:7 ("today") to the exhortations of Deuteronomy (cf. Deut 4:40; 5:3; 6:6; 7:11; 9:3; esp., 11:2) might support the view that this is Levitical preaching style; although von Rad (1966a: 12, 18) proposed a cultic background for Deuteronomy as well. Therefore, Psalm 95 is not necessarily the result of an exposition of Deuteronomy, rather both could have emerged from a similar setting. Other verbal links between Deuteronomy and Psalm 95 are not extensive. The Book of Jeremiah shows allusion to deuteronomistic tradition similar to Psalm 95 within the context of genuine prophetic speech (Jer 42:18-22).[77] What weighs in favour of genuine prophecy in Ps 95:7b-11 is the first-person divine speech which the introduction anticipates ("hear his voice", followed by the divine speech).

As mentioned above, it is questionable whether a preacher would dare to imitate divine speech in this manner. Upon hearing the formulation of Ps 95:7 followed by divine speech, it seems unlikely that the audience would imagine the psalmist "imitating" a prophet. Perhaps they might think of a secondary citation of a prophetic oracle. In this case, the original setting of Ps 95:7b-11 could be questioned but not prophetic authenticity. If the psalm merely cites the prophetic speech from another context, it would still be recognisable as genuine prophetic speech and would be so construed by the audience. However, the expression, "today", is strong evidence that the second half of the psalm was "live" prophetic performance at least in the first instance. As Davies observes:

> "The Psalm closes in v. 7c-11 with an oracular warning in prophetic style. Gunkel described these verses as in content and form an imitation of prophetic speech. But if we are to regard the first part of the Psalm as a 'cultic reality', then consistency suggests that v. 7c-11 are not a literary composition, or a 'poetic fiction' but an actual

---

[77] While Jeremiah 42 consists of a prose account of his oracles, it probably preserves genuine material from the prophet (Holladay 1989: 286); however, McKane (1996: 1037-39) argues that the shorter LXX, which excludes the phrase "I have declared to you today", is superior. Another example in prophetic style is Zech 9:12, but this is not accompanied by an allusion to deuteronomistic tradition.

oracle spoken by some one [sic] in the courtyard, i.e., either a cultic prophet or a preaching priest" (Davies 1973: 192).

Gerstenberger (2001: 184) emphasises that the "exegetical" characteristic of Ps 95:7b-11 points to a homiletical genre instead of prophetic speech. However, prophetic exposition of older tradition is a common characteristic of OT prophets (e.g., Hos 2:16-17; 11:1-11; Amos 4:10-11; 5:25-27; Isa 1:9-10; 10:24). Also, Gerstenberger's citation of 2 Chr 30:6-9 as an illustration of homiletical use of the tradition referred to in Psalm 95 is unconvincing. The royal dispatch in Chronicles is different in both form and function, so the presence of first-person divine speech in Psalm 95 cannot be disregarded as easily as Gerstenberger asserts.

As for Gunkel's observations on the rather general nature of the admonition in Psalm 95, perhaps Jeremias's suggestion regarding the difference between cultic prophecy and classical judgment prophecy is helpful. Given the setting of worship in the temple, one should expect a different emphasis in prophetic proclamation. Specific accusations could come from the mouth of a cult prophet (e.g., Psalms 50 and 81); however, on festive occasions (covenant renewal being only one possibility) a general exhortation to obedience would be very appropriate. The specific listing of offences is not necessary. The basic role of prophecy in the cult, illustrated by Psalm 95, is to sustain or support the worshipping community rather than criticise it with blanket judgment. In addition, generality may be due to the fact that specific stipulations had already been recited in the liturgy (cf. Ps 50:16b). Similarly, flexibility in prophetic style can account for the lack of "sharpness" observed by Tate. Therefore, these arguments based on a narrow expectation of prophetic style need not bear on the issue of the nature of the divine speech in the psalm.

The question of date must remain open. Arguments based upon theorised theological developments (e.g., creation theology or universal kingship of Yahweh above the gods) are too speculative.

4.2.6.4 Conclusion

The framed divine speech in Ps 95:7b-11 suggests a prophetic functionary as the source, speaking in the cultic setting of the psalm. The similarity of Psalm 95 to Psalms 50 and 81 leads to the suggestion that they share a similar cultic setting and origin. If, as has been argued, Psalms 50 and 81 are not Levitical imitation of prophetic style or post-exilic sermons, then the attempt to classify Psalm 95 in this genre largely fails. Conversely, if Psalm 50 and 81 are regarded as cultic prophecy, then this strengthens the likelihood that Psalm 95 is as well. These three psalms are very unlike the prose sermons of Chronicles and should not be placed in the same milieu, even if the latter constitutes a valid genre.

4.2.7 Conclusion

As noted above, Hossfeld suggests that the question of origin for divine speech in the Asaphite psalms rests ultimately on examination of the psalms themselves. The Asaphite psalms and Psalm 95 present first-person divine speech, prophetic form, and prophetic phrases and theology. The texts are also framed as divine speech, i.e., allusion to Sinai revelation and pattern of remembrance in Psalm 81; theophany in Psalm 50; heavenly court scene in Psalm 82; and a framing at the end of divine speech in Psalm 75; exhortation to hear God's voice in Psalm 95. The audience would have understood a prophet speaking in the first performance of these psalms ("real cultic presence" in Nasuti's terms); and they would have understood a singing performance of prophetic speech on subsequent occasions, or perhaps a prophetic liturgist breathed into the speech a new freshness on the occasion of each performance. It is unlikely that any ordinary preacher would have dared to take on the prophetic mantle so clearly indicated in these psalms, and efforts to equate these psalms with a style of post-exilic preaching found in Chronicles are unconvincing. Furthermore, these psalms are consistent with the style of Assyrian cultic prophecy. Dating is not certain for any of these psalms; although Psalm 81 is likely pre-exilic, and arguments that the Asaphite psalms address the needs of northern refugees post-722 and that the collection as a whole was formed before the close of the exilic period have merit. At the least, a post-exilic context cannot be assumed for the sake of arguing a post-exilic style of psalmody. In sum, Psalms 50, 75, 81, 82 and 95 should be regarded as incorporating cultic prophecy, extending from pre-exilic times onward.

Chapter 5
Laments, Hymns and Songs of Confidence

5.1 Introduction

As discussed in the last chapter, Asaphite psalms offer two examples (Psalms 75 and 82) where divine speech occurs in what may have been a prophetic lament liturgy. This chapter opens with discussion of Psalms 12 and 60, which are also set in contexts of lament and preserve a response in the form of first-person divine speech. Considered next is Psalm 91, which does not exhibit features of a lament; nevertheless, it contains a divine response to a worshipper with promise of protection. The fourth psalm discussed, Psalm 68, preserves two possible oracles, one of which is introduced by a citation formula. Psalm 46 contains a very brief exhortation in first-person divine speech and Psalm 87 might present a report from the divine council, but because these two psalms are probably not examples of cultic prophecy they receive only short discussion. Finally, five psalms (Psalms 14[53]; 27; 62; 101; and 105), which contain divine speech that is not prophetic, are listed with a brief comment.

5.2 Psalm 12

5.2.1 Psalm 12 as Cultic Prophecy

Form-critically, the psalm consists of three (or four) parts: 1) a lament consisting of an opening cry for help (Ps 12:2-3) and a prayer for intervention (Ps 12:4-5); 2) an oracle of intervention

(Ps 12:6); and 3) a confessional hymn of trust (Ps 12:7-9).[1] This mixture of forms is regarded by numerous commentators as a prophetic lament liturgy.[2] There are three possible models for the liturgical performance of the psalm: 1) the prophetic liturgy involves a lamenting individual with an oracle of intervention spoken either by a prophet or priest[3]; 2) the prophetic liturgy involves the lamenting congregation with an oracle of intervention spoken either by a prophet or priest[4]; 3) the entire psalm was spoken by a single prophetic representative of the congregation.[5]

An important question in considering the individual or communal backdrop for the psalm is whether one adopts a singular or a plural reading of the suffix on תצרנו in Ps 12:8 (individual "him" or communal "us"). The other variants in verse 8, תשמרם or תשמרנו, support a communal reading either way; although the third-person plural is more difficult and strengthens the case for a prophetic/priestly individual interceding on behalf of the

---

1 Gunkel (1926: 43-44); Anderson (1972: 124); Kraus (1978a: 234; 1988: 207); Gerstenberger (1988: 80).
2 Mowinckel (1923: 62); Jeremias (1970: 113); Anderson (1972: 126); Bellinger (1984: 61-63); Weiser (1962: 159-160; 1987: 107-108); Kraus (1978a: 234-35; 1988: 207-208); Zenger (Hossfeld and Zenger 1993: 93); Seybold (1996: 62). Küchler (1918: 299) lists Psalm 12 as an example of a priestly oracle in a lament context. Gunkel (1926: 43; 1933: 138, 410; 1998: 97, 315) thinks of a divine revelation coming to a priest in a manner similar to a prophet, so with this qualification he classifies Psalm 12 as an "imitation of prophetic liturgy". Gunkel also cites his discussion of Psalm 20 in this connection. While refusing to use the word "prophet", he nevertheless describes the cultic functionary as speaking divine words under inspiration.
3 Mowinckel (1921: 147; 1923: 62-63) prefers an individual lament, rejecting the view of some of the older commentators of his time who thought the individual reference is "collective" or an adoption of an older oracle. Seybold (1996: 62-63) speaks in terms of an individual afflicted by the slander of the wicked. Gerstenberger (1988: 82-83) prefers an individual lament in the original setting but a corporate use at a later time. Küchler (1918: 299), who suggests a priestly oracle for Psalm 12, does not specify whether the context is individual or communal lament.
4 Anderson (1972: 126); Bellinger (1984: 61-63); Weiser (1962: 160; 1987: 108). Gunkel (1926: 43-44; 1933: 138, 410; 1998: 97, 315) likewise stresses the communal nature of the psalm.
5 Jeremias (1970: 113); Kraus (1978a: 234-35; 1988: 207-208); Zenger (Hossfeld and Zenger 1993: 93).

group.⁶ In view of the plural readings on the first verb (תשמרנו/תשמרם), the third-person singular for תצרנו is also more difficult and therefore preferred. However, this does not preclude a corporate concern, since the singular would be generic, like חסיד in Ps 12:2 (cf. parallel to the plural אמונים). Mowinckel (1923: 62-63) maintained that acceptance of a singular or a plural reading of תצרנו depends in large measure on the individual or communal background presupposed for the lament. For him, a communal interpretation is based upon an incorrect understanding of the nature of the "enemies", who should rather be seen as sorcerers afflicting the individual (Mowinckel 1921: 147; 1923: 62). As support for the individual interpretation, Mowinckel observed that unlike Psalm 14, which also expresses an oracle against the wicked, Psalm 12 is closer to the individual lament psalm in that it expresses a direct lament concerning an enemy together with a request for help. Gerstenberger (1988: 82), who also argues for an originally individual backdrop for the psalm, points to the singular references in Ps 12:2, 6 and 8. He explains the plural references, especially Ps 12:6, as later remodelling of the psalm for community use. But none of these arguments is convincing. The sorcery backdrop is a rather speculative construct; and even if true, there might be a corporate concern for this social evil. A simpler assumption is socio-economic oppression so frequently denounced by the prophets. Resorting to a later redaction to account for the plural references is also speculative, and the failure of consistency in the plural redaction remains to be explained.⁷ It is better to interpret the singular references as generic for the collective poor of the community, as suggested above. Finally, Mowinckel's appeal to the petition element of the psalm as evidence for an individual lament is countered not only by Jeremias's arguments for prophetic lament liturgy, but also by the presence of petition in communal laments. For example, Ps 44:27 is especially relevant with the request for God to "Rise up!", similar to Yahweh's oracle of intervention in Ps 12:6.

---

6   No readings reflect a third-person singular understanding of the suffix. It is more likely that the consonants תשמרנו resulted from a mistaken first-person plural reading of תצרנו than that the third-person plural form תשמרם arose from either a first-person plural or third-person masculine singular of תצרנו.
7   There are no plural variants for the singular referent in verses 2 and 6.

Jeremias (1970: 113) argues for a corporate concern by a representative prophet in Psalm 12. In his view, the similarity between Psalm 12 and Habakkuk 1 establishes Psalm 12 as a prophetic liturgy performed by the prophet; not only the words of Ps 12:6 but the psalm as a whole: 1) the use of שד (Hab 1:6; in Psalms, only in Ps 12:6); 2) the "we complaint" is missing as well as the first-person suffixes on the verbs, which would point to the individual praying as the one in need; 3) no response of Yahweh to the individual or the corporate people and the trust statement is without personal tone. The prophetic psalmist, as representative of the people, expresses social concern over the radical derangement of public policy similar to that found in the prophets (Jeremias 1970: 113-14). Jeremias (1970: 114) prefers the third-person suffixes in Ps 12:8 to first-person plural, which reinforces his opinion that a prophet, as representative of the assaulted people, is speaking rather than the community lamenting as a whole. He likens the trust section of Ps 12:7-9 to Hab 3:18. Kraus (1988: 235-38) maintains that intercession was a chief function of a cult prophet, which fits the role of a prophet speaking in Psalm 12 as a corporate representative. Whether the psalm was spoken in parts by the community with a prophetic functionary announcing the oracle (mixed liturgy), or, as Jeremias argues, a single prophetic spokesman interceded for the disenfranchised of the congregation, a corporate context rather than individual lament is in view. Although he prefers a more complex history of multiple settings for the psalm, Gerstenberger (1988: 82) observes that classifying the psalm as a cult prophetic liturgy potentially merges the individual and communal aspects which otherwise remain in opposition.

5.2.2 Psalm 12 as Poetic Citation of a Divine Saying

The majority of commentators maintain that Psalm 12 contains prophetic speech, either in the form of an oracle in Ps 12:6 spoken within the broader liturgical context of the psalm or in the form of a prophetic lament liturgy in which the psalm as a whole is viewed as prophetic speech. However, several scholars argue that the psalmist adopts the style of first-person divine speech for rhetorical purposes. Craigie (1983: 137) acknowledges that Ps 12:6 might be an oracle delivered by a prophet or priest, but he adds:

> "But even this cannot be certain, for the use of direct speech is a useful poetic device and need not imply an additional participant in a cultic context; the imagined words of the enemy have already been utilized in v 5, and it is entirely natural, simply from a literary perspective, to balance them with the divine words of v 6."

In similar fashion, Prinsloo (1998) maintains on the basis of antithetical poetic structure that the divine speech is a literary device:

> "The introduction of direct speech from Yahweh is normally taken as an indication that a cultic prophet or priest utters an oracle at this point. However, this is by no means a foregone conclusion. A shift from description to direct speech of Yahweh occurs in many psalms (cf. Ps 2,5-9; 50,4ff.; 60,8-10; 81,7-15; 82,6-7; 89,20ff.; 91,14ff.). It is a poetic technique to introduce Yahweh on the scene: It is an allusion to the countless examples where Yahweh acted on behalf of his people in distress" (Prinsloo 1998: 398).

For Prinsloo, the psalm is not a prophetic liturgy performed in the cult "but a prayer by a socially bereaved follower of Yahweh that a reversal of fortunes might occur" (Prinsloo 1998: 401). Van der Ploeg (1971: 91) opines that the introduction to divine speech in Ps 12:6 is not a technical form, so the citation of divine words is not a direct oracle from Yahweh; rather, the psalmist formulates the wording according to the thoughts of God as expressed in, for example, Isa 33:10.

5.2.3   Evaluation

It is possible that Ps 12:6 records a citation of prophetic-like language, such as Isa 33:10, especially in view of the brevity of the citation compared to other psalms that have been discussed thus far. However, contrary to Craigie's and Prinsloo's argument, there is no evidence that introducing Yahweh on the scene is a common poetic device.[8] The psalms offered by Prin-

---

[8] Kim (1984: 107-126; 1999: 78-79) doubts that an intervening oracle can explain the mood change within lament psalms. In his view, even Harner's

sloo as examples of such a technique are evidence to the contrary.⁹ Van der Ploeg's suggestion that the divine speech in Ps 12:6 is not introduced by a technical formula is countered by his own observation of the similarity of this expression to Isa 33:10.¹⁰ If the psalm as a whole were spoken by a prophetic functionary, then the divine speech itself would have appeared less "brief" in the sense that the entire psalm would be construed as prophetic. Thus, the framed divine speech in itself, if not the performance of the whole psalm as a genre, would have signalled to the original audience that they were encountering prophetic speech.

As discussed in the second chapter, Assyrian prophetic sources offer many examples of prophetic response to prayer and lament; and similar activity is also illustrated in the Zakkur Inscription, Mari letters, *Papyrus Amherst 63* (a communal liturgy), and Hittite prayers. Therefore, this phenomenon in psalms is consistent with cultural expectations for prophetic activity in other ancient Near Eastern contexts. The emphasis on individual oracles in contrast to community address in the Assyrian oracles could be due to their royal character. Thus, the absence of prophetic response to communal lament may be an accident of preservation. The likelihood of this is supported indirectly in the sources. One royal oracle, not from a lament context, does address the community (SAA 9 3.2), and public pro-

---

appeal to Assyrian evidence to support Begrich's priestly salvation oracle fails, since no such oracles appear in the lament psalms except Psalms 12, 60 and 89. Because the oracles in these three psalms do not change the mood from lament to thanksgiving, he suggests that they are adaptations of ancient oracles and not fresh prophecies. A secondary citation is possible in Psalm 60 and especially Psalm 89 (see discussion of these respective psalms). However, Kim's objection is not necessarily a problem. The return to complaint in Ps 12:9 is not incompatible with reception of the oracle. The oracle has instilled confidence (Ps 12:7-8); and by reasserting his anxious concern (Ps 12:9), the speaker implicitly presses for immediate deliverance. Similarly, in Ps 60:11-13, the psalmist states his request that Yahweh act immediately in keeping with the promise just given (Ps 60:8-10), the confidence in which is declared in v. 14.

9 Psalms 2, 50, 81, 82, and 89 have been discussed above, and Psalms 60 and 91 will be discussed below.
10 See also Isa 1:11, 18; 41:21; and 66:9.

phetic activity is evident from the role of a prophetess in the substitute king ritual (SAA 13 37; cf. SAAS 7 4.2). The efficacy of public, prophetic address in Assyria to move the masses is implicit in Esarhaddon's instructions to report treasonous prophets (SAA 2 6:116-17; cf. SAAS 7 7).

It is granted that the introduction formula יאמר יהוה in Ps 12:6 is unusual for prophetic speech.[11] However, in one Assyrian oracle, SAA 9 8:2, the corresponding present tense form of the Akkadian verb (*iqabbi*) is used as an introduction to divine speech. The metaphor of the deity "rising" to deliver the endangered king occurs in SAA 9 1.1 i 24-27.[12]

5.2.4   Conclusion

Psalm 12 preserves an example of prophetic speech uttered in response to lament in the cult, either a brief oracle in Ps 12:6 or, more likely, the performance of the entire psalm by a prophetic functionary on behalf of the lamenting community. Nothing in the psalm provides reliable clues as to the date. Inclusion in the first Davidic Psalter might in itself suggest that it was among pre-exilic psalms collected early in the formation of the Psalter.

5.3   Psalms 60 and 108

5.3.1   The Question of Intertextuality

These two psalms are grouped together due to the parallel between Ps 60:7-14 and Ps 108:7-14. While variations occur in Ps 60:10/Ps 108:10[13] and Ps 60:11/Ps 108:11[14], they are of no consequence to the question of the nature of the divine speech. Psalm 108 as a whole is composed of parallel texts from not only

---

11   Outside of Psalm 12, it occurs as an introduction formula only in the Book of Isaiah (Isa 1:11, 18; 33:10; 41:21; 66:9).
12   A closer parallel is SAA 9 7 r. 1 if one accepts Ringgren's (1983: 91, 93) reconstruction [e]-ta-al-la ("I will arise") over Parpola's [ma]-a ta-al-la (meaning obscure).
13   "because of me, shout O Philistia"/"over Philistia I will shout"
14   מצור "fortification"/מבצר "fortress"

Ps 60:7-14 but also Ps 57:8-12. The secondary status of Ps 108:7-14 is indicated by the fact that Ps 108:7 has been separated from the preceding verse couplet in its original context of lament (i.e., Ps 60:3-6) and inserted after the praise excerpt from Ps 57:8-12 (cf. Gunkel 1926: 475). This transposition is more likely than the reverse insertion into a lament context. The significance of this intertextual example is that it illustrates the secondary use of oracular speech in a psalm. The relevance of this for the prophetic speech in the psalms is discussed below.

5.3.2 Psalm 60 as Cultic Prophecy

Psalm 60 is generally regarded as composed of three parts: 1) communal lament with complaint and petition (Ps 60:3-7); 2) a divine speech (Ps 60:8-10); and 3) a renewed lament with closing confession of faith (Ps 60:11-14).[15] Both Mowinckel (1923: 65-66) and Gunkel (1926: 257; 1933: 139, 410-11; 1998: 98, 315) maintain that Ps 60:8-10 is an oracle spoken by a priest or prophet in the context of liturgical lament. Gunkel (1926: 257) uncharacteristically uses the term "prophet" as a possible agent for this oracle delivered in the temple. The two differ, however, on the question of whether the oracle originated in the same context as the lament portions of the psalm or is a citation of an older oracle. Mowinckel (1923: 66) argues that Ps 60:8-10 is fresh prophetic revelation in the cult, since an older oracle would be introduced by a formula indicating that it is secondary, such as in Ps 89:20. The freshness of the oracle is also evident in that it responds to a plea for God to answer in a present historical situation (Mowinckel 1923: 71). Mowinckel's view finds support in Jeremias's model of prophetic lament liturgies where the prophet offers both the lament and prophetic response in the same liturgical act. Jeremias (1970: 147, 149) cites Psalm 60 as a possible example of prophetic lament performed on special days of fasting. Gunkel (1926: 258; 1933: 139; 1998: 98), on the other hand, maintains that Ps 60:8-10 is

---

15 E.g., Gunkel (1926: 256); Gerstenberger (1988: 239-40).

a citation of an older oracle.¹⁶ For him, the difference in poetic metre between the oracle and the two framing laments is evidence that the oracle was drawn into the context by the presenter of the psalm. He also observes that the content of the oracle (conquest of the land) does not match exactly the situation of the lament (fugitives from defeat).¹⁷ Evaluation of the merits of these two interpretations will be taken up after presentation of the view that the divine speech in Ps 60:8-10 is not oracular at all but poetic/homiletical rhetoric.

5.3.3 Psalm 60 as Poetic Rhetoric

Gerstenberger (1988: 240) challenges the legitimacy of a cult prophetic interpretation of Psalm 60. He argues that rather than prophetic or priestly style, אלהים דבר is used in the psalms (other than Ps 60:8/108:8, it appears only in Pss 50:1 and 62:12) as a homiletic device similar to narrative style in the Pentateuch, which in Deuteronomy and P is technical language for Yahweh's communication to his people.¹⁸ Gerstenberger suggests that the imperfect form, ידבר (Pss 2:5; 85:9; 99:7), and also אמר (Pss 2:7; 12:6; 33:9; 50:16; 68:22; 106:33) are similarly used. He summarises the point,

> "[The formula] stands out as a characteristic figure of speech to introduce important messages to the community. The formula thus seems to be an assertion of divine communication, a reference to well-known fact, almost like later reference to Scripture. It is not a prophetic messenger or legitimation formula" (Gerstenberger 1988: 240).

Because of the strong nationalistic interpretation of Israel's covenant reflected in the use of ידידך (Ps 60:7), Ogden (1985:

---

16   Also, Weiser (1962: 438; 1987: 296); Anderson (1972: 441, 444); Kraus (1978b: 586; 1989: 2-3); Seybold (1996: 237). Zenger (Hossfeld and Zenger 2000: 157-59; 2002: 367) proposes that an older oracle (vv. 8-10) was combined with a royal prayer (vv. 11-14) in late pre-exilic times, to which was prefixed a communal lament (vv. 3-7) in the post-exilic period.
17   Weiser (1962: 438; 1987: 296) and Kraus (1978b: 586; 1989: 3) argue in a similar fashion.
18   Gerstenberger cites as examples Gen 12:4; 17:23; 18:19; 21:1-2; 24:7, 51; 35:13-14; Deut 1:6, 11, 21; and with human agents, Gen 23:16; 24:30; 42:30; 44:2; 45:27.

87; cf. Tate 1990: 106) argues that Ps 60:8-11 does not give God's own address but rather the nation's attempt to remind God of his commitment.[19] Thus, the form of divine address is rhetorical, drawing on the ideology of older traditions as a motive underlying the petition for God to act (cf. Gen 49:10; Num 24:17-19; Deut 31:1-10).

---

[19] Both Ogden (1985: 83-84) and Gerstenberger (1988: 241) prefer to view verse 11 as a continuation of the speech in verses 6-10, thus closing the second part of the psalm. The basis of this suggestion is two-fold. First, the use of אלהים (Ps 60:3, 8, 12) serves to divide the psalm into its three constituent parts, therefore, a new section must begin with verse 12. Second, the first-person pronouns in verse 11 continue the first-person speech of the previous verses. According to Gerstenberger, Yahweh asks through his speaker for Israel's active participation in the task (cf. Isa 48:14-16; 49:1-4; 50:10; 59:16; 63:5). Ogden (1985: 87) appears, however, to view the questions in verse 11 as words of the psalmist spoken independently from those placed in the mouth of Yahweh (although comments on structure are unclear regarding this distinction, Ogden 1985: 83-84). While the observation that the use of the divine name at the beginning of the three parts is helpful, it is not necessary to suppose that it must mark the first verse line of each part. Ogden suggests that the dual question, "Who . . . who?" (Ps 60:11), ends the second part and is coordinated with the double use of the divine name at the outset of the third part. However, this coordination of dual question with double reference to God is more easily understood as a verse couplet which together opens the resumed lament in the psalm. This is confirmed by the difficulty that this suggestion poses for understanding the first-person pronouns in verse 11. Regarding Gerstenberger's view, it is highly unlikely that God, whose *leadership* over the armies of Israel is deemed necessary (Ps 60:12), would ask to be led into battle against Edom (Ps 60:11). Gerstenberger's appeal to the servant passages in Second Isaiah shows only Yahweh's willingness to enlist agents of his work, but there is nothing in these passages analogous to the request for leadership in Ps 60:11. Ogden's change in speaker does not provide a satisfactory solution. Without a clearly understood break between the divine speech (Ps 60:8-10) and the person speaking at the beginning of the next section (Ps 60:11), the listener/reader is presented with a confusing discourse. Therefore, it is better to regard Ps 60:10 as the end of the divine speech.

5.3.4 Evaluation

The arguments of Ogden and Gerstenberger that the divine speech in Ps 60:8-10 is a rhetorical/homiletical device are unconvincing. First, Gerstenberger's analysis of the introductory formula אלהים דבר is problematic. With the exception of Gen 24:7 and Deut 1:6, none of his narrative examples introduce direct discourse. The use of דבר in Gen 24:7 and Deut 1:6 is part of a formula introducing direct discourse; therefore, it actually counters Gerstenberger's point that it can be a mere rhetorical device in Ps 60:8. Furthermore, the context in both instances is different from one in which a prophetic functionary might be the speaker, particularly in a non-narrative frame such as Psalm 60. The examples of the prefix form ידבר in Pss 85:9 and 99:7 are also not relevant to discussion of introductory formulas, although his example from Ps 2:5 actually supports the uses of this verb to introduce oracular speech. The use of אמר in Pss 2:7; 12:6; and 50:16 are also counter-examples to his argument, since the presence of a prophetic speaker is most likely in these cases. In Ps 68:22, the verb introduces an oracle, not homiletical rhetoric. Pss 33:9 and 106:33 are not relevant to the discussion. It is also important to consider forms other than third-person. For example, the second-person form of the verb in Ps 89:20 provides an example of the use of דבר to introduce oracular speech (דברת בחזון).[20] In sum, Gerstenberger has not demonstrated the existence of a special homiletical device used to introduce important messages to the community. Particularly difficult for his view is the presence of first-person divine speech framed by דבר.

Second, it does not follow from Ogden's idea that Ps 60:8-11 expresses nationalistic interest that these verses must be rhetorical rather than citation of divine speech. It may be that this oracle is used rhetorically to remind Yahweh of his promises in the context of lament, but it does not follow that this section of the psalm must be other than oracular. Understanding the divine speech as a secondary citation of an older oracle is completely compatible with this rhetorical function, if in fact this is

---

20 Other examples discussed below illustrate that the formula in Ps 60:8 can be characterised as prophetic style.

the pragmatic use of the oracle and it is not a prophetic word of encouragement. But the change in mood to confidence in Ps 60:14 strongly suggests that the oracle functions to fortify Israel's confidence in war, not as a reminder to motivate Yahweh to action.

More difficult to judge is the point of disagreement between Mowinckel and Gunkel. Unlike Ps 12:6, where the verb ידבר (imperfect aspect) implies reception of the revelation in the present, the perfect aspect in Ps 60:8 might suggest citation of an oracle spoken in the more distant past. Both Mowinckel and Gunkel cite Ps 89:20 as evidence for their position. Mowinckel (1923: 66) draws attention to the *difference* between Ps 60:8 and Ps 89:20. In the latter case the citation formula (דברת accompanied by אז and ותאמר) indicates that an older oracle (or possibly oracle tradition) is being cited. Conversely, Gunkel (1926 258) uses Ps 89:20 to illustrate that older oracles are sometimes cited in the context of a psalm and so Ps 60:8 could be such a case. Similarly, Mowinckel (1923: 65, 71) contrasts Ps 60:8-10 with Ps 108:8-10 to illustrate that citation of an older oracle is evident in such a text. However, were it not for preservation of the oracle in Ps 60:8-10, there would be no way of knowing that its use in Ps 108:8-10 is secondary. It remains a possibility that Ps 60:8-10 could also be a secondary citation from the same prophetic tradition (cf. Anderson 1972: 441).

Examination of the use of דבר in other psalms and prophetic literature does not settle the issue of secondary citation conclusively, but it does lend considerable support to Mowinckel's view that the perfect aspect can be used to introduce fresh revelation and that secondary citations are generally indicated as such in the context. The use of דבר in the perfect to introduce prophetic speech in a present context is illustrated in Ps 50:1 where it expresses divine speech emanating from a theophany. In a prophetic call to attention, functionally similar to the theophany report in Ps 50:1, it introduces divine speech in Isa 1:2; Jer 10:1 (Jer 13:15?); and Amos 3:1. The weakness of this comparison to Ps 60:8 is that the verb in these examples occurs in a broader call to attention formula. Other examples are even less close due to the first-person form of the verb or, with the exception of Ezek

38:19, is a closing formula (e.g., Isa 1:20; Jer 34:5; Ezek 26:14; Joel 4:8; Obad 18; Mic 4:4).[21] One example closer to Ps 60:8 is Jer 42:19. In the context of the verse, Jeremiah has been asked to inquire of the Lord as to whether the remnant should remain in the land or flee to Egypt (Jer 42:1-6). After ten days (Jer 42:7), Jeremiah responds with an oracle from God (Jer 42:9-22). Nested within a series of introduction formulas (כה־אמר יהוה Jer 42:9, 15, 18) are two other expressions introducing divine speech in Jer 42:15 and 42:19. The use of דבר in Jer 42:19 ("Yahweh has spoken against you, O remnant of Judah") is parallel to the prophetic call to attention in Jer 42:15 ("hear the word of Yahweh, O remnant of Judah"). As noted above, דבר is used in tandem with שמע in the prophetic call to attention in Isa 1:2; Jer 10:1; and Amos 3:1; however, in the case of Jer 42:19 it is used independently to announce divine speech. That this divine speech was performed in the present is evident from the expression "this day" in Jer 42:19 as well as in Jer 42:21.

Two other examples illustrate the use of דבר to introduce divine speech. Isa 16:13-14 is particularly interesting in that דבר is used to refer to new revelation in contrast to what Yahweh spoke (דבר) in the past. The last example, Jer 23:17, is complicated for two reasons. First, in the LXX, דבר is translated as a construct noun in the phrase "word of Yahweh", while the MT presents the word דבר as a verb in the phrase, "Yahweh spoke", introducing the divine words "It shall be well with you". The MT reading presents the second problem in that the citation of Yahweh's words appears to be something repeated. Thus, this example might actually illustrate how דבר can be used to introduce an older or standard expression of divine speech.

As noted by Gunkel, Ps 89:20 offers an example where דבר introduces citation of an older oracle into the context. In addition to the possibility of Jer 23:17, discussed above, several other examples are relevant. In Ps 62:12, דבר introduces a statement of God's promise; however, the proverbial style of the passage not only makes it clear that this is a secondary citation rather than oracular speech, but it also renders Ps 62:12 a poor parallel to Ps 60:8. Two examples from prophetic literature (Isa

---

21 See also Isa 21:17; 22:25; 24:3; 25:8; 40:5; 58:14; Ezek 5:15, 17; 17:21, 24; 21:22, 37; 22:14; 23:34; 24:14; 28:10; 39:5.

20:2; Hos 1:2) use דבר to refer to older oracular speech, but they are narrative introductions of prophetic speech that is secondary (i.e., "old") from the standpoint of the compiler of the prophetic collection. Therefore, they are not analogous to Ps 60:8. Jer 30:4 might also be regarded in a similar manner, although here דבר may introduce a fresh prophetic speech. Already noted above is Isa 16:13, which refers to past divine speech using a temporal particle (מאז), similar to Ps 89:20. But in so doing, the use of דבר to introduce fresh prophetic revelation is highlighted in the next verse, Isa 16:14.

In every case where דבר introduces an older citation of divine speech, it is specified as such by temporal particles (or in the case of Ps 62:12 by a proverbial style). In every case without such indications, דבר can be understood by context to introduce fresh prophetic revelation. This does not prove that the formula אלהים דבר in Ps 60:8 must introduce a fresh oracle according to Mowinckel's model of cult prophecy. But the evidence is sufficient to show that the perfect form of דבר is not out of place as an introduction to prophetic speech (contra Gerstenberger[22]) and that there is a good possibility that Mowinckel's interpretation is correct over against the majority who favour viewing Ps 60:8-10 as a secondary citation of an older oracle.[23] However, Mowinckel's (1923: 71) point that the oracle comes in response to the need of an immediate situation does not bear on the question of freshness versus secondary citation. Quoting an older oracle to remind Yahweh of his commitment is as appropriate to

---

[22] "The citation formula "God speaks/spoke" (v. 3a) certainly is neither prophetic nor priestly in origin" (Gerstenberger 1983: 240).

[23] Booij (1978: 132, 137-39) does not accept arguments for citation of an older oracle based upon different meter or mismatch of historical details from the lament portions of the psalm. However, while arguing for fresh divine speech, he also stresses that Ps 60:8-10 lacks a direct promise of deliverance, which he expects of prophecy as normally conceived. In Psalm 60 there is only a proclamation of the triumph of Yahweh. For him, this is evidence that Ps 60:8-10 is a "singer oracle" which freshly adapts prophetic style to the present liturgical need. Following Booij, Tournay (1991: 177-78) attributes Psalm 60 to a Levitical singer acting as a cultic prophet. However, Ps 60:8-10 is similar to other oracles of Yahweh's dealing with nations (cf. Isa 9:1-4; Joel 4:16; Amos 1:2; Obad 19-21; Zeph 3:9-10). A general statement of triumph does not detract from prophetic authenticity.

the context of lament as would be a fresh cult-prophetic response.

Another issue relevant to the question of cultic prophecy in Ps 60:8-10 is the prepositional phrase בקדשו ("in his sanctuary" or "in his holiness"). The use of קדש with the prepositional prefix ב can refer either to the sanctuary (Ps 150:1; Num 4:16)[24] or to Yahweh's holiness (Ps 89:36; Amos 4:2). The latter meaning is necessitated by the oath formula introduced by שבע. So, one might argue that Ps 60:8 should be translated, "God spoke by his holiness" on analogy with Ps 89:36 and Amos 4:2. But the presence of דבר instead of שבע in Ps 60:8 distinguishes it from the examples of the oath formula (cf. Booij 1978: 332 n. 300). It is the absence of a sense of oath here that weighs in favour of the translation, "in his sanctuary". In either case, this expression supports the view that Ps 60:8 is an introduction to prophetic speech, and if קדש denotes the sanctuary it offers strong evidence for the function of cultic prophecy, even if secondary.[25]

The Assyrian prophecies provide some insight for this discussion. With respect to Psalm 12, it was noted that the Assyrian prophetic sources illustrate the dynamic of prophetic response to lament; and some evidence supports the role of Assyrian prophets in public life, even in community worship in the case of the substitute king ritual. While Psalm 60 is primarily communal[26], there is also a human individual who speaks. This could be the cult prophet, who intercedes for the community, or the king, or other military leader.[27] As noted above, the extant Assyrian oracles are often addressed to the king in the context of military challenges. Also of relevance to Ps 60:8-10, Assyrian prophets would specifically mention foreign peoples

---

[24] Exod 26:36, "in the holy of holies", is closely related; and perhaps also Num 18:10, although this might be rendered "as a most holy thing" (ב *essentiae*).

[25] It is still a possibility that the prophet or priest on the field of battle received the oracle, and the reference to the sanctuary merely acknowledges the earthly place from which God speaks, akin to "holy hill" in Ps 3:5. Assyrian prophets accompanied the army on campaign, thus, Psalm 60 could be a lament liturgy taking place in the field.

[26] The community concern is indicated by the "we" (Ps 60:2, 5, 12-14) as well as the plural forms (ליראיך, v. 6; ידידיך, v. 7).

[27] Singular suffixes in Ps 60:7 (the singular reading, וענני, has strong textual support and in view of the plural ידידיך יחלצון, it is the more difficult reading) as well as Ps 60:11.

(SAA 9 2.3 ii 15-16; 2.4 iii 12-15; 3.2 ii 1-7 [note community address in the opening line]; SAA 9 7:12-r 5; SAA 9 8). Assyrian oracles could function to bolster the courage of the troops as well; although the possibility exists that some of these reports are mere literary creations produced for propagandistic purposes or interpretive expansions of omens.[28] Thus, Assyrian prophetic sources reinforce the suggestion that Psalm 60 preserves a prophetic oracle delivered in the context of a military crisis (cf. Ps 60:3, 6, 12-14 and superscription). The applicability of Assyrian sources in this comparison is reinforced by parallels from outside the book of psalms which illustrate the interplay between the lamenting community, the interceding king and a responding prophet (2 Chr 20:13-17 and Isa 37:6-7, 21-35 [2 Kgs 19:6-7, 20-34]).[29]

5.3.5 Conclusion

Psalm 60 provides an example of a prophetic lament liturgy, either as a whole psalm or at least in the preservation of the prophetic response in Ps 60:8-10. Even if verses 8-10 are only the citation of an older oracle, it still constitutes evidence for cultic prophecy, particularly if the prepositional phrase בקדשו is translated "in his sanctuary". In any case, Psalm 108 demonstrates that oracles were reused in a secondary citation in cultic song. The dating of Psalm 60 is elusive, and if the oracle is a secondary citation then the problem arises of determining the date of its origin before being incorporated into the psalm. Kraus

---

28 Nissinen (1998b: 57-61). The use of prophecy to encourage troops is a reasonable inference based upon the report of a revelation to Assurbanipal's troops in a corporate dream. Divine encouragement was not just for the private benefit of the king, but was put to use more broadly to lift military morale.

29 Christensen (1975: 121-27) suggests that cultic prophecy in Psalm 60 contributed to the prophetic use of war oracles against the nations in the prophetic literature. Perhaps it is better simply to view war oracles as a standard type of prophetic speech which is preserved in Psalm 60 as well as other OT literature. Others have also observed this role of prophetic speech and psalms (Hayes 1968; Ogden 1982).

(1978b: 587; 1989: 3) understands from the psalm that the Northern Kingdom is in enemy hands and that perhaps Jerusalem has fallen (cf. Tate 1990: 104). Gunkel (1933: 139; 1998: 98) also views the oracle as originating some time after the downfall of the north. Jeremias (1970: 149) imagines the post-586 days as a likely time when such prophetic lament liturgies were spoken. However, Weiser (1962: 440; 1987: 297-98) is impressed by the fact that Israelite armies are conceived as under the command of Yahweh and therefore proposes a pre-exilic date. Mowinckel (1923: 66-68) correctly notes that Ephraim is not an object of re-conquest; rather, the northern territories together with Judah are Yahweh's weapons, pointing possibly to the time of David or Solomon. He also proposes the possibility of the loss of Edom under Joram (2 Kgs 8:20-22). Seybold (1996: 237, 239) argues that, after the time of Solomon, the oracle part can only point to the territorial expansion program of Josiah. Zenger (Hossfeld and Zenger 2000: 157-59; 2002: 367) also prefers an older pre-exilic oracle adapted to the psalm in a post-600 setting. Their views illustrate the complexity that secondary citation of the oracle poses, since the final form of the psalm might date after the origin of the oracle. But a pre-exilic date for the oracle seems to fit best the political realities reflected in the whole psalm. Military application of the oracle *by an Israelite army* against Edom is difficult to imagine post-586, even though hostilities were high during the exile (cf. Obadiah).

5.4 Psalm 91

5.4.1 Psalm 91 as Cultic Prophecy

Psalm 91 is generally regarded as consisting of two principal parts. The first part (Ps 91:1-13) is a blessing (or possibly a didactic poem) addressed to a worshipper in the second-person singular with reference to Yahweh in the third person. The second part (Ps 91:14-16) is an oracle of first-person divine speech referring to the worshipper in the third person.[30] Mowinckel (1923: 103-104) suggests that the entire psalm was part of a longer liturgy, the first part answering a prayer with a blessing followed by a divine confirmation of these human words in the second part, both of which accompanied cultic acts and were spoken by one or two priests. He argues that if, contrary to his view, the psalm is regarded as a didactic poem, then Ps 91:14-16 must be assumed to be a cultic oracle assimilated secondarily into the poem, yet with the same force as a fresh word of God (Mowinckel 1923: 104-105). Gunkel (1904: 169; 1926: 405-406) also stresses the liturgical performance of the psalm in which a priestly official answers the prayer of a worshipper with a didactic poem followed by a divine oracle.[31] Gunkel (1904: 169 n. 4)[32] illustrates the setting by reference to the *Dialogue Between Assurbanipal and Nabû* (SAA 3 13) where the prayer of the worshipper interchanges with divine response in the form of first-person speech. Therefore, in the case of Psalm 91, Gunkel thinks of the divine speech in terms of a cultic address by God

---

[30] E.g., Mowinckel (1923: 103); Gunkel (1904: 162-63; 1926: 403); Tate (1990: 450); Booij (1994: 112) Seybold (1996: 362); Gerstenberger (2001: 163-64). As several commentators note, the opening participle and first-person verbs and suffixes in verse 2 set Ps 91:1-2 apart from the following verses as an introduction. While recognising that scholars generally find a liturgical origin for the psalm, Zenger (Hossfeld and Zenger 2000: 619-20; 2002: 500) thinks it is possible that the psalm merely imitates old liturgical rituals for private recitation, either within or outside the temple.

[31] Burrelli's (1993: 139) study of Psalm 91 focused on its possible apotropaic purpose and assumed Gunkel's view that Ps 91:14-16 is a priestly oracle.

[32] Cf. Gunkel (1933: 178 n. 9; 1998: 125 n. 22).

through his spokesman.[33] Weiser (1962: 79; 1987: 54) points to Psalms 12 and 60 and Booij (1994: 112) cites Psalms 81 and 95 as examples of similar changes from human to genuine divine speech in the course of a psalm.[34] On the basis of a comparison between Psalm 91 and Psalm 34, Kraus (1978b: 807-808; 1989: 224-25) suggests the possibility that a pious person, who had experienced God's protective care, now in turn encourages another person with the divine words he himself had received on a previous occasion. While he appears to favour a priestly oracle in the present context of the psalm, his alternative solution still involves the delivery of a genuine cultic oracle in the past. In either case, he affirms that the statement is not "poetic dress" (Kraus 1978b: 804; 1989: 221).

5.4.2   Psalm 91 as Didactic Style

Gerstenberger (2001: 166-67) argues that Ps 91:14-16 is not a direct oracle. Rather, a speaker not manifest in verses 1-13 now reveals himself and reflects on his motivation for speaking blessing to the supplicant. The voice can only be Yahweh's, but the form and situation imply that the first-person speech is rhetorical. It parts from true oracular form in that the individual is not addressed directly but in the third person. The audience being addressed is the congregation or the cultic functionary through whom Yahweh communicates. Gerstenberger (2001: 167) stresses the importance to him of this form-critical observation by contrasting the divine assurance of Ps 91:14-16 with the unchanged oracle form of Isa 41:10-14; 43:1, 5; 44:2; 51:7; and 54:4. He argues that the change to third person in Ps 91:14-16 signals that the whole is a form of benediction. The "oracle" pro-

---

[33] Gunkel appears to be inconsistent here. He illustrates the dynamic of the change from human to divine speech in Ps 91:14 by reference to Pss 75:3 and 95:8 (Gunkel 1926: 405). However, in his separate discussion of these two psalms, he considers them to be poetic adaptation of prophetic speech. For Psalm 75:3, see Gunkel (1933: 370-72), for Ps 95:6, see Gunkel (1904: 176; 1926: 419). He is unclear in his commentary on the source of the oracle in Ps 75:3 (Gunkel 1926).

[34] For Booij, however, the divine words are those of a Levitical singer and not a prophet.

vides the "profile" of a righteous man and confirms the benedictions of verses 3-13. Thus, the whole psalm is a benediction preached to the community in worship. Tate (1990: 451-52, 457) affirms the possibility that Ps 91:14-16 was spoken by a priest or prophet in the course of a liturgy, but he prefers the idea that the speaker was a teacher respected for wisdom.[35]

5.4.3 Evaluation

In considering the Asaphite psalms, the presence or absence of prophetic introduction formulas is a major issue relative to the question of genuine prophecy versus poetic rhetoric. This issue hardly receives mention in commentaries on Psalm 91, although it merits consideration.[36] As discussed in the chapter on Asaphite psalms, the important question is not the presence or absence of a formula introducing prophetic speech, since divine speech can be framed by means other than technical formulas and in some cases needs no frame at all. Non-verbal signals such as liturgical transitions might also function to introduce prophetic speech.[37] More important than a mere formula is what the audience's expectation would have been for prophetic speech and how the performance of the psalm would have informed them of its presence. In his discussion of Psalm 75, Gerstenberger (2001: 82) mentions Psalm 91 as an example of "unmarked" (i.e., unframed) prophetic speech. He also suggests that in similar cases of divine discourse such as Psalms 50, 81, 82, and 95, one cannot take the "divine oratory" at face value "because human mediation is always an integral part of God's mes-

---

35 Tate (1990: 450, 458) considers this similar to the case of Ps 95:7-11 which in his view is sermonic.
36 Gunkel (1926: 405) compares the rapid change in voice with Pss 12:6; 20:7-9; 75:3; 85:9 and 95:8. His inconsistency in this comparison has already been noted. Tate (1990: 450, 458) notes the similar structure of Psalm 91 to Psalm 95, but he does not elaborate on the implications for genuineness of prophetic speech. As noted above, Booij (1994: 112) compares Psalm 91 to Psalms 81 and 95 to discount the possibility of mere poetic freedom in Ps 91:14-16.
37 See especially the discussion of Psalm 75.

sages" (Gerstenberger 2001: 184). Therefore it is not theologically legitimate to treat the discourse in Ps 91:14-16 as genuine divine speech (Gerstenberger 2001: 166). In his model, human speakers could freely adapt divine speech in their homiletical discourses. However, divine authority is implicit in the use of oracles, and it is doubtful anyone would venture to use first-person divine speech without the authorisation of a prophetic mantle. Apart from these debated psalms, no illustrations of such homiletical use are extant. Whether or not divine beings actually communicate through human agents is not the issue here; rather, it is ascertaining the reality perceived by the audience in the worship setting of the psalm.

Psalm 91 poses a particularly difficult case in that there is no introduction formula or other framing device, such as a portrayal of a theophany, to signal the appearance of prophetic speech in the psalm. One factor is the relative length of Ps 91:14-16 compared to other brief citations of divine speech (e.g., Ps 46:11). It may be that an extended divine speech would be implicitly understood by the audience as an oracle. Another possibility is that the words of Ps 91:14-16 might have been a common dictum amenable to repeated use (e.g., Ps 62:12, although here the proverbial formula suggests that it does not involve prophetic speech). Probably the function of the psalm as a whole, that is, the intermediary nature of Ps 91:3-13 in the context of liturgical performance (cf. Ps 91:1-2), supports the heuristic expectation that the first-person divine speech in Ps 91:14-16 is genuine prophetic speech.[38] Liturgical action, such as the appearance of a prophetic functionary, would have made this more clear to the original audience. Admittedly, this unframed speech is difficult; but Gerstenberger's (2001: 167) suggestion that Ps 91:14-16 constitutes another example of sermonic style ("a benediction preached to the community in worship") is less cogent. Tate's preference for a sage as the speaker is something of a compromise between prophet/priest and preacher; however, this also depends on the first-person divine speech being understood as an original prophetic address

---

[38] De Regt (2000: 231-32) cites the person shift in Ps 91:14 as indicating a major structural change in the psalm. This does not exclude a possible change in the ritual at this point.

drawn into the wisdom tradition. In essence, this would be a variation of Kraus's suggestion.

The Assyrian sources offer evidence to support the possibility that Psalm 91 was regarded as prophetic and not merely didactic rhetoric. As noted above, Gunkel observed the relevance of the *Dialogue Between Assurbanipal and Nabû* (SAA 3 13 r. 1-11) to Psalm 91. Both texts contain divine response to a devoted worshipper seeking the deity for blessing and safety.[39] The oracle report SAA 9 9, which shares literary affinities with SAA 3 13 as well as the same cultic context,[40] displays promise of blessing for the king in third person (SAA 9 9:3-7), followed by first-person divine speech addressing the king in second person (SAA 9 9:8-28), then a benedictory prayer for the king in third person (SAA 9 9 r. 1-3). Psalm 91 differs in combining the first-person divine speech with third-person reference to the worshipper in the same section of the psalm (vv. 14-16), but SAA 9 9 illustrates that third-person address is compatible with prophetic style. Other Assyrian prophecies combine second-person address to the king with third-person address within the same oracle (SAA 9 1.2 [third person in line i 33?]; 1.6; 2.2; 2.4). This supports the possibility that Psalm 91 is a form of prophetic promise of safety throughout.[41] The shift to third-person address in Ps 91:14 does bring a wider audience into view but this does not preclude there being a continuation of the prophetic encouragement to the individual seeking divine protection.

---

39 Aside from the question of prophetic speech, this text might shed light on the difficult, rapid shift from third person to first person in Ps 91:1-2, which is sometimes explained as a liturgical change of speaker. According to this view, a priest's invitation to the worshipper to approach God was followed by the worshipper's profession of faith. But SAA 3 13 r. 1-4 shows a similarly rapid shift in persons (although within a prayer section), followed by confirmation in first-person divine speech addressing the king in the second person (SAA 3 13 r. 6 is likely the deity). This supports the possibility that Ps 91:1-2 could be spoken by the same person; and therefore, the attempts by translators (e.g., LXX) to smooth out this transition are unnecessary.
40 See the discussion in Chapter 2.
41 The use of imperfect verbs instead of jussives in Ps 91:3-13 weakens the benedictory illocution and strengthens the possibility of direct prophetic assurance.

There are additional reasons why the didactic thrust of Ps 91:14-16 is compatible with the genre of prophetic speech. The announcement of deliverance for the suffering servant in Isa 53:12 utilises first-person divine speech, refers to the one delivered in the third-person singular, and at the same time functions didactically for the community. Other prophetic announcements of salvation in Second Isaiah also incorporate the third-person plural (e.g., Isa 41:17-20; 42:14-17).[42] While not a prophetic text, *Assurbanipal's Coronation Hymn* (SAA 3 11) combines second- and third-person address to the king in a prayer of benediction (SAA 3 11:1-r. 2). Even though the third-person references add to the hymn a didactic function (i.e., for the benefit of the congregation), they still convey to the king the message of blessing. Similarly, a switch from second to third person in Ps 91:14 simply adds a didactic emphasis to the divine speech but does not necessarily make Ps 91:14-16 any less prophetic.

The promise of long life (Ps 91:16) finds a close parallel in Assyrian prophetic texts SAA 3 13:18, 24; SAA 9 9:9, 16, 20-21, r. 1-3 as well as the benediction in SAA 3 11:21 (note other blessings in lines 21-r. 2, 15-16). Possibly, Psalm 91 was first and foremost (but not exclusively) a royal prayer, and then blessings that attend a life of wisdom are expecially fitting (SAA 3 11 is royal). But wisdom themes also appear in classical prophetic texts (e.g., Isa 2:3; 40:14; Zeph 3:2). Therefore, wisdom themes and a didactic thrust do not necessarily point to a rhetorical use of first-person divine speech in Psalm 91.[43]

---

42 Thus, if there is any modification here of the salvation oracle, it is not from second- to third-person address (Gerstenberger 2001: 167) rather from plural to singular.

43 Because of the hortatory nature of Ps 32:8-9, some argue that it records divine speech. However, the form-critical explanation, that this is the place in the individual thanksgiving psalm where the psalmist exhorts the congregation, is probably the best solution. The didactic nature of Psalm 91 lends itself to comparison with Psalm 32 in this regard. However, the genre of Psalm 91 is quite different (benedictory prayer or prophetic announcement versus individual thanksgiving psalm).

5.4.4 Conclusion

While the unframed nature of the first-person divine speech in Ps 91:14-16 is problematic, there is reason to accept a cult-prophetic explanation as the best solution. A liturgical setting in which God responds to a devoted worshipper through the mouth of a prophetic functionary was common in both OT and ancient Near Eastern contexts; and this is a reasonable explanation for the mediation of divine blessing in Psalm 91. Thus, the function of the psalm as a whole, that is, the mediatory nature of Ps 91:3-13 in the context of liturgical performance (cf. Ps 91:1-2), supports the assumption that first-person divine speech in Ps 91:14-16 is genuinely prophetic. Comparative Assyrian sources demonstrate that a shift in persons addressed or a didactic function do not preclude prophetic speech. The explanation that Ps 91:14-16 preserves a common dictum that originated from prophetic speech in the cult remains a possibility. However, the proposal that Psalm 91 preserves prophetic mediation, delivered by a priest or prophet in a liturgy, is most likely. Nothing in the Psalm helps in setting a date, unless it is assumed that the application was first royal, in which case the psalm originated during the monarchy.

5.5 Psalm 68

5.5.1 Psalm 68 Contains Cultic Prophecy

Psalm 68 preserves at least one oracle (Ps 68:23-24) and possibly two if Ps 68:12b-15 is regarded as the content of a divine speech announced in Ps 68:12a. Kraus (1978b: 629; 1989: 48) regards both excerpts as divine speeches. Ps 68:12-14[44] contains a statement from God drawing on traditions found in Judges 5 or possibly preserving a very ancient oracle (Kraus 1978b: 633; 1989: 52). Ps 68:23-24 is a general oracle of victory that serves as the reason for the preceding praise (Kraus 1978b:

---

44 For Kraus, verse 15 is only a report of the outcome of the battle.

636; 1989: 55). Anderson (1972: 488, 494) and Weiser (1962: 486, 488-89; 1987: 331-33) also understand the formula אמר אדני (Ps 68:23) as an introduction to an oracle in verses 23-24, but they interpret the phrase אדני יתן־אמר (Ps 68:12) as merely Yahweh's voice in thunder, not a reference to prophetic speech (cf. Ps 68:34). Thus, while Anderson and Weiser do not consider Ps 68:12-15 as divine speech and Kraus holds open the possibility that it only preserves a secondary citation, all three view Ps 68:23-24 as oracular. It is unclear whether they view the latter as cultic prophecy originating in the ritual procession of the psalm or possibly a case of secondary citation of an earlier oracle. Booij (1978: 78) recognises both possibilities, either a direct divine speech or citation of an earlier oracle. However, for Booij, even a direct divine speech in this case would be only a type of "prophesying" whereby praise comes out in a divine word.

5.5.2 Psalm 68 as Poetic Adaptation

For Gunkel (1926: 283) the entire psalm has been influenced by prophetic style. It contains prophecies ("*Weissagungen*", e.g., vv. 2-3, 22, 24) but belongs to the category of eschatological hymns which only imitate genuine prophecy (cf. Gunkel and Begrich 1933: 79-80; 1998: 55). Ps 68:10-12 is a prophecy ("Weissagung") utilising imagery from the wilderness tradition similar to Isa 41:17-20, 44:3, 48:21, 49:10 (Gunkel 1926: 284). Since the imagery of bloody carnage in Ps 68:22-24 is not carried throughout the psalm, he conceives of these verses as promises spoken at one time by God but cited here secondarily from pre-existing material (Gunkel 1926: 285). In his view, the psalm depends on the same theology as Deutero-Isaiah and therefore must have originated at a very late date (Gunkel 1926: 283-84, 286-87). Tate (1990: 178) interprets Ps 68:12a as an introduction to a divine message, the content of which extends through verse 15; however, it is not direct divine speech but rather a report of the message Yahweh has proclaimed (the doves of v. 14 are the messengers). In his view, it is doubtful that אָמַר could be used of an oracle (Tate 1990: 164). His translation of Ps 68:23, "(He is) the Lord who says", frames the divine words as the kind of thing Yahweh says but excludes the possibility of divine speech originating in the performance setting of this psalm. Gerstenberger (2001: 39) observes that the phrase אדני יתן אמר is not likely a formula to introduce an oracle, since this would necessitate a "hearer" (e.g., Balaam in Num 24:4, 16), which is missing in the context of this psalm. He recognises that Ps 68:23 begins an oracle of God, using a less elaborate formula אמר אדני (Gerstenberger 2001: 40). However, he asks,

> "But can we count on prophets delivering messages in cultic assemblies? We probably should first opt for the more neutral designation 'mediator', avoiding the stereotyped and much later concept of the canonical 'Word-of-God messenger', and then freely admit communication from God to his people by way of priests or liturgists in early Jewish assemblies. Consequently, we may identify two cultic but probably 'nonprophetic' oracles in Psalm 68, namely, vv. 12-15 and 23-24" (Gerstenberger 2001: 40-41).

Similar to Gerstenberger (2001: 43-44), who posits that the divine speeches were shaped from pre-exilic fragments that preserve older traditions, Hossfeld (Hossfeld and Zenger 2000: 248-50, 253-54; 2002: 393-94) argues that Ps 68:12-15 and 20-24 form part of a pre-exilic core. The first divine speech (Ps 68:12-15) echoes a type of war oracle similar to 1 Kgs 20:13-15. The prophetic word itself is not cited, rather women appear as victory messengers. Parallel to the divine message in Ps 68:12-15, a new divine speech occurs in Ps 68:23 referring to the same battle.

5.5.3 Evaluation

The view that Ps 68:12-15 preserves a divine oracle is unlikely. The absence of first-person divine speech, while a general criterion for limiting the scope of this study, is not necessarily proof against this possibility. However, the presence of messengers (whether the feminine plural המבשרות refers to women, doves or a gender-neutral collective plural) makes the content in Ps 68:13-15 a divinely commissioned report of victory but not direct divine speech. Ps 68:23, on the other hand, begins with the direct citation formula אמר אדני. Gerstenberger's (2001: 40) placement of this form in "more ancient times, before more elaborate formulas were applied to prophetic words" is unnecessary. This expression, compounded with another divine name, occurs in the prophets as a closing frame (Isa 22:14; Amos 1:8, 7:6) and the form אמר יהוה as a closing frame is common (e.g., Amos 1). The formula נאם יהוה can be used as an opening frame with or without the particle כה (e.g., Num 24:3-4; Jer 9:21; Isa 1:24; 56:8; Zech 12:1-2; Ps 110:1) as well as a closing frame (e.g., Amos 2:16; 3:15; Jer 5:11).[45] In view of this interchangeable use of נאם יהוה it is not surprising to find אמר אדני (a common closing frame) used as an opening frame in Ps 68:23. Therefore, Ps 68:23-24 is a prophetic oracle with formal introduction and first-person divine speech; however, this does not resolve the question whether Ps 68:23-24 is a fresh oracle (in the first instance of performance) or the citation of an older one (perhaps announced before or in the field of battle).

Psalm 68 differs from Psalms 12, 60, and 91 in genre. These latter three originated as lament (or prayer) liturgies in which one expects a "live" performance of prophetic response. In contrast, Psalm 68 is set in the context of festive procession but the dominant theme is retrospective praise for victory in battle. The context of the oracle is a benediction (cf. Ps 68:20), it is followed by a portrayal of cultic procession to the sanctuary, and as Hossfeld notes, the oracle parallels the victory proclaimed in Ps 68:12-15. So secondary citation of an oracle assuring victory before battle is likely. But one might also argue that the psalm celebrates the timeless character of God as just judge and sovereign victor and so expresses hope that victory will always be assured. In this setting, the appearance of a prophetic liturgist is possible, announcing a promise that undergirds all victories, whether past or future. A final determination of the origin of the oracle is not possible, but the context suggests that a secondary citation is more likely.

---

45 See Meier (1992: 304-314) for the flexible use of this formula, although his conclusion regarding the diachronic development of framing formulas in prophetic speech is questionable.

5.5.4 Conclusion

Psalm 68 offers two potential examples of cultic prophecy (Ps 68:12-15 and 23-24). It appears unlikely that Ps 68:12-15 contains direct divine speech, rather it reports a divinely authorised proclamation of victory. In spite of the prophetic formula framing Ps 68:23-24, it is more likely that it introduces a secondary citation of divine speech within the context of praise (Ps 68:20). If this is the case, the original setting for the oracle is unknown. It could have been in the cult, but other possibilities include the court of the king (cf. 1 Kings 22) or on the field of battle.

5.6 Psalm 46

Psalm 46 is a song of confidence containing an exhortation with first-person divine speech and self-presentation of God (Ps 46:11). The prophetic style and contents of the psalm as a whole are emphasised by Gunkel (1904: 110; 1926: 197-99) but explained as the product of prophetic theology expressed in an eschatological hymn (cf. 1962: 366-67; cf. Weiser 1987: 247). Anderson (1972: 354) thinks that verse 11 only "resembles" a prophetic oracle (cf. Craigie 1983: 343), and Zenger (Hossfeld and Zenger 1993: 288) suggests that the lead singer is speaking in direct divine speech as an explication of the voice of God reported in verse 7. Gerstenberger (1988: 193) thinks that the self-presentation formula in Ps 46:11 had come to be "formalized to such an extent that it became an accepted phrase even in exhortatory discourse to the congregation". Kraus (1978a: 497, 501; 1988: 461, 464) represents a minority opinion when he entertains the possibility that Ps 46:11 is an "oracle of salvation and of being heard".

In view of the strong prophetic style in the psalm as a whole, Ps 46:11 could be a prophetic proclamation from the mouth of a prophetic functionary. In addition to Gunkel's observations, it was noted under discussion of the Asaphite psalms that the self-presentation formula is standard prophetic style. However, the brevity of the expression coupled with the absence of any frame to indicate that a prophetic proclamation is being issued leaves the prophetic identity of the speaker open to doubt. The notion that a non-prophetic singer would create a first-person divine speech for this psalm, even if explicating the voice of God in verse 7 as Zenger suggests, is still difficult to accept. Imitation of prophetic style is one thing, but presumption to speak in the divine voice without an authorised prophetic identity is another matter.[46] More likely, a prophetic aphorism is being cited secondarily, in which case it is still unknown whether or not the oracle originated in a cultic setting.

5.7 Psalm 87

Ps 87:4 and 6 contain a report of divine speech. First-person divine speech appears in verse 4, and the introductory phrase יהוה יספר in verse 6 might be the functional equivalent of an introductory prophetic speech formula. Kraus (1978b: 767-68; 1989: 186-87) suggests the possibility that a prophetic tradition stands in the background or that a prophet is speaking who had audience in the divine council. But others modify the cult-prophetic explanation or avoid it altogether. Booij (1978: 79) understands the divine word as a "prophetic" contribution, exhibiting the "vision and breath of prophetic and poetic-like ecstasy", and he explains the short unframed oracle in verse 4 by analogy to Ps 46:11 and 75:3-4 (Booij 1987: 19). But his view appears to fall short of a cultic prophecy model. Anderson (1972: 621) regards verse 4 as a "form of direct divine utterance" while verses 5-6 are prophetic exposition, however he does not elaborate further. For Weiser (1962: 582; 1987: 397) the psalm only portrays in a cultic scene what the prophets spoke in eschatological hope. Even Mowinckel (1923: 50) regarded the type of cult oracle as unclear, not introduced expressly but in a po-

---

46 Gerstenberger imagines that a preacher might voice the self-presentation formula in a formalised manner. This is not far removed from the idea that a prophetic aphorism is cited secondarily. However, the statements of intent to intervene in Ps 46:11 are distinctly prophetic and inappropriate as a homiletical creation.

etic manner as though Yahweh himself were speaking. In his view, the psalm might best be thought of as poetic fiction.

Kraus's suggestion that the psalm reflects a prophetic vision of the divine council is possible. However, the passive construction of the speech frames in Ps 87:3[47] and 5 suggests that the statements which follow only envisage the kind of thing that might be said.[48] Booij (1994: 63) observes a progression in speakers: Yahweh himself (v. 4), words humans might say (v. 5), words written by God (v. 6), and words sung at the festival (v. 7). This seems to support the idea that the speech is a literary portrayal.

5.8 Other Psalms

5.8.1 Psalm 14 (53)

As discussed in relation to Psalm 12 and prophetic lament liturgies, Jeremias includes Psalm 14 in this category. It does not contain first-person divine speech, unless the reference to "my people" may be an equivalent, as Jeremias argues. But this is tenuous evidence (cf. Ruth 1:16).

5.8.2 Psalm 27

Ps 27:8 ("Come, says my heart, 'Seek my face'") could be a secondary citation of prophetic exhortation delivered in the cult (plural imperative, בקשׁו). Such forms are known in prophetic speech (e.g., Amos 5:4, 6; Zeph 2:3). Although, it may simply be a well-known call to piety originating from such speeches.

---

[47] For a defense of the passive construction including concordance between the plural subject and singular participle, see Booij (1987: 18-19).

[48] The indirectness of the speech frames appears to be what moved Mowinckel away from a typical cult prophetic explanation in the case of Psalm 87.

5.8.3   Psalm 62

Ps 62:12 contains a report of proverbial divine speech.

5.8.4   Psalm 101

Kselman (1985) argues that Ps 101:6-7 is an oracle of divine response to the king's words. However, the absence of any indication that the identity of the speaker in the first person has changed makes this doubtful. Kselman's (1985: 49) observation regarding the appearance of a non-verbal sentence in Ps 101:6 is not adequate reason to postulate a change, and עיני most likely denotes the eyes of the king as in verse 3.

5.8.5   Psalm 105

Ps 105:11 and 15 contain first-person divine speech introduced with the discourse marker לאמר. Both are set within a narrative context reporting God's revelation to the patriarchs. Therefore, these short oracles are secondary citations drawn from older tradition.

5.9   Conclusion

Psalms 12 and 60 are prophetic lament liturgies which contain divine affirmations in response to community distress. The divine words in Ps 12:6 and Ps 60:8-10 may have been spoken by a prophetic functionary in response to the lament uttered by a different individual, but the possibility exists that the whole of both psalms is the word of a prophetic intermediary. The role of prophetic response to lament conforms to the social expectation for prophets in Assyria and elsewhere in the ancient Near East. Ps 60:8-10 may be a secondary citation of a prophetic oracle (as in Psalm 108), but in any event, the reference to the sanctuary locates the origin of the divine word in the cult. While the unframed form of first-person divine speech in Ps 91:14-16 is problematic, the liturgical context of divine response to a devoted worshipper points to the view that these verses preserve words of a prophetic intermediary. The similar pattern of response to lament with unframed divine speech in Assyrian sources lends support to this possibility. Because of the historical retrospect in Psalm 68, the oracle introduced with a citation formula in verse 23 is probably secondary, in which case the location of the original citation is unknown. The brevity and lack of speech frame suggests that Ps 46:11 is most likely a secondary citation of a prophetic aphorism; and because of the passive verb frames, Psalm 87 probably only reports the sort of thing Yahweh would say about his beloved city rather than actual prophetic speech.

Chapter 6
Conclusion

6.1 The Central Question

A strong case can be made that prophets participated in worship from pre-exilic to post-exilic times. However, even if this is granted, the question remains: what traces of this prophetic speech are preserved in psalms? Two competing traditions of interpretation have developed. Mowinckel attempted to explain many psalms as a result of prophetic activity in the cult. Gunkel doubted that prophets contributed directly to psalmody, arguing that free, spontaneous prophecy is incompatible with a fixed liturgical agenda. Poetic or homiletical adaptation of prophetic style might account for such elements as first-person divine speech. Some recent scholarship has stressed the unified composition of psalms containing divine speech and argued for composition of the whole prior to performance in worship, without the involvement of actual prophets. Assyrian prophetic sources are relevant to this discussion. They attest to the existence of cult prophets in a culture relatively close to that of the OT, thereby inviting functional, form-critical, and thematic comparisons. The Assyrian prophetic collections and their use also invite comparison to literary composition and subsequent performance of psalms.

6.2 Cultic Functions of Assyrian Prophets and the OT

Temples played an important role in state politics. Since Assyrian prophets were often located in temple communities, it is not surprising that their prophecies functioned to legitimise the relationship between the king and the divine realm. In addition, Assyrian cult prophets advocated the maintenance of temples and sacrifices. They gave divine response to inquiry and lament from the king, which may have included communal concerns. Evidence also suggests that the role of cultic mediator was a general one not limited to royal service. These functions correspond to descriptions of prophets in the OT as voices of divine authority in royal affairs and as intermediaries who sometimes functioned at shrines. One might then expect psalms containing prophetic words that legitimise royal power (Psalms 2; 89; 110; 132), advance cultic orthodoxy and practices (Psalms 50; 68; 81; 95; 132) or address prayers and laments (Psalms 12; 60; 75; 82; 91; 132) to arise from this setting, even as Assyrian cultic prophecy functioned in similar ways.

6.3 Comparison of Assyrian Prophecies and Psalms

Because Assyrian prophecies concern the king, some royal psalms are their closest counterpart in the Psalter, corresponding not only in form-critical style and thematic content but also in function. The correspondence in both form and function strengthens the legitimacy of the comparison. Psalms 2 and 110 grant divine authority to the king and are best understood as part of enthronement ritual. The form, style and function of Assyrian cultic prophecies (particularly SAA 9 2.4; 3.3; and SAA 9 7, but also Egyptian enthronement oracles) support this interpretation. While Psalm 132 does not correlate structurally with any single Assyrian oracle, the thematic and stylistic elements are similar. As in Psalm 132, Assyrian prophecy played a role in royal prayers, cultic initiatives and the unification of the political and religious spheres. Psalm 89 shares many themes and phrases with Assyrian oracles, and the order of many elements corresponds to SAA 9 1.6. Regarding Psalm 89, the importance of Assyrian prophecy in royal lament is also noteworthy. The presence of Assyrian cultic prophecy in a seventh-century monarchic context lends support to arguments that prophets served the king in pre-exilic Israel as well. Psalms 110, 2, 132 and 89 likely preserve elements of this royal cultic prophecy.

The Asaphite psalms 50, 75, 81 and 82 (together with Psalm 95) contain framed, first-person divine speech as well as prophetic form and content. While the similarities to Assyrian prophetic texts are not as clear as for royal psalms, several features of Assyrian oracles support the prophetic authenticity of these psalms. First, the common use of the divine self-identification formula in Assyrian prophecies associates the similar use in Psalms 50 and 81 with prophetic speech. On the basis of form-critical similarity, SAA 9 3 may support the prophetic origin of Psalm 81, both having functioned as part of covenant renewal. Concern for cultic affairs among Assyrian prophets supports the idea that cultic exhortations in Psalm 50 are prophetic, not necessarily priestly. Both Psalm 50 and SAA 9 3.3 utilise theophany in the proclamation of divine self-identification. No form-critical correlations exist between Assyrian oracles and Psalm 75; however, the deity's commitment to cosmic stability and the promise to cut off enemies are themes common to both. The concern for cosmic order appears in Psalm 82 as well as the revelation of proceedings in the divine council, which appears in SAA 9 9. Yahweh's judgment of other deities in Psalm 82 is mirrored to a degree by Ištar's implicit warning in SAA 9 3.4. These similarities support the argument that prophetic speech is the proper context in which to understand the psalm. The classification of Psalms 50 and 81 as "sermons", whether Levitical or deuteronomistic, fails for lack of clear genre characterisation. On the other hand, the stylistic similarities with Assyrian prophecies point to an origin in cultic prophecy. Therefore, Psalms 50, 75, 81 and 82 are best understood as the product of cultic prophecy. If Psalms 50 and 81 are considered prophetic, then the possibility remains that the closely related Psalm 95 originated from cultic prophecy as well.

The role of Assyrian prophets as intermediaries in contexts of lament provides comparative evidence for a similar setting of Psalms 12, 60 and 91. In addition, form-critical comparisons exist for the introduction formula of Ps 12:6 as well as use of the metaphor of "arising". Assyrian oracles offer a close thematic parallel to Psalm 60 in the encouragement of troops during military crisis and the naming of foreign enemies. While the unframed nature of first-person divine speech in Psalm 91 is problematic, Assyrian sources offer support for the view that it may be prophetic. Blessing with didactic intent in response to prayer and a shift in the person addressed are not incompatible with prophetic speech. Therefore, cultic prophecy offers the best explanation for the divine speech in these three psalms.

6.4 Psalm Composition and Performance

For some of the psalms examined in this study, the text points to a real cultic setting (e.g., in sanctuary [Ps 60:8], to worshippers [Ps 89:20], during ark procession [Ps 132:8], worship context [Ps 50:5; 75:2; 81:2-4]; and in other cases, a cultic setting is implied by the form and contents (lament [Psalms 12; 82; 89], coronation [Psalms 2; 110], blessing/apotropaic ritual [Psalm 91]). Therefore, framed first-person divine speech and other prophetic elements of style and content in these psalms need to be explained in a cultic setting.

Gunkel doubted that spontaneous prophetic speech in the cult resulted in psalmody; and even if a psalm contains words of God spoken prophetically in the first performance, subsequent performances would only be regarded as secondary citations. Other scholars point to the unified composition of psalms with diverse genre elements and argue that such compositions cannot be accounted for by cult prophetic speech. Therefore, the imitation of prophetic style by temple singers or congregational preachers who composed psalms in advance of performance has been suggested. However, there are several ways to envision the relationship between prophecy and psalmody that overcome objections to the incorporation of cultic prophecy in psalms. The following suggestions illustrate that actual prophetic composition and performance are not necessarily incompatible with liturgical settings.

First, as Mowinckel suggested, a prophet scheduled to appear at a fixed point in worship could easily prepare in advance an address that would be appropriate to the context. A composition prepared in advance, *to whatever degree*, is not incompatible with genuine prophetic phenomena.[1] Its original performance in worship classifies it as cultic prophecy. A prophet might be asked to contribute to a coronation ceremony in the temple (e.g., Psalm 110). Given the prophetic stature of a king, his own discourse might bring a prophetic element to the festivities (e.g., Psalm 2). Where intertextual unity between the divine speech and other component parts of the psalm is not an issue, psalm composition could incorporate elements that were originally voiced by different functionaries but redacted into a unified psalm after the original performance of these elements in worship. Psalm 81 incorporates an extended prophetic speech on covenant fidelity (Ps 81:5-17) as a response to a call to worship, possibly a festival celebrating the covenant (Ps 81:2-4). The conjunction between the two parts (כי, Ps 81:5) could be a scribal addition drawing two parts together that were originally perhaps more extensive and voiced by separate functionaries. The transitions in Ps 75:3 and Ps 95:7 present a similar possibility; however, in all three cases a single prophetic speaker could be responsible for the whole. In some cases where there is intertextual unity, cultic prophecy delivered in the course of worship is still possible. For Psalm 132, a prophet might respond to the prayer of Ps 132:1-10 with the corresponding words of Ps 132:11-18, knowing in advance the outline of the prayer that would be offered.

Second, a prophet's contribution to a psalm must not be restricted to first-person divine speech only. This consideration is important when there is tight intertextual unity between different parts of a psalm. Psalm 12 is likely a prophetic lament, the whole of which was offered by a single prophetic speaker. Similarly, Psalm 89 as a whole may be a prophetic adaptation of the lament form performed by one individual. In each case, the integration of divine speech with the remaining parts of the psalm is understandable if the speaker of the whole is a prophet. The transition in Psalm 91 from second-person address to third-person, incorporating promissory elements in a didactic man-

---

[1] The reports of prior composition and subsequent delivery of prophetic speech in Jeremiah are illustrative of this type of prophecy, regardless of whether these are genuine prophecies of Jeremiah or reconstructed prose sermons (2:1-2; 7:1-2; 11:6; 17:19-21; 18:1-5; 19:1-3, 14-15; 22:1-2; 26:1-2; 27:1-4; 39:15-16).

ner, is not incompatible with a single spokesperson. Psalms 50 and 82 present no difficulty for imagining a single prophetic speaker. The prophet in these cases is responsible for the composition and performance of the whole psalm.

Third, granting a high degree of rhetorical skill, a prophet might be able to address a situation at hand by spontaneous oral composition, in some circumstances echoing very closely the themes and phrases of other functionaries in the setting. While none of the psalms studied necessarily originated in this way, it cannot be ruled out as a possibility.[2]

Fourth, Psalm 108 demonstrates the reality of secondary citation of prophetic speech in a psalm. If a psalm contains a secondary citation, the citation may not have originated in the cult. Ps 68:23-24 offers an example of secondary citation for which the original setting of the prophecy is unknown. However, in the case of Ps 108:8-10, the source from which it was drawn (Ps 60:8-10) was probably cultic prophecy. Even though Ps 60:8-10 might itself be a secondary citation, it attests to its own origin in the sanctuary.

Assyrian prophecy makes a significant contribution to the question of cultic prophecy, textual composition, and subsequent performance of biblical psalms. Assyrian prophetic oracles displaying considerable rhetorical sophistication were delivered orally and immediately recorded in a temple setting. Even though Assyrian prophecies were deposited in the royal archive, they nevertheless illustrate a process whereby oral cultic prophecy became inscribed for future use.[3] In the case of SAA 9 3, additional redactional activity is evident. Here, separate oracles from two different deities were collected on one tablet with liturgical instructions inserted. This is significant because it illustrates the movement from oral to written composition for the

---

[2] Oral composition commonly involves creation of new poems, even to suit particular occasions, based upon stock phrases and accepted patterns, the presence of which points to the cultic origin of some types of psalms (Culley 1967: 6-7, 29, 112-13). While Culley does not include any of the psalms examined in this monograph (cf. his chart on p. 103), one might presume that oral composition is possible in the case of some cultic prophecy and that subsequent recording of such compositions is also possible.

[3] However, FLP 1674 was deposited in the temple archive.

purpose of subsequent liturgical performance.[4] Another significant example is SAA 3 13, which illustrates the incorporation of cultic prophecy with royal prayer in what probably reflects a real cultic situation. On the basis of the inclusion of an oracle of salvation in the Akitu kingship ritual, van der Toorn (1987: 93) suggested that such oracles were placed into frozen liturgical form for such occasions. Indeed, repeat performances of prophetic words could retain a degree of freshness (cf. Jeremiah 36). During repeated performances of Psalm 2, the divine words must have been construed as a fresh oracle able to renew divine legitimation of kingship, not unlike SAA 9 3, which Parpola (1997: LXIV) proposed was performed live by the prophet at the enthronement ceremony. The Akitu and Assyrian enthronement rituals suggest that a renewal festival might be the type of setting in which prophetic words originating in the cult could be reused and performed by either a prophet or priest. Psalms 50, 81 and 95 are appropriate to this context, as is Psalm 132 to a festival involving the ark. In this respect, one might wish for more light on the role of Assyrian prophets whose cultic activities were frequent enough to merit institutional support in Assyrian temples, since it might illustrate the kinds of activities that engaged Israelite prophets in the cult. Prophetic lament liturgies could be archived for appropriate use during difficult times in the life of the community or an individual (cf. Psalms 12; 60; 91). Assyrian cult prophets appear to have been on call for such occasions, and perhaps archived oracles served as exemplars for such service. Therefore, the possible scenarios of composition and performance are varied enough to accommodate prophecy in both liturgy and psalms.

---

4   Schaper (2003) stresses that written prophecy frequently became the basis of oral delivery (cf. Ezek 2:7-3:4; Hab 2:2). Niditch (1996: 119-20) also stresses that the relationships between oral and written prophecy and performance is rich with possibilities.

6.5 Diachronic Continuity of Cultic Prophecy

Evidence is not sufficient to date the composition of all psalms examined in this study; but the dates that can be suggested are relevant. With the exception of Psalm 89, which may be early exilic, the royal psalms (Psalms 2; 110; 132) correspond to a real monarchic setting and are therefore pre-exilic. The Asaphite collection (which includes Psalms 50; 75; 81; 82) may have closed, at least preliminarily, in the early exilic period. Psalm 12 is likely pre-exilic by virtue of its place in the first Davidic Psalter. Psalms 60 and 68 are suitable to a pre-exilic military context. Psalms 91 and 95 offer no clues. Therefore, on the basis of Psalms evidence, cultic prophets were active in pre-exilic and exilic times and may have re-emerged in the Second Temple. This is consistent with OT evidence from outside the psalms that there was a continuity of classical prophecy and that prophets were active in the cult before and after the exile.

6.6 Cultic Prophecy in the Psalms

Discussing the real life setting from which psalms arose, Gunkel (1933: 10; 1998: 7) offered the example of a prophet shouting before the congregation gathered in the sanctuary. Ironically, the prophet's liturgical role is eclipsed in Gunkel's ensuing discussions of the origin of prophetic elements in psalms. Doubts about the contribution of cult-prophetic speech to psalmody remain in current debate. Examination of psalms containing first-person divine speech has demonstrated their authentic prophetic character. Complementing the first-person divine speech are framing devices, formal structure, rhetoric, themes, as well as life settings, which conform to what ancient Israelite worshippers would have expected of actual prophetic speech. Alternative explanations of prophetic speech in psalms, such as the sermon or poetic imitation, lack comparable examples external to psalms. On the other hand, Assyrian cultic prophecies, arising from a culture not far removed from ancient Israel, parallel the characteristics of prophetic speech found in psalms. In addition, the Assyrian sources support possible composition and performance scenarios that overcome objections raised against the compatibility of genuine prophecy with psalmody. In conclusion, a model of cultic prophecy remains the best explanation for the origin of psalms containing first-person divine speech.

Bibliography

Ackroyd, Peter R. (1968). *Exile and Restoration: A Study of Hebrew Thought of the Sixth Century BC*, OTL, London: SCM Press.

Adler, Hans-Peter (1976). *Das Akkadische des Königs Tušratta von Mitanni*, AOAT 201, Neukirchener: Butzon and Bercker.

Allen, Leslie C. (1983). *Psalms 101-150*, WBC 21, Waco: Word Books.

Anderson, A. A. (1972). *The Book of Psalms*, NCB, London: Marshall, Morgan & Scott.

Baines, John (1995). "Kingship, Definition of Culture, and Legitimation", *Ancient Egyptian Kingship*, David B. O'Connor and David P. Silverman, eds. (Probleme der Ägyptologie 9; Leiden, New York, Köln: E. J. Brill): 3-47.

Baines, John (1998). "Ancient Egyptian Kingship: Official Forms, Rhetoric, Context", *King and Messiah in Israel and the Ancient Near East: Proceedings of the Oxford Old Testament Seminar*, John Day, ed. (JSOTSup 270; Sheffield: Sheffield Academic Press): 16-53.

Balentine, Samuel E. (1997). "'You Can't Pray a Lie': Truth and Fiction in the Prayers of Chronicles", *The Chronicler as Historian*, M. Patrick Graham, Kenneth G. Hoglund and Steven L. McKenzie, eds. (JSOTSup 238; Sheffield: Sheffield Academic Press): 246-267.

Barstad, Hans M. (1993). "No Prophets? Recent Developments in Biblical Research and Ancient Near Eastern Prophecy", *JSOT* 57: 39-60.

Becking, Bob (1990). "'Wie Töpfe Sollst Du Sie Zerschmeißen'. Mesopotamische Parallel zu Psalm 2,9b", *ZAW* 102: 59-79.

Begrich, Joachim (1934). "Das priesterliche Heilsorakel", *ZAW* 54: 81-92.

Bell, Lanny (1985). "Luxor Temple and the Cult of the Royal Ka", *JNES* 44: 251-294.

Bellinger, W. H., Jr. (1984). *Psalmody and Prophecy*, JSOTSup 27, Sheffield: JSOT Press.

Ben Zvi, Ehud and Michael H. Floyd, eds. (2000). *Writings and Speech in Israelite and Ancient Near Eastern Prophecy*, SBLSS 10, Atlanta: Society of Biblical Literature.

Booij, Thijs (1978). *Godswoorden in de Psalmen: Hun Funktie en Achtergronden*, Amsterdam: Rodopi.

Booij, Thijs (1984). "The Background of the Oracle in Psalm 81", *Bib* 65: 465-475.

Booij, Thijs (1987). "Some Observations on Psalm LXXXVII", *VT* 37: 16-25.

Booij, Thijs (1991). "Psalm CX: 'Rule in the Midst of Your Foes!'", *VT* 41: 396-407.

Booij, Thijs (1994). *Psalmen deel III (81-110)*, De Prediking van het Oude Testament, Nijkerk: G. F. Callenbach B. V.

Borger, Riekele (1967). *Die Inschriften Asarhaddons Königs von Assyrien*, Archiv für Orientforschung Beiheft 9, Osnabrück: Biblio-Verlag.

Breasted, James Henry (1906a). *Ancient Records of Egypt II*, Ancient Records 2, Chicago: The University of Chicago Press.

Breasted, James Henry (1906b). *Ancient Records of Egypt III*, Ancient Records 3, Chicago: The University of Chicago Press.

Burrelli, Robert Joseph Jr. (1993). "A Study of Psalm 91 With Special Reference to the Theory That It Was Intended as a Protection Against Demons and Magic", Ph.D. Dissertation, University of Cambridge, Cambridge.

Buss, Martin J. (1963). "The Psalms of Asaph and Korah", *JBL* 82: 382-392.

Butler, S. A. L. (1998). *Mesopotamian Concepts of Dreams and Dream Rituals*, AOAT 258, Münster: Ugarit-Verlag.

Christensen, Duane L. (1975). *Transformations of the War Oracle in Old Testament Prophecy: Studies in the Oracles*

Against the Nations, Harvard Dissertations in Religion 3, Missoula: Scholars Press.
Clements, Ronald E. (1965). *Prophecy and Covenant*, London: SCM Press.
Clements, Ronald E. (1976). *A Century of Old Testament Study*, Guildford and London: Lutterworth Press.
Clifford, Richard J. (1980). "Psalm 89: A Lament Over the Davidic Ruler's Continued Failure", *HTR* 73: 35-47.
Cole, Steven W. and Peter Machinist (1998). *Letters from Priests to the Kings Esarhaddon and Assurbanipal*, SAA 13, Helsinki: University of Helsinki Press.
Cooper, Jerrold (2000). "Assyrian Prophecies, the Assyrian Tree, and the Mesopotamian Origins of Jewish Monotheism, Greek Philosophy, Christian Theology, Gnosticism, and Much More", *JAOS* 120: 430-444.
Craigie, Peter C. (1983). *Psalms 1-50*, WBC 19, Waco: Word Books.
Croft, Steven J. L. (1987). *The Identity of the Individual in the Psalms*, JSOTSup 44, Sheffield: JSOT Press.
Cross, Frank Moore (1973). *Canaanite Myth and Hebrew Epic: Essays in the History of the Religion of Israel*, Cambridge: Harvard University Press.
Cryer, Frederick (1994). *Divination in Ancient Israel and Its Near Eastern Environment*, JSOTSup 142, Sheffield: JSOT Press.
Crystal, David (1997). *A Dictionary of Linguistics and Phonetics*, 4th Edition, Oxford: Blackwell.
Culley, Robert C. (1967). *Oral Formulaic Language in the Biblical Psalms*, Near and Middle Eastern Series 4, Toronto: University of Toronto Press.

Davies, G. Henton (1973). "Psalm 95", *ZAW* 85: 183-195.
Day, John (1998). "The Canaanite Inheritance of the Israelite Monarchy", *King and Messiah in Israel and the Ancient Near East: Proceedings of the Oxford Old Testament Seminar*, John Day, ed. (JSOTSup 270; Sheffield: Sheffield Academic Press): 72-90.

Day, John (2004). "How Many Pre-exilic Psalms Are There?", *In Search of Pre-exilic Israel: Proceedings of the Oxford Old Testament Seminar*, John Day, ed. (JSOTS 406; London, New York: T.& T. Clark): 225-250.
Delitzsch, Franz (1894). *Biblical Commentary on the Psalms I*, David Eaton, trans., London: Hodder and Stoughton.
Delitzsch, Franz (1902). *Biblical Commentary on the Psalms II*, David Eaton, trans., London: Hodder and Stoughton, 2nd Edition.
Dever, William G. (1971). "Archaeological Methods and Results: A Review of Two Recent Publications", *Or* 40: 459-471.
Dijk, J. J. A. van (1962). *XVIII. vorläufiger Bericht über die von dem Deutschen Archäologischen Institut und der Deutschen Orient-Gesellschaft aus Mitteln der Deutschen Forschungsgemeinschaft unternommenen Ausgrabungen in Uruk-Warka*, Berlin: Deutsches Archäologisches Institut.
Dijkstra, Meindert (1980). *Gods voorstelling: Predikatieve expressie van zelfopenbaring in oudoosterse teksten en Deutero-Jesaja*, Dissertationes Neerlandicae, Series Theologica 2, Kampen.
Duhm, B. (1899). *Die Psalmen*, Leipzig: J. C. B. Mohr.
Durand, Jean-Marie (1988). *Archives épistolaires de Mari I/1*, Archives Royales de Mari 26, Paris: Éditions Recherche sur les Civilisations.

Eaton, John H. (1976). *Kingship and the Psalms*, Studies in Biblical Theology, London: SCM Press.
Eerdmans, B. D. (1947). *The Religion of Israel*, Leiden: Universitaire Pers Leiden.
Eichrodt, Walther (1933). *Theologie des Alten Testaments*, Leipzig: Hinrichs'sche Buchhandlung.
Eichrodt, Walther (1961). *Theology of the Old Testament*, J. A. Baker, trans., London: SCM Press.
Eissfeldt, Otto (1934). *Einleitung in das Alte Testament*, Tübingen: J. C. B. Mohr.
Eissfeldt, Otto (1948). "Alfred Haldar: Associations of Cult Prophets among the Ancient Semites", *TLZ* 73: cols. 151-155.

Ellis, Maria deJong (1987). "The Goddess Kititum Speaks to King Ibalpiel: Oracle Texts from Ishchali", *MARI* 5: 235-266.
Ellis, Maria deJong (1989). "Observations on Mesopotamian Oracles and Prophetic Texts: Literary and Historiographical Considerations", *JCS* 41: 127-185.
Emerton, J. A. (1971). "The Riddle of Genesis XIV", *VT* 21: 403-439.

Fales, F. M. and J. N. Postgate (1992). *Imperial Administrative Records, Part I: Palace and Temple Administration*, SAA 7, Helsinki: University of Helsinki Press.
Fichtner, J. (1961). "Propheten IIB Seit Amos", *Die Religion in Geschichte und Gegenwart*, Kurt Galling, ed. (Tübingen: J. C. B. Mohr): V, cols. 616-627.
Fishbane, Michael (1985). *Biblical Interpretation in Ancient Israel*, Oxford: Clarendon Press.
Fleming, Daniel (1993). "*Nābû* and *Munabbiātu*: Two New Syrian Religious Personnel", *JAOS* 113: 175-183.
Floyd, Michael H. (1992). "Psalm LXXXIX: A Prophetic Complaint About the Fulfillment of an Oracle", *VT* 42: 442-457.
Fretheim, Terence E. (1967). "Psalm 132: A Form-Critical Study", *JBL* 86: 289-300.

Gakuru, Griphus (2000). *An Inner-Biblical Exegetical Study of the Davidic Covenant and the Dynastic Oracle*, Mellen Biblical Press Series 58, Lewiston: The Edwin Mellen Press.
Gerstenberger, Erhard S. (1988). *Psalms Part 1 with an Introduction to Cultic Poetry*, FOTL XIV, Grand Rapids: Eerdmans.
Gerstenberger, Erhard S. (1997). "Predigt II", *Theologische Realenzyklopädie*, Gerhard Müller ed. (Berlin, New York: Walter de Gruyter): XXVII, 231-235.
Gerstenberger, Erhard S. (2001). *Psalms Part 2 and Lamentations*, FOTL XV, Grand Rapids: Eerdmans.

Gordon, Robert P. (1995). "Where Have All the Prophets Gone? The 'Disappearing' Israelite Prophet Against the Background of Ancient Near Eastern Prophecy", *BBR* 5: 67-86.

Goulder, Michael D. (1996). *The Psalms of Asaph and the Pentateuch: Studies in the Psalter, III*, JSOTSup 233, Sheffield: Sheffield Academic Press.

Grabbe, Lester L. (1993). "Prophets, Priests, Diviners and Sages in Ancient Israel", *Of Prophets' Visions and the Wisdom of Sages: Essays in Honour of R. Norman Whybray on his Seventieth Birthday*, Heather A. McKay and David J. A. Clines, eds. (JSOTSup 162; Sheffield: JSOT Press): 43-62.

Grabbe, Lester L. (1995). *Priests, Prophets, Diviners, Sages: A Socio-historical Study of Religious Specialists in Ancient Israel*, Valley Forge: Trinity Press International.

Gressmann, Hugo (1914). "Die literarische Analyse Deuterojesajas", *ZAW* 34: 254-297.

Gunkel, Hermann (1904). *Ausgewählte Psalmen*, Göttingen: Vandenhoeck and Ruprecht.

Gunkel, Hermann (1913). "Psalmen", *Die Religion in Geschichte und Gegenwart*, Friedrich Michael Schiele and Leopold Zscharnack, eds. (Tübingen: J. C. B. Mohr): IV, cols. 1927-49.

Gunkel, Hermann (1926). *Die Psalmen*, Göttingen: Vandenhoeck and Ruprecht.

Gunkel, Hermann and Joachim Begrich (1933). *Einleitung in die Psalmen: Die Gattungen der religiösen Lyrik Israels*, Göttingen: Vandenhoeck and Ruprecht.

Gunkel, Hermann and Joachim Begrich (1998). *Introduction to Psalms: The Genres of the Religious Lyric of Israel*, James D. Nogalski, trans., Macon: Mercer University Press.

Haldar, Alfred (1945). *Associations of Cult Prophets Among the Ancient Semites*, Uppsala: Almquist and Wiksells Boktryckeri Ab.

Hämeen-Anttila, Jaakko (2000). *A Sketch of Neo-Assyrian Grammar*, SAAS 13, Helsinki: University of Helsinki Press.

Haney, Randy G. (2002). *Text and Concept Analysis in Royal Psalms*, Studies in Biblical Literature 30, New York: Peter Lang.

Harner, Philip B. (1969). "The Salvation Oracle in Second Isaiah", *JBL* 88: 418-434.

Harris, James G. III (1970). "Prophetic Oracles in the Psalter", Th.D. Dissertation, Southern Baptist Theological Seminary, Louisville.

Hayes, J. H. (1968). "The Usage of Oracles Against Foreign Nations in Ancient Israel", *JBL* 87: 81-92.

Heim, Knut M. (1998). "The (God-)Forsaken King of Psalm 89: A Historical and Intertextual Enquiry", *King and Messiah in Israel and the Ancient Near East: Proceedings of the Oxford Old Testament Seminar*, John Day, ed. (JSOTSup 270; Sheffield: Sheffield Academic Press): 296-322.

Herrmann, Siegfried (1986). "Die Königsnovelle in Ägypten und in Israel: Ein Beitrag zur Gattungsgeschichte in den Geschichtsbüchern des Alten Testaments", *Gesammelte Studien zur Geschichte und Theologie des Alten Testaments*. (Theologische Bücherei 75; München: Chr. Kaiser Verlag): 120-144.

Heschel, Abraham J. (1962). *The Prophets*, New York and Evanston: Harper and Row.

Hesse, Franz (1953). "Wurzelt die prophetische Gerichtsrede im israelitischen Kult?", *ZAW* 65: 45-53.

Hilber, John W. (2003). "Psalm cx in the Light of Assyrian Prophecies", *VT* 53: 353-366.

Hillers, Delbert R. (1968). "Ritual Procession of the Ark and Ps 132", *CBQ* 30: 48-55.

Hoffmeier, James K. (1997). "The King as God's Son in Egypt and Israel", *JSSEA* 24: 28-38.

Holladay, William L. (1989). *Jeremiah 2*, Hermeneia, Minneapolis: Fortress Press.

Hölscher, Gustav (1914). *Die Propheten: Untersuchungen zur Religionsgeschichte Israels*, Leipzig: J. C. Hinrichssche Buchhandlung.

Hossfeld, Frank-Lothar (1994). "Psalm 95: Gattungsgeschichtliche, kompositionskritische und bibeltheologische Anfragen", *Neue Wege der Psalmenforschung: Für Walter Beyerlin*, Klaus Seybold and Erich Zenger, eds. (HBS 1; Freiburg, Basel, Wien: Herder): 29-44.

Hossfeld, Frank-Lothar (1998). "Das Prophetische in den Psalmen: Zur Gottesrede der Asafpsalmen im Vergleich mit der des ersten und zweiten Davidpsalters", *Ich bewirke das Heil und erschaffe das Unheil (Jesaja 45, 7). Studien zur Botschaft der Propheten: Festschrift für Lothar Ruppert zum 65. Geburtstag*, Friedrich Diedrich and Bernd Willmes, eds. (FB 88; Wurzburg: Echter).

Hossfeld, Frank-Lothar and Erich Zenger (1993). *Die Psalmen I (Psalm 1-50)*, NEchtBAT, Würzburg: Echter.

Hossfeld, Frank-Lothar and Erich Zenger (2000). *Psalmen 51-100*, HTKAT, Freiburg, Basel, Wien: Herder.

Hossfeld, Frank-Lothar and Erich Zenger (2002). *Die Psalmen II (Psalm 51-100)*, NEchtBAT, Würzburg: Echter.

Huffmon, Herbert B. (1968). "Prophecy in the Mari Letters", *BA* 31: 101-124.

Huffmon, Herbert B. (2000). "A Company of Prophets: Mari, Assyria, Israel", *Prophecy in Its Ancient Near Eastern Context: Mesopotamian, Biblical, and Arabian Perspectives*, Martti Nissinen, ed. (SBLSS 13; Atlanta: Society of Biblical Literature): 47-70.

Hunger, Hermann (1992). *Astrological Reports to Assyrian Kings*, SAA 8, Helsinki: Helsinki University Press.

Hupfeld, Hermann (1888). *Die Psalmen*. 3rd Edition, Vol. 1, Gotha: Friedrich Andreas Perthes.

Hurowitz, Victor (1998). "True Light on the Urim and Thummim", *JQR* 88: 263-274.

Illman, Karl-Johan (1976). *Thema und Tradition in den Asaf-Psalmen*, Publications of the Research Institute of the Åbo Akademi Foundation 13, Åbo: Stiftelsens för Åbo Akademi.

Ishida, Tomoo (1977). *The Royal Dynasties in Ancient Israel: A Study on the Formation and Development of Royal-Dynastic Ideology*, BZAW 142, Berlin, New York: Walter de Gruyter.

Jacquet, Louis (1975). *Les Psaumes et le coeur de l'Homme: Etude textuelle, littéraire et doctrinale (Psaumes 1 à 41)*, Belgium: Duculot.

Jacquet, Louis (1979). *Les Psaumes et le coeur de l'Homme: Etude textuelle, littéraire et doctrinale (Psaumes 101 à 150)*, Belgium: Duculot.

Japhet, Sara (1993). *I & II Chronicles: A Commentary*, OTL, Louisville: Westminster John Knox Press.

Jensen, Joseph E. (2001). "Psalm 75: Its Poetic Context and Structure", *CBQ* 63: 416-429.

Jeremias, Jörg (1970). *Kultprophetie und Gerichtsverkündigung in der späten Königzeit Israels*, WMANT 35, Neukirchen-Vluyn: Neukirchener Verlag.

Johnson, Aubrey R. (1935/36). "The Prophet in Israelite Worship", *ExpTim* 47: 312-19.

Johnson, Aubrey R. (1955). *Sacral Kingship in Ancient Israel*, Cardiff: University of Wales Press.

Johnson, Aubrey R. (1962). *The Cultic Prophet in Ancient Israel*. 2nd Edition, Cardiff: University of Wales Press.

Johnson, Aubrey R. (1979). *The Cultic Prophet and Israel's Psalmody*, Cardiff: University of Wales Press.

Jones, G. H. (1965). "'The Decree of Yahweh (Ps. II 7)'", *VT* 15: 336-344.

Jong, Matthijs de (2001). "Prophecy in Context", M.St. Dissertation, University of Oxford, Oxford.

Joüon, Paul and T. Muraoka (1996). *A Grammar of Biblical Hebrew-Part Three: Syntax*, T. Muraoka, trans., Subsidia Biblica 14/II, Rome: Pontifical Biblical Institute.

Kataja, L. and R. Whiting (1995). *Grants, Decrees and Gifts of the Neo-Assyrian Period*, SAA 12, Helsinki: University of Helsinki Press.

Keel, Othmar (1978). *The Symbolism of the Biblical World: Ancient Near Eastern Iconography and the Book of Psalms*, New York: Seabury Press.

Kelso, James Leon (1993). "Bethel", *The New Encyclopedia of Archaeological Excavations in the Holy Land*, Ephraim

Stern, ed. (Jerusalem: The Israel Exploration Society & Carta): I, 192-194.

Kemp, Barry J. (1991). *Ancient Egypt: Anatomy of a Civilization*, London, New York: Routledge.

Kim, Ee Kon (1984). "A Study of the Rapid Change of Mood in the Lament Psalms, with Special Inquiry into the Impetus for its Expression", Ph.D. Dissertation, Union Theological Seminary, Richmond.

Kim, Ee Kon (1999). "Holy War Ideology and the Rapid Shift of Mood in Psalm 3", *On the Way to Nineveh: Essays in Honor of George M. Landes*, Stephen L. Cook and S. C. Winter, eds. (ASOR Books 4; Atlanta: Scholars Press): 77-93.

Kirkpatrick, A. F. (1898). *The Book of Psalms: Books II & III*, Cambridge: Cambridge University Press, 1898.

Klatt, Werner (1969). *Hermann Gunkel*, Göttingen: Vandenhoeck and Ruprecht.

Klein, Ralph W. (1995). "Reflections on Historiography in the Account of Jehoshaphat", *Pomegranates and Golden Bells: Studies in Biblical, Jewish, and Near Eastern Ritual, Law and Literature in Honor of Jacob Milgrom*, David P. Wright, David Noel Freedman and Avi Hurvitz, eds. (Winona Lake: Eisenbrauns): 643-657.

Klein, W. C. (1963). "Prophecy, Prophets", *Dictionary of the Bible*, Frederick C. Grant and H. H. Rowley, eds. (Edinburgh: T.& T. Clark): 800-809.

Kleinig, John W. (1993). *The Lord's Song: The Basis, Function and Significance of Choral Music in Chronicles*, JSOTSup 156, Sheffield: JSOT Press.

Knoppers, Gary N. (1997). "Ancient Near Eastern Royal Grants and the Davidic Covenant: A Parallel?", *JAOS* 116: 670-697.

Koch, Klaus (2002). "Der König als Sohn Gottes in Ägypten und Israel", *"Mein Sohn bist du" (Ps 2,7): Studien zu den Königspsalmen*, Hans-Josef Klauck and Erich Zenger, eds. (SBS 192; Stuttgart: Katholisches Bibelwerk): 1-32.

Koenen, Klaus (1996). *Gottesworte in den Psalmen: Eine formgeschichtliche Untersuchung*, Biblische-Theologische Studien 30, Neukirchen-Vluyn: Neukirchener Verlag.

Kraus, Hans-Joachim (1961). *Psalmen I*. 2nd Edition, BKAT 15/1, Neukirchen-Vluyn: Neukirchener Verlag.
Kraus, Hans-Joachim (1966). *Worship in Israel: A Cultic History of the Old Testament*, Oxford: Basil Blackwell.
Kraus, Hans-Joachim (1978a). *Psalmen 1-59*. 5th Edition, BKAT 15/1, Neukirchen-Vluyn: Neukirchener Verlag.
Kraus, Hans-Joachim (1978b). *Psalmen 60-150*. 5th Edition, BKAT 15/2, Neukirchen-Vluyn: Neukirchener Verlag.
Kraus, Hans-Joachim (1988). *Psalms 1-59*, C. Oswald Hilton, trans., Minneapolis: Augsburg.
Kraus, Hans-Joachim (1989). *Psalms 60-150*, C. Oswald Hilton, trans., Minneapolis: Augsburg.
Kselman, John S. (1985). "Psalm 101: Royal Confession and Divine Oracle", *JSOT* 33: 45-62.
Küchler, Friedrich (1918). "Das priesterliche Orakel in Israel und Juda", *Abhandlungen zur semitischen Religionskunde und Sprachwissenschaft: Wolf Wilhelm Grafen von Baudissin zum 26. September 1917*, Wilhelm Frankenberg and Friedrich Küchler, eds. (BZAW 33; Giessen: Alfred Topelmann Verlag): 285-301.

Laato, Antti (1992). "Psalm 132 and the Development of the Jerusalemite/Israelite Royal Ideology", *CBQ* 54: 49-66.
Laato, Antti (1996). *History and Ideology in the Old Testament Prophetic Literature: A Semiotic Approach to the Reconstruction of the Proclamation of the Historical Prophets*, ConBOT 41, Stockholm: Almquist and Wiksells Boktryckeri Ab.
Laato, Antti (1997). *A Star Is Rising: The Historical Development of the Old Testament Royal Ideology and the Rise of the Jewish Messianic Expectations*, University of South Florida International Studies in Formative Christianity and Judaism 5, Atlanta: Scholars Press.
Laato, Antti (1998). "The Royal Covenant Ideology in Judah", *"Lasset uns Brücken bauen." Collected Communications to the XVth Congress of the International Organization for the Study of the Old Testament, Cambridge 1995*,

K. D. Schunck and M. Augustin, eds. (Beiträge zur Erforschung des Alten Testaments und des Antiken Judentums 42; Frankfurt: Peter Lang): 93-100.

Lafont, Bertrand (1985). "Le roi de Mari et les prophètes du dieu Adad", *RA*: 7-18.

Lambert, W. G. (1998). "Kingship in Ancient Mesopotamia", *King and Messiah in Israel and the Ancient Near East: Proceedings of the Oxford Old Testament Seminar*, John Day, ed. (JSOTSup 270; Sheffield: Sheffield Academic Press): 54-70.

Lambert, W. G. (2001/2002). "Review of Simo Parpola, *Assyrian Prophecies* (SAA 9)", *AfO* 48/49: 208-211.

Lemaire, André (1977). *Inscriptions Hébraïques. Tome I Les Ostraca*, Paris: Les éditions du Cerf.

Lemaire, André. (1986). "'Avec un sceptre de fer'. Ps. II,9 et l'archéologie", *BN* 32: 25-30.

Lindblom, J. (1962). *Prophecy in Ancient Israel*, Oxford: Basil Blackwell.

Lion, Brigitte (2000). "Les mentions de 'prophètes' dans la seconde moitié du IIe millénaire av. J.-C", *RA* 94: 21-32.

Livingstone, Alasdair (1989). *Court Poetry and Literary Miscellanea*, SAA 3, Helsinki: Helsinki University Press.

Loretz, Oswald (2002). *Psalmstudien: Kolometrie, Strophik und Theologie ausgewählter Psalmen*, BZAW 309, Berlin, New York: Walter de Gruyter.

Luukko, Mikko and Greta van Buylaere (2002). *The Political Correspondence of Esarhaddon*, SAA 16, Helsinki: University of Helsinki Press.

Mason, Rex (1982). "The Prophets of the Restoration", *Israel's Prophetic Tradition: Essays in Honour of Peter R. Ackroyd*, Richard Coggins, Anthony Phillips and Michael Knibb, eds. (Cambridge: Cambridge University Press): 137-154.

Mason, Rex (1990). *Preaching the Tradition: Homily and Hermeneutics after the Exile*, Cambridge: Cambridge University Press.

Mathias, Dietmar (1984). "'Levitische Predigt' und Deuteronomismus", *ZAW* 96: 23-49.

Mathys, Hans-Peter (2001). "Prophetie, Psalmengesang und Kultmusik in der Chronik", *Prophetie und Psalmen: Festschrift für Klaus Seybold zum 65. Geburtstag*, Beat Huwyler, Hans-Peter Mathys and Beat Weber, eds. (AOAT 280; Münster: Ugarit-Verlag): 281-96.

McDowell, A. G. (1990). *Jurisdiction in the Workmen's Community of Deir El-Medîna*, Leiden: Nederlands Instituut voor het Nabije Oosten.

McKane, William (1986). *Jeremiah*, ICC 1, Edinburgh: T.& T. Clark.

McKane, William (1996). *Jeremiah*, ICC 2, Edinburgh: T.& T. Clark.

Meier, Samuel A. (1992). *Speaking of Speaking: Marking Direct Discourse in the Hebrew Bible*, VTSup 46, Leiden, New York, Köln: E. J. Brill.

Melville, Sarah C. (1999). *The Role of Naqia/Zakutu in Sargonid Politics*, SAAS 9, Helsinki: Helsinki University Press.

Menzel, Brigitte (1981). *Assyrische Tempel: Untersuchungen zu Kult, Administration und Personal*, Studia Pohl: Series Maior 10/1, Rome: Biblical Institute Press.

Millard, Alan R. (1985). "La prophétie et l'écriture: Israël, Aram, Assyrie", *RHR* 202: 125-145.

Millard, Alan R. (1988). "King Og's Bed and Other Ancient Ironmongery", *Ascribe to the Lord: Biblical and Other Studies in Memory of Peter C. Craigie*, Lyle Eslinger and Glen Taylor, eds. (JSOTSup 67; Sheffield: JSOT Press): 481-492.

Miller, Cynthia L. (1996). *The Representation of Speech in Biblical Hebrew Narrative: A Linguistic Analysis*, Harvard Semitic Monographs 55, Atlanta: Scholars Press.

Miller, J. Maxwell (1970). "The Korahites of Southern Judah", *CBQ* 32: 58-68.

Moran, William L., ed. (1992). *The Amarna Letters*, Baltimore, London: Johns Hopkins University Press.

Moran, William L. (1993). "An Ancient Prophetic Oracle", *Biblische Theologie und gesellschaftlicher Wandel (Fest-*

schrift N. Lohfink), George Braulik, Walter Groß and Sean McEvenue, eds. (Freiburg: Herder): 252-59.

Motyer, J. A. (1962). "Prophecy, Prophets", *New Bible Dictionary*, J. D. Douglas, ed. (London: The Inter-Varsity Fellowship): 1036-1046.

Mowinckel, Sigmund (1921). *Psalmenstudien I: Āwän und die Individuellen Klagepsalmen*, Repr. Amsterdam: BRG / P. Schippers N.V., 1966.

Mowinckel, Sigmund (1922). *Psalmenstudien II: Das Thronbesteigungsfest Jahwäs und der Ursprung der Eschatologie*, Repr. Amsterdam: BRG / P. Schippers N.V., 1966.

Mowinckel, Sigmund (1923). *Psalmenstudien III: Kultprophetie und Prophetische Psalmen*, Repr. Amsterdam: BRG / P. Schippers N.V., 1966.

Mowinckel, Sigmund (1924). *Psalmenstudien VI: Die Psalmdichter*, Repr. Amsterdam: BRG / P. Schippers N.V., 1966.

Mowinckel, Sigmund (1951). *Offersang og Sangoffer*, Oslo: H. Aschehoug & Co.

Mowinckel, Sigmund (1962a). *The Psalms in Israel's Worship I*, D. R. Ap-Thomas, trans., Oxford: Blackwell.

Mowinckel, Sigmund (1962b). *The Psalms in Israel's Worship II*, D. R. Ap-Thomas, trans., Oxford: Blackwell.

Murnane, William J. and Edmund S. Meltzer (1995). *Texts from the Amarna Period in Egypt*, Writings from the Ancient World 5, Atlanta: Scholars Press.

Murray, Robert (1982). "Prophecy and Cult", *Israel's Prophetic Tradition: Essays in Honour of Peter R. Ackroyd*, Richard Coggins, Anthony Phillips and Michael Knibb, eds. (Cambridge: Cambridge University Press): 200-216.

Nasuti, Harry P. (1988). *Tradition History and the Psalms of Asaph*, SBLDS 88, Atlanta: Scholars Press.

Niditch, Susan (1996). *Oral World and Written Word: Ancient Israelite Literature*, Library of Ancient Israel, Louisville: Westminster John Knox Press.

Nissinen, Martti (1991). *Prophetie, Redaktion und Fortschreibung im Hoseabuch: Studien zum Werdegang eines Prophetenbuches im Lichte von Hos 4 und 11*, AOAT 231, Kevelaer.

Nissinen, Martti (1993). "Die Relevanz der neuassyrischen Prophetie für die alttestamentliche Forschung", *Mesopotamica, Ugaritica, Biblica: Festschrift für Kurt Bergerhof zur Vollendung seines 70. Lebensjahres am 7. Mai, 1992*, Manfred Dietrich and Oswald Loretz, eds. (AOAT 232; Kevelaer: Butzon and Bercker): 217-258.

Nissinen, Martti (1998a). "Prophecy Against the King in Neo-Assyrian Sources", *"Lasset uns Brücken bauen." Collected Communications to the XVth Congress of the International Organization for the Study of the Old Testament, Cambridge 1995*, Klaus-Dietrich Schunk and Matthias Augustin, eds. (Beiträge zur Erforschung des Alten Testaments und des antiken Judentum 42; Frankfurt: Peter Lang): 157-170.

Nissinen, Martti (1998b). *References to Prophecy in Neo-Assyrian Sources*, SAAS 7, Helsinki: University of Helsinki Press.

Nissinen, Martti, ed. (2000a). *Prophecy in Its Ancient Near Eastern Context: Mesopotamian, Biblical, and Arabian Perspectives*, SBLSS 13, Atlanta: Society of Biblical Literature.

Nissinen, Martti (2000b). "The Socioreligious Role of the Neo-Assyrian Prophets", *Prophecy in Its Ancient Near Eastern Context: Mesopotamian, Biblical, and Arabian Perspectives*, Martti Nissinen, ed. (SBLSS 13; Atlanta: Society of Biblical Literature): 89-114.

Nissinen, Martti (2000c). "Spoken, Written, Quoted, and Invented: Orality and Writtenness in Ancient Near Eastern Prophecy", *Writings and Speech in Israelite and Ancient Near Eastern Prophecy*, Ehud Ben Zvi and Michael H. Floyd, eds. (SBLSS 10; Atlanta: Society of Biblical Literature): 235-271.

Nissinen, Martti (2001). "City as Lofty as Heaven: Arbela and Other Cities in Neo-Assyrian Prophecy", *'Every City Shall Be Forsaken': Urbanism and Prophecy in Ancient Israel and the Near East*, Lester L. Grabbe and Robert D. Haak, eds. (JSOTSup 330; Sheffield: Sheffield Academic Press): 172-209.

Nissinen, Martti (2003a). "Das kritische Potential in der altorientalischen Prophetie", *Propheten in Mari, Assyrien und Israel*, Matthias Köckert and Martti Nissinen, eds. (FRLANT 201; Göttingen: Vandenhoeck and Ruprecht): 1-32.

Nissinen, Martti (2003b). "Fear Not: A Study on an Ancient Near Eastern Phrase", *The Changing Face of Form Criticism for the Twenty-First Century*, Marvin A. Sweeney and Ehud Ben Zvi, eds. (Grand Rapids, Cambridge: Eerdmans): 122-161.

Nissinen, Martti, C. L. Seow, et al. (2003). *Prophets and Prophecy in the Ancient Near East*, Writings from the Ancient World 12, Atlanta: Society of Biblical Literature.

O'Connor, David B. (1995). "Beloved of Maat, The Horizon of Re: The Royal Palace in New Kingdom Egypt", *Ancient Egyptian Kingship*, David B. O'Connor and David P. Silverman, eds. (Probleme der Ägyptologie 9; Leiden, New York, Köln: E. J. Brill): 263-300.

O'Connor, Michael (1980). *Hebrew Verse Structure*, Winona Lake: Eisenbrauns.

Oded, Bustenay (1992). *War, Peace and Empire: Justifications for War in Assyrian Royal Inscriptions*, Wiesbaden: Ludwig Reichert Verlag.

Oeming, M. (1989). "צוּר", *Theologisches Wörterbuch zum Alten Testament* (Stuttgart, Berlin, Köln: W. Kohlhammer): VI, cols. 930-936.

Ogden, Graham S. (1982). "Prophetic Oracles Against Foreign Nations and Psalms of Communal Lament: The Relationship of Psalm 137 to Jeremiah", *JSOT* 24: 89-97.

Ogden, Graham S. (1985). "Psalm 60: Its Rhetoric, Form, and Function", *JSOT* 31: 83-94.

Otto, Eckart (2002). "Politische Theologie in den Königpsalmen zwischen Ägypten und Assyrien. Die Herrscherlegitimation in den Psalmen 2 und 18 in ihren altorientalischen Kontexten", *"Mein Sohn bist du" (Ps 2,7): Studien zu den Königspsalmen*, Hans-Josef Klauck and Erich Zenger, eds. (SBS 192; Stuttgart: Katholisches Bibelwerk): 33-65.

Parkinson, R. B. (1991). *Voices from Ancient Egypt: An Anthology of Middle Kingdom Writings*, London: British Museum Press.

Parpola, Simo (1983). *Letters from Assyrian Scholars to the Kings Esarhaddon and Assurbanipal*, AOAT 5/2, Kevelaer: Butzon and Bercker.

Parpola, Simo (1993). *Letters from Assyrian and Babylonian Scholars*, SAA 10, Helsinki: University of Helsinki Press.

Parpola, Simo (1997). *Assyrian Prophecies*, SAA 9, Helsinki: Helsinki University Press.

Parpola, Simo (2000). "Monotheism in Ancient Assyria", *One God or Many? Conceptions of Divinity in the Ancient World*, Barbara N. Porter, ed. (Transactions of the Casco Bay Assyriological Institute): 165-209.

Parpola, Simo and Kazuko Watanabe (1988). *Neo-Assyrian Treaties and Loyalty Oaths*, SAA 2, Helsinki: University of Helsinki Press.

Pedersen, J. (1940). *Israel: Its Life and Culture*, III-IV, London: Oxford University Press.

Petersen, Allan Rosengren (1998). *The Royal God: Enthronement Festivals in Ancient Israel and Ugarit?*, JSOTSup 259, Sheffield: Sheffield Academic Press.

Petersen, David L. (1977). *Late Israelite Prophecy: Studies in Deutero-Prophetic Literature and in Chronicles*, SBLMS 23, Missoula: Scholars Press.

Petersen, David L. (2000). "Defining Prophecy and Prophetic Literature", *Prophecy in Its Ancient Near Eastern Context: Mesopotamian, Biblical, and Arabian Perspectives*, Martti Nissinen, ed. (SBLSS 13; Atlanta: Society of Biblical Literature): 33-44.

Ploeg, J. P. M. van der (1971). *Psalmen*, De Boeken van het Oude Testament VIIb, Roermond: J. J. Romen & Zonen.

Plöger, Otto (1951). "Priester und Prophet", *ZAW* 63: 157-192.

Pongratz-Leisten, Beate (1999). *Herrschaftswissen in Mesopotamien: Formen der Kommunikation zwischen Gott und König im 2. und 1. Jahrtausend v. Chr.*, SAAS 10, Helsinki: University of Helsinki Press.

Porteous, N. W. (1950-51). "Prophet and Priest in Israel", *ExpTim* 62: 4-9.

Porter, Barbara N. (1999). "Review of *Assyrian Prophecies*", *BO* 61: 685-690.

Porter, Barbara N. (2000). "The Anxiety of Multiplicity: Concepts of Divinity as One and Many in Ancient Assyria", *One God or Many? Concepts of Divinity in the Ancient World*, Barbara N. Porter, ed. (Transactions of the Casco Bay Assyriological Institute): 211-271.

Prinsloo, Gert T. M. (1998). "Man's Word-God's Word: A Theology of Antithesis in Psalm 12", *ZAW* 110: 390-402.

Pritchard, James B., ed. (1969). *Ancient Near Eastern Texts Relating to the Old Testament*, 3rd Edition, Princeton: Princeton University Press.

Quell, Gottfried (1956). "Der Kultprophet", *TLZ* 81: cols. 401-404.

Rad, Gerhard von (1933). "Die falschen Propheten", *ZAW* 51: 109-120.

Rad, Gerhard von (1947). "Das judäische Königsritual", *TLZ* 72: cols. 211-216.

Rad, Gerhard von (1966a). *Deuteronomy*, OTL, London: SCM Press.

Rad, Gerhard von (1966b). "The Royal Ritual in Judah", *The Problem of the Hexateuch and Other Essays* (Edinburgh and London: Oliver & Boyd): 222-231.

Redford, Donald B. (1992). *Egypt, Canaan, and Israel in Ancient Times*, Princeton: Princeton University Press.

Regt, Lénart de (2000). "A Genre Feature in Biblical Prophecy and the Translator: Person Shift in Hosea", *Past, Present, Future: The Deuteronomistic History and the Prophets*, Johannes C. de Moor and Harry F. van Rooy, eds. (Oudtestamentische Studiën 44; Leiden, Boston, Köln: E. J. Brill): 230-250.

Regt, Lénart de (2001). "Person Shift in Prophetic Texts: Its Function and its Rendering in Ancient and Modern Translations", *The Elusive Prophet: The Prophet as a Historical Person, Literary Character and Anonymous Artist,*

Johannes C. de Moor, ed. (Oudtestamentische Studiën 45; Leiden, Boston, Köln: E. J. Brill): 214-231.

Rendtorff, Rolf (1959). "προφήτη"/נביא", *Theologisches Wörterbuch zum Neuen Testament* (Stuttgart: W. Kohlhammer): VI, 796-813.

Rendtorff, Rolf (1985). *Das Alte Testament: Eine Einführung*, Neukirchen-Vluyn: Neukirchener Verlag.

Renz, Johannes (1995). *Die Althebräischen Inschriften*, Handbuch der Althebräischen Epigraphik 1, Darmstadt: Wissenschaftliche Buchgesellschaft.

Ringgren, Helmer (1966). *Israelite Religion*, David Green, trans., London: SPCK.

Ringgren, Helmer (1983). "Psalm 2 and Bāli:'s Oracle for Ashurbanipal", *The Word of the Lord Shall Go Forth: Essays in Honor of David Noel Freedman in Celebration of His Sixtieth Birthday*, Carol L. Meyers and M. O'Connor, eds. (Winona Lake: Eisenbrauns): 91-95.

Robert, André (1953). "L'exégèse des psaumes selon les méthodes de la 'formgeschichteschule': Exposé et critique in curante", *Miscellanea Biblica B. Ubach*, Dom. Romualdo M. Díaz, ed. (Barcelona: Montserrat): 211-226.

Roberts, J. J. M. (2002). "The Mari Prophetic Texts in Transliteration and English Translation", *The Bible and the Ancient Near East: Collected Essays* (Winona Lake: Eisenbrauns): 157-253.

Rooke, Deborah W. (1998). "Kingship and Priesthood: The Relationship between the High Priesthood and the Monarchy", *King and Messiah in Israel and the Ancient Near East: Proceedings of the Oxford Old Testament Seminar*, John Day, ed. (JSOTSup 270; Sheffield: Sheffield Academic Press): 187-208.

Rowley, H. H. (1945). "The Nature of Prophecy in the Light of Recent Study", *HTR* 38: 1-38.

Rowley, H. H. (1950). "Melchizedek and Zadok", *Festschrift Alfred Bertholet*, W. Baumgartner, ed. (Tübingen: J. C. B. Mohr): 461-72.

Rowley, H. H. (1963). "Ritual and the Hebrew Prophets", *From Moses to Qumran: Studies in the Old Testament.* (London: Lutterworth Press): 111-138.

Rowley, H. H. (1967). *Worship in Ancient Israel: Its Forms and Meaning,* London: SPCK.

Sarna, N. M. (1963). "Psalm 89: A Study in Inner Biblical Exegesis", *Biblical and Other Studies,* Alexander Altmann, ed. (Cambridge, MA: Harvard University Press): 29-46.

Schaper, Joachim (2003). "Exilic and Post-exilic Prophecy and the Orality/Literacy Problem", International Meeting of the Society of Biblical Literature, Cambridge, unpublished paper.

Schelling, Pieter (1985). *De Asafspsalmen: hun Samenhang en Achtergrond,* Dissertationes Neerlandicae, Series Theologica, Kampen: J. H. Kok.

Schniedewind, William M. (1997). "Prophets and Prophecy in the Books of Chronicles", *The Chronicler as Historian,* M. Patrick Graham, Kenneth G. Hoglund and Steven L. McKenzie, eds. (JSOTSup 238; Sheffield: Sheffield Academic Press): 204-224.

Scott, R. B. Y. (1944). *The Relevance of the Prophets,* New York: The Macmillan Company.

Seitz, Christopher R. (1990). "The Divine Council: Temporal Transition and New Prophecy in the Book of Isaiah", *JBL* 109: 229-247.

Seow, C. L. (1989). *Myth, Drama, and the Politics of David's Dance,* Harvard Semitic Monographs 44, Atlanta: Scholars Press.

Seybold, Klaus (1994). "Das 'Wir' in den Asaph-Psalmen: Spezifische Probleme einer Psalmgruppe", *Neue Wege der Psalmenforschung: Für Walter Beyerlin,* Klaus Seybold and Erich Zenger, eds. (HBS 1; Freiburg, Basel, Wien: Herder): 143-155.

Seybold, Klaus (1996). *Die Psalmen,* HAT I/15, Tübingen: J. C. B. Mohr.

Singer, Itamar and Harry A. Hoffner Jr., eds. (2002). *Hittite Prayers,* Writings from the Ancient World 11, Atlanta: Scholars Press.

Spieckermann, Hermann (1994). "Rede Gottes und Wort Gottes in den Psalmen", *Neue Wege der Psalmenforschung: Für Walter Beyerlin*, Klaus Seybold and Erich Zenger, eds. (HBS 1; Freiburg, Basel, Wien: Herder): 157-173.

Starbuck, Scott R. A. (1999). *Court Oracles in the Psalms: The So-Called Royal Psalms in their Ancient Near Eastern Context*, SBLDS 172, Atlanta: Society of Biblical Literature.

Starr, Ivan (1990). *Queries to the Sungod: Divination and Politics in Sargonid Assyria*, SAA 4, Helsinki: Helsinki University Press.

Steiner, Richard C. (1997). "The Aramaic Text in Demotic Script", *The Context of Scripture I: Canonical Compositions from the Biblical World*, William W. Hallo and K. Lawson Younger, Jr., eds. (Leiden, New York, Köln: E. J. Brill): 309-327.

Steymans, Hans Ulrich (2002). "'Deinen Thron habe ich unter den großen Himmeln festgemacht': Die formgeschichtliche Nähe von Ps 89,4-5.20-38 zu Texten vom neuassyrischen Hof", *"Mein Sohn bist du" (Ps 2,7): Studien zu den Königspsalmen*, Hans-Josef Klauck and Erich Zenger, eds. (SBS 192; Stuttgart: Katholisches Bibelwerk): 184-251.

Sweeney, Marvin A. (1996). *Isaiah 1-39 with an Introduction to Prophetic Literature*, FOTL XVI, Grand Rapids: Eerdmans.

Tadmor, Hayim (1975). "Assyria and the West: The Ninth Century and Its Aftermath", *Unity and Diversity: Essays in the History, Literature, and Religion of the Ancient Near East*, Hans Goedicke and J. J. M. Roberts, eds. (Baltimore: Johns Hopkins University Press): 36-48.

Tate, Marvin (1990). *Psalms 51-100*, WBC 20, Waco: Word Books.

Throntveit, Mark A. (1997). "The Chronicler's Speeches and Historical Reconstruction", *The Chronicler as Historian*, M. Patrick Graham, Kenneth G. Hoglund and Steven L.

McKenzie, eds. (JSOTSup 238; Sheffield: Sheffield Academic Press): 225-245.

Toorn, Karel van der (1987). "L'oracle de victoire comme expression prophétique au Proche-Orient ancien", *RB* 94: 63-97.

Toorn, Karel van der (1991). "The Babylonian New Year Festival: New Insights from the Cuneiform Texts and Their Bearing on Old Testament Study", *Congress Volume Leuven (1989)*, J. A. Emerton, ed. (VTSup 43; Leiden, New York, Copenhagen, Köln: E. J. Brill): 331-344.

Toorn, Karel van der (2000a). "From Oral to the Written: The Case of Old Babylonian Prophecy", *Writings and Speech in Israelite and Ancient Near Eastern Prophecy*, Ehud Ben Zvi and Michael H. Floyd, eds. (SBLSS 10; Atlanta: Society of Biblical Literature): 219-234.

Toorn, Karel van der (2000b). "Mesopotamian Prophecy between Immanence and Transcendence: A Comparison of Old Babylonian and Neo-Assyrian Prophecy", *Prophecy in Its Ancient Near Eastern Context: Mesopotamian, Biblical, and Arabian Perspectives*, Martti Nissinen, ed. (SBLSS 13; Atlanta: Society of Biblical Literature): 71-87.

Tournay, Raymond J. (1960). "Le Psaume CX", *RB* 67: 5-41.

Tournay, Raymond J. (1991). *Seeing and Hearing God with the Psalms: The Prophetic Liturgy of the Second Temple in Jerusalem*, J. Edward Crowley, trans., JSOTSup 118, Sheffield: JSOT Press.

Tournay, Raymond J. (1998). "Les Relectures du Psaume 110 (109) et l'allusion à Gédéon", *RB* 105: 321-331.

Treves, Marco (1965). "Two Acrostic Psalms", *VT* 15: 81-90.

Uchelen, N. A. van (1977). *Psalmen deel II (41-80)*, De Prediking van het Oude Testament, Nijkerk: G. F. Callenbach B. V.

Van Seters, John (2000). "Prophetic Orality in the Context of the Ancient Near East: A Response to Culley, Crenshaw and Davies", *Writings and Speech in Israelite and Ancient Near Eastern Prophecy*, Ehud Ben Zvi and Michael H. Floyd, eds. (SBLSS 10; Atlanta: Society of Biblical Literature): 83-88.

Vaux, Roland de (1961). *Ancient Israel: Its Life and Institutions*, John McHugh, trans., London: Darton, Longman and Todd.
Veijola, Timo (1982). *Verheissung in der Krise: Studien zur Literatur und Theologie der Exilszeit anhand des 89. Psalms*, Suomalaisen Tiedeakatemian Toimituksia B 220, Helsinki: Suomalainen Tiedeakatemia.
Vriezen, Theodore C. (1958). *An Outline of Old Testament Theology*, Oxford: Basil Blackwell.

Wagner, Andreas (2002). "Die Stellung der Sprechakttheorie in Hebraistik und Exegese", *Congress Volume Basel 2001*, André Lemaire, ed. (VTSup 92; Leiden, Boston: E. J. Brill): 55-83.
Waltke, Bruce K. and M. O'Connor (1990). *An Introduction to Biblical Hebrew Syntax*, Winona Lake: Eisenbrauns.
Ward, James M. (1961). "The Literary Form and Liturgical Background of Psalm LXXXIX", *VT* 11: 321-339.
Weber, Beat (2001). "Der Asaph-Psalter — eine Skizze", *Prophetie und Psalmen: Festschrift für Klaus Seybold zum 65. Geburtstag*, Beat Huwyler, Hans-Peter Mathys and Beat Weber, eds. (AOAT 280; Münster: Ugarit-Verlag): 117-141.
Weinfeld, M. (1970). "The Covenant of Grant in the Old Testament and the Ancient Near East", *JAOS* 90: 184-203.
Weippert, Manfred (1972). "'Heiliger Krieg' in Israel und Assyrien: Kritische Anmerkungen zu Gerhard von Rads Konzept des 'Heiligen Krieges im alten Israel'", *ZAW* 84: 460-493.
Weippert, Manfred (1981). "Assyrische Prophetien der Zeit Asarhaddons und Assurbanipals", *Assyrian Royal Inscriptions: New Horizons in Literary, Ideological and Historical Analysis*, F. M. Fales, ed. (Orientis Antiqui Colectio 18; Rome: Istituto per L'Orient): 71-115.
Weippert, Manfred (1985). "Die Bildsprache der neuassyrischen Prophetie", *Beiträge zur Prophetischen Bildsprache in Israel und Assyrien.* (Orbis Biblicus et Ori-

entalis 64; Gottingen: Vandenhoeck and Ruprecht): 55-93.

Weippert, Manfred (1988). "Aspekte israelitischer Prophetie im Lichte verwandter Erscheinungen des Alten Orients", *Ad bene et fideliter seminandum: Festgabe für Karlheinz Deller zum 21. Februar 1987*, Gerlinde Mauer and Ursula Magen, eds. (AOAT 220; Neukirchen-Vluyn: Kevelaer): 287-319.

Weippert, Manfred (1993). "Königsprophetie und Königsideologie in Juda zur 'Nathansweissagung' 2 Sam 7,4-17", *Spuren eines Weges: Freundesgabe für Bernd Janowski zum 50. Geburtstag am 30. April 1993*, T. Podella and P. Riede, eds. (Heidelberg): 291-302.

Weippert, Manfred (1997). "'Das Frühere, siehe, ist eingetroffen.' Über Selbstzitate im altorientalischen Prophetenspruch", *Oracles et prophéties dans l'antiquité: Actes du colloque de Strasbourg 15-17 juin 1995*, Jean-Georges. Heintz, ed. (Travaux du Centre de Recherche sur le Proche-Orient et la Grèce Antiques 15; Paris: Université des Sciences Humaines de Strasbourg): 147-169.

Weippert, Manfred (2001a). "'Ich bin Jahwe' - 'Ich bin Ishtar von Arbela': Deuterojesaja im Lichte der neuassyrischen Prophetie", *Prophetie und Psalmen: Festschrift für Klaus Seybold zum 65. Geburtstag*, Beat Huwyler, Hans-Peter Mathys and Beat Weber, eds. (AOAT 280; Munster: Ugarit-Verlag): 31-59.

Weippert, Manfred (2001b). "Prophetie im Alten Orient", *Neues Bibel-Lexikon*, Manfred Görg and Bernhard Lang, eds. (Düsseldorf, Zürich: Benziger): III, cols. 196-200.

Weippert, Manfred (2002). "'König, fürchte dich nicht!' Assyrische Prophetie im 7. Jahrhundert v. Chr", *Or* 71: 1-54.

Weiser, Artur (1962). *The Psalms*, Herbert Hartwell, trans., OTL, London: SCM Press.

Weiser, Artur (1987). *Die Psalmen*. 8th Edition, ATD 14/15, Göttingen and Zürich: Vandenhoeck and Ruprecht, 1987.

Williamson, H. G. M. (1982). *1 and 2 Chronicles*, NCB, Grand Rapids, London: Eerdmans, Marshall, Morgan & Scott.

Willis, John T. (1990). "A Cry of Defiance—Psalm 2", *JSOT* 47: 33-50.

Wilson, Robert R. (1980). *Prophecy and Society in Ancient Israel*, Philadelphia: Fortress Press.

Würthwein, Ernst (1952). "Der Ursprung der Prophetischen Gerichtsrede", *ZTK* 44: 1-16.

Zimmerli, Walther (1953). "Ich bin Jahwe", *Geschichte und Altes Testament*, Gerhard Ebeling, ed. (Beiträge zur Historischen Theologie 16; Tübingen: J. C. B. Mohr): 179-209.

Zimmerli, Walther (1982). "I Am Yahweh", *I Am Yahweh*, Walter Brueggemann, ed. (Atlanta: John Knox Press): 1-28.

Index of Texts

1) Bible

Genesis
11:1	154
11:7	155
12:4	194
15:1	46
17:23	194
18:19	194
21:1-2	194
23:16	194
24:7	194, 196
24:30	194
24:51	194
25	100
25:23	101
25:28	113
27:7	113
31:13	133
35:13-14	194
42:30	194
44:2	194
45:27	194
48:17-18	79
49:10	195

Exodus
3:6	133
6:30	155
15:17	107
20:2	133, 164
24	166
26:36	200
32:13	101
34:10-16	164

Leviticus
13:36	32
19	162

Numbers
10:35	110
11	30
11:16	200
11:24-30	9, 30
14:20-35	106
18:10	200
23:1, 14	4
23:29	4
24:3-4	76, 212
24:4, 16	155, 211
24:15-16	76
24:17-19	195
25:7-8	167

Deuteronomy
Book of	106, 120, 182, 194
1:6	194, 196
1:8	106
1:11	194
1:21	194
4:33	155
4:36	155
4:40	182
5:3	182
5:6	133
5:21	96
5:24	155
6:6	182
7:11	182
9:3	182
11:2	182
13	41
17:14-20	48
18:9-14	20
18:15, 18	141
20:3-4	31
31:1-10	195
31:9-13	163
32:1	162

Index of Texts

33:8	131	23	120
		23:1-2	76
Joshua		23:1-7	120
9:5, 12, 14	113	23:5	49
Judges		*1 Kings*	
2:1b-2	158	1:38, 45	83
4:14, 20	31	1:39	83
4:28	31	1:40, 46	83
5	209	2:19	79
6:8b-10	158	2:26-27	27
7:8	113	8	109
20:28	46	8:2	109
		8:15-16	109
Ruth		8:16	110
1:16	215	8:20-21	109
		8:27-32	99
1 Samuel		8:64	109
1:13	154	11	47
3:7	152, 155	11:36	104
3:21	9	14:5	62
4:17	11	18	7, 26
9:6-20	62	18:16	7
9:9	31	18:16-39	4
10	30	18:40	167
10:5	4, 7, 9, 26, 27, 36	19:10	9, 26
10:5-6	30	20:3	46
19	30	20:13-15	211
19:19	4, 7	21:21-22	139
22:10	113	22	7, 213
22:12	86	22:5ff	31
23:4	46	22:5-12	63
25:25	86	22:6	31
		22:12-15	46
2 Samuel		22:14	30
1:10	86	22:19	176
2:1-2	64	22:19-23	176, 178
3:9	106		
5	48	*2 Kings*	
5:23-24	4, 32	1:2-4	62
6	109	2:3	4, 26
6-7	106, 110	2:5	4
7	43, 47-48, 104, 120, 121-22	3	137
		3:11ff	31
7:12, 16	48	3:11-12	63
7:14	48	3:15	4, 7, 27, 36
7:14-15	120	3:17	138
16:23	76	3:18	137

4:23	9, 26	29:30	136
4:38	4, 7, 26	30:6-9	183
8:20-22	202	34:30	35
9:11	31	34:31	83
11	48		
11:12, 17	85, 90	*Ezra*	
11:14	83	Book of	22
11:19	83	5:2	34
16:15	32	6:14	34
17:13-15	158		
18:20	154	*Nehemiah*	
19:6-7	201	Book of	22
19:8-37	136	6:7, 14	34
19:20-34	201	6:10-12	5
22:6	58	8:8, 18	163
23:2	35	13:15	113
23:3	83		
25	118	*Job*	
		1:6-12	176
Chronicles		4:12-16	153
Book of	21-23, 31, 33, 35-37, 98, 134, 136, 139, 147, 156-57, 180, 183-84	4:16	155
		12:20	154
		26:14	155
		32:17-22	164
		33:14-18	153
1 Chronicles		38:31	113
12:19	157	38:39	113
15	7	38:41	113
15:22, 27	4, 35		
16	135	*Psalms*	
22:6-16	157	1	94
25	28, 35-36	2	2, 18, 23, 48, 50, 76-77, 79, 86-87, **89-101**, 118, 127, 138-39, 191, 219-22, 224-25
25:1-3	2, 36, 38, 135-36		
25:1, 6-7	35, 136		
28:2-10	157		
		2:1	100
2 Chronicles		2:1-3	90, 99
5:3	109	2:1-11	95
6:41-42	107, 109, 111	2:4-5	99
8:11	111	2:4-9	100
12:5-8	157	2:5-9	190, 194, 196
15:1-7	157	2:6	96
20	4, 8, 21, 35, 37, 63, 136	2:6-9	95, 97-98, 107
		2:7	48, 91, 96, 126-27, 194, 196
20:14-17	35, 136, 157, 201		
20:37	157	2:7-8	97, 99
21:12-15	157	2:7-9	2, 22, 95-96, 137
24:20-22	157	2:8-11	87
25:15	157	2:9	99-100
26:16	87		

2:10-12	94	32:5	169
2:12	100	32:8-9	208
3:2	89	32:8-11	147
3:5	96, 200	32:9-12	169
5:4	32	33	24
7:7, 9	99	33:9	194, 196
10:1	89	34	204
12	129, 139, **186-92**, 200, 204, 212, 215-16, 219, 220, 221-22, 224-25	35:3	18, 22
		36:2	76
		37:28	124
		38:17	169
12:2-5	186, 188	39:2	169
12:6	1, 14, 17, 130, 137, 147, 153, 170, 172-73, 175, 187-92, 194, 196-97, 205, 220	40:7-9	165
		40:11	169
		41:5	169
		44	24
		44:27	188
12:7-8	191	45:10	79
12:7-9	187-88	46	186, **213-14**
12:8	187-89	46:7	214
12:9	191	46:11	22, 137, 171-72, 206, 213-14, 217
13:2	89		
14	17, 129, 186, 188, **215**	47	109
		47:5	107
14:4	130, 147, 174	48	107
14:6	130, 175	48:7	145
15	11	48:13-14	145
15:1	89, 96	49:5	4, 27
16:8	80	50	7, 11, 24, 18, 21, 24, 94 128-35, 140-43, 149-50, **162-66**, 171, 176, 179–81, 183–85, 191, 205, 219–21, 223–25
18:48-51	87, 99		
19:4	155		
20	77, 101, 107, 187		
20:3	83, 96		
20:7-9	205		
21:2-8	48		
21:9-13	87	50:1	163, 194, 197
22:23-27	169	50:1–6	164
24	11, 111	50:2	140, 166
27	186, **215**	50:4	162
27:4	32	50:4ff	190
27:8	147, 215	50:4–7	170
30:5	124	50:5	124, 166
30:7	169	50:7	133, 142, 162-63, 166
31:5	169		
31:15	173	50:9–13	165
31:19	154	50:10-12	163
31:24	124	50:11	135
32	208	50:14	145

Index of Texts

50:14–15	7	68	18, 21, 147, 186, **209-13**, 217, 219, 225
50:15	163, 165		
50:16	132, 162, 165, 183, 194, 196		
		68:10-12	210
50:16–20	7	68:12-14	147
50:18-20	163	68:12-15	209-13
50:22	162	68:20	212-13
50:22–23	7	68:20-24	211
50:23	163	68:22	194, 196, 1-2, 211, 217
51:18-21	165	68:23	109, 137, 209-210, 212-13, 223
52:9	124	68:23-24	
53	186, **215**		
53:1-6	7	68:22-24	210
53:5	147	69:32	165
53:6	7	72: 8-11	87, 99
56	24	73	128, 142, 144
56:8	99	73:15	169
57:8-12	193	74	118, 136, 141-44
58	175	74:1	24
59: 6, 9	99	74:2, 7	140
60	5, 13, 18, 21, 24, 120, 139, 147, 186, 191, **192-202**, 204, 212, 216, 219, 220, 224-25	74:8	140-41
		74:9	135, 148
		75	11, 18, 21, 129-31, 134-35, 138, 140-42, 149-50, **167-74**, 177, 181, 184-86, 205, 219-20, 225
60:2, 5	200		
60:3	201, 195		
60:3-7	193	75:2	129, 221
60:6	201	75:3	2, 204-05, 222
60:7	2, 200	75:3-4	129, 168, 172-74, 214
60:7-14	192-93		
60:8	2, 195-99, 221	75:4	130, 174
60:8-10	2, 8, 137, 147, 190-91, 193, 194-97, 199, 200, 201, 216, 223	75:5	167, 173
		75:5-6	174
		75:5-7	173
		75:5-8	129-30
60:11	195, 200	75:5-9	174
60:8-11	195-96	75:9	129-30, 172
60:11-13	191	75:10	172-73
60:11-14	193	75:10-11	129, 174
60:12	195	75:11	130
60:12-14	200-01	76	41-42
60:14	191, 197	76:4	144-45
62	186, **216**	76:12	145
62:12	153, 194, 198-99, 206, 216	77	141
		77:9	148
		77:16	135
66:16-19	169	78	107, 141, 157
		78:1-2	141

Index of Texts

78:25	113		**174-79**, 180-81,
78:60	107		185-86, 191, 205,
78:67	135		219-221, 223,
78:67-72	107, 145	82:1	225
79	118, 136, 141-45	82:1-2	176
79:2	124	82:2	170-71
79:10	90	82:3-4	130, 174
79:13	24	82:5	7, 130, 174
80	136, 143	82:6	130, 174
80:2	24, 135, 145	82:6-7	173
80:3	144	82:7	190
80:14	135	82:8	130
80:18	79	83	130
81	18, 21, 24, 94,	83:2	113, 144, 136
	129-35, 140-43,	83:3-5	148
	149, **150-61**, 162-	83:18	90
	63, 165-66, 176,	85	112
	179-81, 183-85,	85:5-8	25
	191, 204-05, 219-	85:9	102
	20, 222, 224-25		11, 124, 194, 196,
81:1-3	144		153, 205
81:2-4	24, 150, 221-22	87	186, **214-15**, 217
81:5	222	87:3, 5	215
81:5-6	90	87:4	137
81:5-17	150, 222	87:4, 6	214
81:6	1, 11, 36, 135,	87:4-7	215
	141, 149-56, 163	89	18, 49-50, 76, 86,
81:6-8	151		104, 107, **115-26**,
81:6-9	170		172, 191, 219-22,
81:7	2		225
81:7-11	152	89:2-3	120
81:7-15	190	89:2-5	123
81:7-17	154-56, 158-59	89:3	169
81:8	163	89:3-4	115, 117
81:9	142, 159, 163	89:3-5	137
81:9-11	151	89:4	115, 116
81:9-12	7	89:4-5	120-22, 124-26,
81:10	163		171-72
81:11	133, 142, 152,	89:4-6	119
	154-56, 163	89:5	48, 115, 121
81:12-13	151	89:6	121
81:12-17	152	89:6-19	98, 121
81:14	7	89:16-19	119, 120, 124
81:14-15	151	89:19	117
81:16-17	151	89:20	119, 127, 193,
82	7, 11, 18, 129-31,		196-99, 221
	134-35, 140-42,	89:20ff	190
	149-50, 167, 171,	89:20-35	120

258   Index of Texts

89:20-38	115, 117, 119, 121-26, 172	105	24, 142, 147, 186, **216**
89:23-24	116	105:10	90
89:25, 29	116	105:11	216
89:26-27	116	105:15	171-72, 216
89:27-28	115	105:17	135
89:27-30	48	106	24, 142
89:30, 37	115	106:33	194, 196
89:31-33	116	108	192-93, 201, 216, 223
89:33-38	120		
89:34-35	116	108:7-14	192-93
89:35-36	49	108:8	194
89:36	82, 116, 200	108:8-10	137, 197, 223
89:36-38	120	110	2, 48, 50, **76-88**, 94, 96-97, 100, 120, 127, 138-39, 219-22, 225
89:41-42	118-19		
89:47-52	117		
90:3	22		
91	8, 180, 186, 191, **203-09**, 212, 219-222, 224-25	110:1	2, 36, 77, 79-80, 83, 86, 95, 126-27, 212
91:1-2	203, 206-07, 209	110:2	83
91:1-13	203	110:3	79
91:3-13	206-07, 209	110:4	78, 82, 84, 106, 120, 127, 137
91:14	137, 204, 206-07		
91:14ff	190	110:6	78
91:14-16	171-72, 203-06, 208-09, 216	110:7	83
		114:1	155
92:8	112	116:11	169
95	7-8, 21, 24, 129-31, 148-50, 163, **179-84**, 185, 204-05, 219-20, 224-25	116:14	169
		116:15	124
		116:18	169
		118:10-12	87, 99
		119	24
95:4-5	163	119:57	169, 174
95:5	137	120:2	154
95:6	204	121	8
95:7	155, 180, 182, 222	122:2	145
		122:4	145
95:7-8	170-71	130:7	112
95:7-11	182-84, 205	131:3	112
95:8	2, 204-05	132	21-22, 48, 76, 86, **101-115**, 120, 122, 126, 138-39, 219-20, 222, 224-25
95:8-11	7		
95:10	163		
97:10	124		
99:7	194, 196		
101	186, **216**	132:1-10	102, 108, 222
101:6-7	216	132:1-12	107
102:14	6	132:2-11	106
102:16-19	6	132:8	110-11, 221
		132:9	124

Index of Texts

132:11	82, 106, 120, 127	9:5	48
132:11-18	102-03, 105-06, 108-09, 137, 222	10:24	183
		14:28	82
132:12	90, 105	16:13-14	198-99
132:13-16	107-08	19:18	154
132:15	113	20:2	198-99
132:16	124	21:17	198
132:17	104	22:1	89, 162
132:17-18	106-07	22:14	212
132:18	104	22:25	198
137	24	24:3	198
140:7	173	25:8	198
142:6	173	26	113
145:10	124	26:4	112
148:14	124	27:1	175
149:1	124	28:7	4, 9, 27
149:5	124	28:11	154
149:9	124	28:14	152
150	130	30:1	77
150:1	200	30:8	44
		30:27	155
Proverbs		33:10	153, 190-92
7:1-3	164	33:19	154-55
10:19	154	34	100
16:10	32	34:4-5	175
30:1	76	37:6-7	201
30:5-6	76	37:21-35	201
		40	176
Isaiah		40-48	45
Book of	18, 24, 43-45, 47, 49-50, 52, 175-77, 195, 208, 210	40-55	42
		40:1-8	176
		40:1-22	176
1:2	162, 197-98	40:5	198
1:2-3	166	40:6-8	24
1:9-10	183	40:14	208
1:11-18	191-92	40:27	89
1:20	198	41:8-13	44
2:3	208	41:10-14	204
3:1-4	81	41:17-20	208, 210
3:15	162	41:21	153, 191-92
6	176	41:21-29	45
6:1	176	42:5-9	45
6:1-13	176, 178	42:14-17	208
6:8	30, 155	42:18-43:7	180
7-8	43	43:1, 5	204
8:16-23	48	43:11	50
8:18	30	43:25-28	180
9:1-4	199	44:1	162

44:2	204	11:16	100
44:3	210	11:18	30
45:1-7	47	11:18-23	45
45:5, 21	50	13:13	9
46:1-2	175	13:15	197
48:1, 12	162	14:18	4, 9, 27
48:3, 6	43	15:10-18	123
48:12-16	45	15:10-21	45
48:14-16	195	15:12	100
48:21	210	15:16	152
49-55	45	17:19-21	222
49:1-4	195	18:1-5	222
49:10	210	18:18	4, 7, 27
50:10	195	19:1-3	222
51:1	162	19:14-15	222
51:7	204	20:1-6	28
51:15-16	164	20:7-13	45
52:15	123	21:1ff	31
53:12	208	22:1-2	222
54:4	204	22:5	82
55:3	49	23:11	9, 28
55:10	24	23:14, 16	28
58:14	198	23:17	29, 198
59:16	195	23:18	155
61:8	164	23:21	28
62:8	82	23:25-32	28
63:1	89	23:34-40	28
63:5	195	25:15-16	130
66:9	153, 191-92	26	7, 107
		26:1-2	222
Jeremiah		26:7	9, 26
Book of	34, 131	27:1-4	222
1:1	4, 27	27:1-11	89
1:6-7	30	27:16	9
1:10	123	28	7
2:1-2	222	29:4-23	177
2:4	162	29:8	32
2:4-14	158	29:26	4, 7, 9, 27-28, 31
2:26	27	30:4	199
4:1-4	156	31:33	180
4:9	9, 27	34:4	9
5:11	212	34:5	198
6:13	4, 9, 27	35:4	28
7:1-2	222	36	7, 44, 224
7:22-25	158	36:1-4	177
8:1	9	36:11-26	42
8:10	9	38:14ff	31
9:21	212	39:15-16	222
10:1	162, 197, 198	41:5	118
11:6	222	42	182

Index of Texts

42:1ff	31	5:14	152
42:1-22	198	6:1	152
42:18-22	182	11:1-2	158
44:7	89	11:1-11	133
46:7	89	12:3	49
49:13	82	12:10	133
51:14	82	13:4	133
		13:4-6	158

Lamentations
2:9	148	*Joel*	
2:20	9, 26, 148	Book of	4-5, 34
4:13	9	4:8	198
		4:16	199

Ezekiel
Book of	34, 133	*Amos*	
1:3	4	1	212
1:28-29	171	1-2	43
2:7-3:4	224	1:2	199
3:5-6	154	1:8	212
3:6	155	2:10-12	158
5:15, 17	198	2:16	212
8:1-3	7	3:1	197-98
11:1, 24	7	3:1-2	156
17:21, 24	198	3:1-7	81
18:2	162	3:15	212
20	159	4:2	82, 200
20:5-8	158	4:10-11	183
20:10-13	198	5:4, 6	215
20:18-21	198	5:18	89
21:22, 37	198	6:8	81-82
22:14	198	7:6	212
23:34	198	8:7	82
24:14	198		
26:14	198	*Obadiah*	
28:10	198	Book of	202
34:11	32	18	198
38:19	197-98	19-21	199
39:5	198		
		Micah	
Hosea		1:3-7	81
Book of	133	3:1, 9	162
1:2	199	3:5-7	9
2:16-17	183	3:6-7	32
3:2-3	156	3:10-11	107
4	44	3:11	4, 7, 9, 27
4:1-10	49	4:4	198
4:4	9	4:9	89
5:1-7	81	4:11-12	89

6:1	166	*Malachi*	
6:1-4	158	Book of	34, 157
		1:1	77
Nahum			
Book of	16		

2) Assyria

Habakkuk		SAA	
Book of	4, 16, 129	2 6	192
1	189	3 3	72, 74, 93-94, 103, 105, 115
1:6	189		
2:1-3	167	3 7	53
2:2	44, 224	3 8	145
2:2-17	123	3 11	94, 171, 208
2:3	129	3 12	74
2:16	130	3 13	53, 60, 70-74, 125, 132, 171, 177, 203, 207-08, 224
2:18-19	89		
3	130		
3:2-19	167		
3:17	129-30, 174	3 31	68
3:18	189	3 33	62, 116
3:18-19	130	3 34	57
		3 35	57
Zephaniah		3 39	104
1-2	176	3 44	116
1:13, 17	156	3 45	69
2:3	215	3 47	59, 69, 177
3:2	208	4 81	64
3:4	9	4 196	62
3:9	154	4 267-69	65
3:9-10	199	4 279	65
		7 9	54, 65
Haggai		9 1	68, 91, 132, 139
Book of	5, 9, 34, 47, 157	9 1.1	53, 55, 67, 80, 90-91, 125, 132, 159, 165, 192
2:1-9	109		
Zechariah		9 1.2	53, 55, 67-68, 74, 78, 90-92, 103, 125, 132, 207
Book of	5, 9, 34, 47, 157		
1:7-17	176		
1:8	176	9 1.3	54, 56
3:1-5	176	9 1.4	53, 55, 71, 77, 80, 86-87, 90, 125, 132, 159, 165, 178
3:11	176		
4:6	77		
7-8	118		
7:1-3	10	9 1.5	53, 55, 132
7:3	4	9 1.6	47-48, 50, 53, 55, 67, 71-72, 78-80, 82, 91, 103-04, 115-17, 125, 132, 165, 178, 207, 219
9:12	182		
12-13	176		
12:1-2	212		
13:2-6	34		

Index of Texts

9 1.7	47, 53, 55, 57, 68, 91	9 3.5	56, 60, 77-78, 80, 103, 116, 132-33, 159, 165
9 1.8	31, 53, 55, 57, 65-68, 72, 79, 91, 103, 132	9 4	55, 80, 92, 116
		9 5	53, 55, 60, 65-66, 77-80, 125, 139
9 1.9	47, 53, 55, 91, 115, 171	9 6	53, 55, 68, 178
9 1.10	43, 47-48, 53, 55, 72, 79, 91, 104, 115, 125, 132, 159	9 7	45, 50, 53, 55, 60, 72, 74, 80, 90-94, 103, 115, 125, 139, 192, 201, 219
9 2	68, 91, 178		
9 2.1	55, 72, 132-33, 139, 178	9 8	55, 68, 192, 201
		9 9	53, 55, 58, 65, 70-74, 78-79, 125-26, 139, 155, 172, 178, 207-08, 220
9 2.2	55, 78-79, 125, 132, 139, 178, 207		
9 2.3	48, 53, 55-56, 65, 67-68, 80, 91-92, 103-04, 115-16, 125, 132, 139, 165, 201, 219	9 10	55
		9 11	55, 66, 79
		10 24	54
		10 109	54, 65
9 2.4	46, 53, 55, 60, 68, 71-72, 77-78, 90, 92, 139, 159, 201, 207, 219	10 111	53
		10 174	58
		10 185	80
		10 284	53
9 2.5	55, 68, 78-79, 91-92, 115-16, 132, 139, 178	10 294	31, 58, 69
		12 69	57-58
		13 37	57, 192
9 2.6	55, 72, 103, 132, 139, 165, 178	13 139	56, 69
		13 144	56
9 3	47-49, 68, 85, 91, 94, 97, 102, 139, 159-61, 165-66, 220, 223-24	13 148	56-57
		16 60	66
		16 61	66
9 3.1	85, 103, 105	*Assurbanipal*	
9 3.2	68, 78-80, 91-92, 116, 139, 159, 171-72, 191, 201	Prism A	65
		Prism B	68
		Prism T	56, 65, 105
9 3.3	45, 47, 53, 67, 78, 85, 90, 102, 116, 125, 132, 139, 160, 165, 220	*Esarhaddon*	
		Ass. A	68
		Nin. A	67-68, 80
9 3.4	47, 49, 53, 60, 77-80, 90, 92, 95, 165, 178, 220	3) Egypt	
		EA 23	59

Hatshepsut	84-85, 96-97	Zakkur Inscription	64, 136, 191
Horemheb	84-85, 96		

7) Mari

Papyrus Amherst 63	64, 191
The King as Sun Priest	79

A.1121+2731	58, 63, 132
A.1968	116

4) Eshnunna

FLP 1674   59, 132, 177, 223

5) Hatti

Kantuzzili's and
Mursili's Prayers   64, 191

6) Levant

Amman Citadel Inscription	64
Arad Ostraca	
No. 49	136
No. 52	113
Mesha Inscription	64

ARM 26/1	
194	132
195	58
196	58, 63
197	63
200	63
202	58
206	58, 63
207	63
208	63
209	58, 63
212	58, 63
213	58
214	58
215	58, 64
216	58, 63
219	58, 64
227	58
233	58
236	58
237	58
371	58

Index of Authors

Ackroyd, P. R.	118	Davies, G. H.	182-83
Adler, H.-P.	59	Day, J	82, 87-88, 114
Allen, L. C.	77, 80, 82, 102, 112	Delitzsch, F.	1-2, 128, 140
		Dever, W. G.	145
Anderson, A. A.	76, 89, 95, 102, 109, 112, 119, 150, 152, 180, 187, 194	Dijk, J. J. A. van,	59
		Dijkstra, M.	45, 70, 74
		Duhm, B.	2, 86, 112
Baines, J.	79, 84, 97	Durand, J.-M.	63-64
Balentine, S. E.	35	Eaton, J. H.	118, 167
Barstad, H. M.	43	Eerdmans, B. D.	14, 28
Becking, B.	99	Eichrodt, W.	14
Begrich, J.	5-6, 11, 14, 44, 191	Eissfeldt, O.	11-12
		Ellis, M. de J.	44, 59, 64, 132
Bell, L.	84, 97	Emerton, J. A.	88
Bellinger, W. H.	16, 20, 187	Fichtner, J.	15
Booij, T.	8, 16, 20-22, 28, 33, 36, 78, 82, 102, 117, 119, 123-24, 155, 158-59, 161, 163, 166, 168, 175, 180, 199-200, 203-05, 210, 214-15	Fishbane, M.	122
		Fleming, D.	63-64
		Floyd, M. H.	118-19, 121-23, 126
		Fretheim, T. E.	101, 108
		Gakuru, G.	43, 47-48, 104, 108, 112, 115, 118, 120, 122
		Gerstenberger, E. S.	76, 81, 86, 89, 98, 100, 106, 110-112, 114, 119, 122, 138, 150, 153, 163-66, 168-73, 176, 180, 183, 187-89, 193-94, 195-96, 199, 203-06, 208, 211, 213-14.
Borger, R.	67, 80		
Breasted, J. H.	84-85, 96-97		
Burrelli, R. J.	203		
Buss, M. J.	128		
Butler, S. A. L.	73		
Christensen, D. L.	201		
Clements, R. E.	1, 13		
Clifford, R. J.	122		
Cooper, J.	51, 91		
Craigie, P. C.	89, 95, 162, 190, 213	Gordon, R. P.	43, 50
Croft, S. J. L.	15	Goulder, M. D.	128, 140, 142, 145, 149, 155
Cross, F. M.	112		
Cryer, F.	16, 20	Grabbe, L. L.	16, 19-20, 41
Crystal, D.	170	Gressmann, H.	44
Culley, R. C.	223		

Index of Authors

Gunkel, H.	1-3, 5-9, 11, 13-14, 16, 18, 24, 26-27, 29, 33, 38, 77, 80, 82, 86-89, 91, 95, 99, 100, 101-02, 109-12, 114, 117-18, 122, 143, 150-53, 155, 162-64, 166, 168, 174-77, 179-80, 182-83, 187, 193, 197-98, 202-05, 207, 210, 213, 218, 221, 225		179, 183, 187-89, 193, 202, 215
		Johnson, A. R.	9-16, 18, 21, 25-27, 33-34, 36, 118
		Jones, G. H.	90
		Jong, M. de	54, 66-67, 73, 160
		Joüon, P. and T. Muaoka	96
		Keel, O.	46, 84, 96
		Kelso, J. L.	145
		Kemp, B. J.	84-85
		Kim, E. K.	190
Haldar, A.	10-12, 15	Kirkpatrick, A. F.	1
Hämeen-Anttila, J.	93	Klatt, W.	6, 8
Haney, R. G.	38	Klein, R. W.	35
Harner, P. B.	44, 190	Klein, W. C.	14, 28
Harris, J. G.	15, 17	Kleinig, J. W.	36
Hayes, J. H.	201	Knoppers, G. N.	104
Heim, K. M.	117	Koch, Klaus	96-97
Herrmann, S.	84	Koenen, K.	15, 18-19, 156-57
Heschel, A. J.	15	Kraus, H.-J.	14, 76, 80, 83, 89, 95, 102, 106, 110-12, 117, 119, 121, 150, 152, 163-64, 167, 175, 177, 179-80, 187, 189, 194, 201, 204, 207, 209-10, 213-15
Hesse, F.	12		
Hilber, J. W.	50, 76		
Hillers, D. R.	110		
Hoffmeier, J. K.	85		
Holladay, W. L.	182		
Hölscher, G.	2		
Hossfeld, F.-L.	16, 25, 120, 128, 142, 146, 149-50, 153, 163-64, 168, 170, 172-73, 176, 179, 181, 184, 211-12		
		Kselman, J. S.	216
		Küchler, F.	2, 22, 187
		Laato, A.	42-43, 48, 50-51, 79-80, 85, 90, 92, 97, 101-04, 107-08, 112, 114
Huffmon, H. B.	40, 63, 132		
Hunger, H.	56		
Hupfeld, H.	2	Lafont, B.	58, 63, 132
Hurowitz, V.	64	Lambert, W. G.	51, 85
Illman, K.-J.	128, 134, 157	Lemaire, A.	99, 113
Ishida, T.	43, 46-48, 85, 115-16	Lindblom, J.	13-14
		Lion, B.	59-60
Jacquet, L.	81, 100	Livingstone, A.	69
Japhet, S.	35-36	Loretz, O.	95
Jensen, J. E.	165	Mason, R.	34, 156-57
Jeremias, J.	15-18, 129-34, 149, 152, 156, 163-64, 167, 169, 172, 174-75, 177,	Mathias, D.	156
		Mathys, H.-P.	36
		McDowell, A. G.	84
		McKane, W.	27-28, 182

Meier, S. A.	138, 170, 212	Plöger, O.	12
Melville, S.	65-66	Pongratz-Leisten,	
Menzel, B.	55	B.	54, 57, 59, 61,
Millard, A. R.	43, 99		63-65, 69, 70, 73-
Miller, C. L.	138, 170, 173		74, 160, 177
Miller, J. M.	136	Porteous, N. W.	12
Moran, W. L.	59	Porter, B. N.	51
Motyer, J. A.	14	Prinsloo,	
Mowinckel, S.	1, 3-9, 11-13, 15-16, 21-23, 25-27, 29, 32-33, 35-36, 38, 77, 82, 86, 89, 95, 102-03, 109-11, 117, 120, 122, 133, 150-51, 153, 162, 164-65, 167, 174, 179-80, 187-88, 193, 197, 199, 202-03, 214-15, 218, 221	G. T. M.	190-91
		Pritchard, J. B.	59
		Quell, G.	13-14, 38
		Rad, G. von	12, 46, 83-84, 90, 182
		Redford, D. B.	99
		Regt, L. de	78, 81, 206
		Rendtorff, R.	13
		Renz, J.	136
		Ringgren, H.	14, 50, 90-93, 192
		Robert, A.	12
Murnane, W. J. and E. S.		Roberts, J. J. M.	58, 132
Meltzer	84-85, 96	Rooke, D. W.	87
Murray, R.	15	Rowley, H. H.	11-12, 14-15, 82
Nasuit, H. P.	128, 132-40, 146-49, 166, 169, 184	Sarna, N. M.	117-18, 122
		Schaper, J.	224
Niditch, S.	224	Schelling, P.	128, 134
Nissinen, M.	31-32, 40-70, 74, 80, 85, 91, 108, 115-16, 126, 201	Schniedewind,	
		W. M.	34-35
		Scott, R. B. Y.	12
O'Connor, D. B.	84	Seitz, C. R.	176-77
O'Connor, M.	170	Seow, C. L.	107-08, 112
Oded, B.	47, 79, 91	Seybold, K.	77, 87, 91, 94-95, 106-08, 111, 118, 120-21, 140, 142-47, 149, 152-53, 163, 167, 175-76, 187, 194, 202-03
Oeming, M.	113		
Ogden, G. S.	194, 195-96, 201		
Otto, E.	93, 96-97, 99		
Parkinson, R. B.	79		
Parpola, S.	40, 46, 50-51, 53-55, 57, 59-60, 64, 66-67, 70, 73-74, 77, 79-80, 85, 91-93, 104, 115, 125-26, 159-60, 192, 224	Singer, I. and H. A.	
		Hoffner	64
		Spieckermann,	
		H	16, 23-25, 142-43, 150
		Starbuck,	
Pedersen, J.	12	S. R. A.	49-50, 85, 119
Petersen, A. R.	109	Starr, I.	32, 62
Petersen, D. L.	30, 35, 43	Steiner, R. C.	64
Ploeg, J. P. M. van der	190-91	Steymans, H. U.	50, 115-16, 118, 120-23

Sweeney, M. A.	113	Ward, J. M.	117, 120, 122, 124
Tadmor, H.	46		
Tate, M.	115, 118, 121, 150, 152, 159, 167, 176-77, 180, 183, 195, 202-03, 205-06, 210	Weber, B.	128, 135, 141-42, 145, 149, 158, 166
		Weinfeld, M.	104
		Weippert, M.	29-31, 40-43, 45-47, 49, 51-52, 60, 64, 69, 73, 91-93, 125
Throntveit, M. A.	35		
Toorn, K. van der	31-32, 42, 46, 48, 50-51, 58-59, 64, 79-80, 85, 92, 105, 109, 115, 224	Weiser, A.	76, 80, 83, 89, 95, 102, 109, 112, 117-18, 150-01, 154, 162, 167, 174, 179, 187, 194, 202, 204, 210, 213-14
Tournay, R. J.	16, 22-23, 81, 86, 98, 100-101, 112-14, 118, 121, 143-44, 150, 163, 199		
		Williamson, H. G. M.	35-36
Treves, M.	86	Willis, J. T.	95
Uchelen, N. A. van	169	Wilson, R. R.	51, 132, 136-38
		Würthwein, E.	11
Van Seters, J.	43	Zenger, E.	94, 98, 100, 179, 187, 194, 202-03, 213-14
Vaux, R. de	14-15, 90		
Veijola T.	118-19		
Vriezen, R. C.	14	Zimmerli, W.	44, 130, 132-33, 156, 164
Wagner, A.	96		
Waltke, B. K. and M. O'Connor	96